SUPER
HOROSCOPE

VIRGO

19 99

August 22 - September 22

B

BERKLEY BOOKS, NEW YORK

The publishers regret that they cannot answer
individual letters requesting personal horoscope information.

1999 SUPER HOROSCOPE VIRGO

PRINTING HISTORY
Berkley Trade Edition / August 1998

The Penguin Putnam Inc. World Wide Web site address is
http://www.penguinputnam.com

ISBN: 0-425-16329-6

PRINTED IN THE UNITED STATES OF AMERICA

10 9 8 7 6 5 4 3 2 1

CONTENTS

THE CUSP-BORN VIRGO

Are you *really* a Virgo? If your birthday falls during the fourth week of August, at the beginning of Virgo, will you still retain the traits of Leo, the sign of the Zodiac before Virgo? And what if you were born late in September—are you more Libra than Virgo? Many people born at the edge, or cusp, of a sign have great difficulty determining exactly what sign they are. If you are one of these people, here's how you can figure it out, once and for all.

Consult the cusp table on the facing page, then locate the year of your birth. The table will tell you the precise days on which the Sun entered and left your sign for the year of your birth. In that way you can determine if you are a true Virgo—or whether you are a Leo or Libra—according to the variations in cusp dates from year to year (see also page 17).

If you were born either at the beginning or the end of Virgo, yours is a lifetime reflecting a process of subtle transformation. Your life on earth will symbolize a significant change in consciousness, for you are either about to enter a whole new way of living or are leaving one behind.

If you were born at the beginning of Virgo, you may want to read the horoscope book for Leo as well as Virgo, for Leo holds the key to much of your complexity of spirit, reflects certain hidden weaknesses and compulsions, and your unspoken wishes. Your tie to Leo symbolizes your romantic dilemma and your unusual—often timid—approach to love. You are afraid of taking a gamble and letting everything ride on your emotions. You may resist giving up the rational, logical, clear-minded approach to life, but you can never really flee from your need for love.

You symbolize the warmth and fullness of a late summer day, a natural ripeness and maturity that is mellow and comfortable to be near.

If you were born sometime after the third week of September, you may want to read the horoscope book for Libra as well as Virgo, for Libra is possibly your greatest asset. Though you are eager to get involved with another person and you crave warmth and companionship, you may hover between stiff mental analyzing and poetic romanticism. You have that Garboesque desire to be secluded, untouched—yet you want to share your life with another. You are a blend of monastic, spartan simplicity with grace,

4

harmony, and gentle beauty. You combine a profound power to sift, purify, and analyze with the sensibilities of recognizing what is right, beautiful, and just. You can be picky and faultfinding, inconsistent and small, needing someone desperately but rejecting the one you love most. Yet you are fundamentally a thoughtful, loving person with the sincere wish to serve and make someone happy.

Developing your capacity to share will aid you in joint financial ventures, bring your values into harmony, and create a balance in your life.

THE CUSPS OF VIRGO

DATES SUN ENTERS VIRGO (LEAVES LEO)

August 23 every year from 1900 to 2000, except for the following:

August 22				August 24
1960	1980	1992	1903	1919
64	84	93	07	23
68	88	96	11	27
72	89	97	15	
76				

DATES SUN LEAVES VIRGO (ENTERS LIBRA)

September 23 every year from 1900 to 2000, except for the following:

September 22				September 24
1948	1968	1981	1992	1903
52	72	84	93	07
56	76	85	96	
60	77	88	97	
64	80	89		

THE ASCENDANT: VIRGO RISING

Could you be a "double" Virgo? That is, could you have Virgo as your Rising sign as well as your Sun sign? The tables on pages 8–9 will tell you Virgos what your Rising sign happens to be. Just find the hour of your birth, then find the day of your birth, and you will see which sign of the Zodiac is your Ascendant, as the Rising sign is called. The Ascendant is called that because it is the sign rising on the eastern horizon at the time of your birth. For a more detailed discussion of the Rising sign and the twelve houses of the Zodiac, see pages 17–20.

The Ascendant, or Rising sign, is placed on the 1st house in a horoscope, of which there are twelve houses. The first house represents your response to the environment—your unique response. Call it identity, personality, ego, self-image, facade, come-on, body-mind-spirit—whatever term best conveys to you the meaning of the you that acts and reacts in the world. It is a you that is always changing, discovering a new you. Your identity started with birth and early environment, over which you had little conscious control, and continues to experience, to adjust, to express itself. The 1st house also represents how others see you. Has anyone ever guessed your sign to be your Rising sign? People may respond to that personality, that facade, that body type governed by your Rising sign.

Your Ascendant, or Rising sign, modifies your basic Sun sign personality, and it affects the way you act out the daily predictions for your Sun sign. If your Rising sign is indeed Virgo, what follows is a description of its effects on your horoscope. If your Rising sign is not Virgo, but some other sign of the Zodiac, you may wish to read the horoscope book for that sign as well.

With Virgo on the Ascendant, that is, in the 1st house, your ruling planet Mercury is therefore in the 1st house. You are known for your inquiring mind, sharp verbal skills, love of learning. Your very appearance—fastidious, lean, efficient—gives the impression of a great openness to the environment; you seem to pick up clues from the most cursory observations, filing them away for future use. Mercury in the 1st house, however, can make you too self-absorbed with your own interests and thus lacking in sympathy for other people. And your quick wit and loquaciousness, if put into the service of petty gossip, could make you a tattletale who gets in trouble with people.

Your striving for perfection and your liking for details make many of you with Virgo Rising master craftspeople. That talent is not restricted to the arts of fashioning jewelry, fabric, metals, food, and other materials of the earth, though you are an earth sign. Mercury, your ruler, gives you a quicksilver mind, and you excel in the mathematical and scientific arts. Your memory is splendid, too. If you are not actually working in complex systems such as computer science or engineering, your talent for organizing details and structuring information certainly benefits your work life, as well as your social life.

Your love of learning has few boundaries, and no limits if you with Virgo Rising consistently apply yourself. You are equally attracted to medicine, art, science, literature. Your analytical mind, scalpel-sharp, can cut through a mass of confused information, selecting the wheat from the chaff, so to speak. Certainly you can distinguish theory from practice, and you know when and how to use the practice. Many of you, for that reason, and also because you like to help people, find yourselves in health and medical service careers.

Personally you are interested in the perfection of the body and the purity of the mind. Translated into everyday activities, you could be very fussy about your diet, your clothes, your living quarters, your spiritual beliefs, your exercise programs. It is not unlikely that you experiment often in these areas, and sometimes you're accused of being a faddist. If you cannot change where you live frequently, you'll be satisfied to take a few long trips and many short ones during your lifetime.

Basically you are patient, methodical, ambitious sometimes in a secretive way. Your caustic wit, which strips the facade from people, hides your true feelings and melancholy of spirit. As much as you like to quip in bright dialogue with others, you like to be alone. Even your travels can be solitary adventures; you commune with the nature around you. Some of these experiences may motivate an in-depth study of art and literature at some point in your lifetime. And you may well become a writer, merging a myriad of facts with personal data you are loathe to talk about.

For you with Virgo Rising, two key words are self-mastery and service. But while you are perfecting your knowledge and skills in serving others, don't forget your own needs. Develop compassion for yourself.

RISING SIGNS FOR VIRGO

Hour of Birth*	Day of Birth		
	August 22–26	August 27–31	September 1–5
Midnight	Gemini	Gemini	Cancer
1 AM	Cancer	Cancer	Cancer
2 AM	Cancer	Cancer	Cancer
3 AM	Leo	Leo	Leo
4 AM	Leo	Leo	Leo
5 AM	Leo	Leo; Virgo 8/31	Virgo
6 AM	Virgo	Virgo	Virgo
7 AM	Virgo	Virgo	Virgo
8 AM	Libra	Libra	Libra
9 AM	Libra	Libra	Libra
10 AM	Libra	Libra; Scorpio 8/29	Scorpio
11 AM	Scorpio	Scorpio	Scorpio
Noon	Scorpio	Scorpio	Scorpio
1 PM	Sagittarius	Sagittarius	Sagittarius
2 PM	Sagittarius	Sagittarius	Sagittarius
3 PM	Sagittarius	Capricorn	Capricorn
4 PM	Capricorn	Capricorn	Capricorn
5 PM	Capricorn; Aquarius 8/26	Aquarius	Aquarius
6 PM	Aquarius	Aquarius	Aquarius; Pisces 9/3
7 PM	Pisces	Pisces	Pisces
8 PM	Aries	Aries	Aries
9 PM	Aries; Taurus 8/26	Taurus	Taurus
10 PM	Taurus	Taurus	Taurus; Gemini 9/3
11 PM	Gemini	Gemini	Gemini

*Hour of birth given here is for Standard Time in any time zone. If your hour of birth was recorded in Daylight Saving Time, subtract one hour from it and consult that hour in the table above. For example, if you were born at 7 PM D.S.T., see 6 PM above.

Hour of Birth*	Day of Birth		
	September 6–10	September 11–15	September 16–24
Midnight	Cancer	Cancer	Cancer
1 AM	Cancer	Cancer	Cancer; Leo 9/21
2 AM	Leo	Leo	Leo
3 AM	Leo	Leo	Leo
4 AM	Leo	Leo; Virgo 9/14	Virgo
5 AM	Virgo	Virgo	Virgo
6 AM	Virgo	Virgo	Virgo; Libra 9/21
7 AM	Libra	Libra	Libra
8 AM	Libra	Libra	Libra
9 AM	Libra	Scorpio	Scorpio
10 AM	Scorpio	Scorpio	Scorpio
11 AM	Scorpio	Scorpio	Scorpio; Sagittarius 9/21
Noon	Sagittarius	Sagittarius	Sagittarius
1 PM	Sagittarius	Sagittarius	Sagittarius
2 PM	Sagittarius	Capricorn	Capricorn
3 PM	Capricorn	Capricorn	Capricorn
4 PM	Capricorn; Aquarius 9/10	Aquarius	Aquarius
5 PM	Aquarius	Aquarius	Pisces
6 PM	Pisces	Pisces	Pisces; Aries 9/21
7 PM	Aries	Aries	Aries
8 PM	Aries; Taurus 9/10	Taurus	Taurus
9 PM	Taurus	Taurus	Gemini
10 PM	Gemini	Gemini	Gemini
11 PM	Gemini	Gemini	Cancer

*See note on facing page.

THE PLACE OF ASTROLOGY IN TODAY'S WORLD

Does astrology have a place in the fast-moving, ultra-scientific world we live in today? Can it be justified in a sophisticated society whose outriders are already preparing to step off the moon into the deep space of the planets themselves? Or is it just a hangover of ancient superstition, a psychological dummy for neurotics and dreamers of every historical age?

These are the kind of questions that any inquiring person can be expected to ask when they approach a subject like astrology which goes beyond, but never excludes, the materialistic side of life.

The simple, single answer is that astrology works. It works for many millions of people in the western world alone. In the United States there are 10 million followers and in Europe, an estimated 25 million. America has more than 4000 practicing astrologers, Europe nearly three times as many. Even down-under Australia has its hundreds of thousands of adherents. In the eastern countries, astrology has enormous followings, again, because it has been proved to work. In India, for example, brides and grooms for centuries have been chosen on the basis of their astrological compatibility.

Astrology today is more vital than ever before, more practicable because all over the world the media devotes much space and time to it, more valid because science itself is confirming the precepts of astrological knowledge with every new exciting step. The ordinary person who daily applies astrology intelligently does not have to wonder whether it is true nor believe in it blindly. He can see it working for himself. And, if he can use it—and this book is designed to help the reader to do just that—he can make living a far richer experience, and become a more developed personality and a better person.

Astrology and Relationships

Astrology is the science of relationships. It is not just a study of planetary influences on man and his environment. It is the study of man himself.

We are at the center of our personal universe, of all our relationships. And our happiness or sadness depends on how we act, how we relate to the people and things that surround us. The emotions that we generate have a distinct effect—for better or worse—on the world around us. Our friends and our enemies will confirm this. Just look in the mirror the next time you are angry. In other words, each of us is a kind of sun or planet or star radiating our feelings on the environment around us. Our influence on our personal universe, whether loving, helpful, or destructive, varies with our changing moods, expressed through our individual character.

Our personal "radiations" are potent in the way they affect our moods and our ability to control them. But we usually are able to throw off our emotion in some sort of action—we have a good cry, walk it off, or tell someone our troubles—before it can build up too far and make us physically ill. Astrology helps us to understand the universal forces working on us, and through this understanding, we can become more properly adjusted to our surroundings so that we find ourselves coping where others may flounder.

The Challenge of Love

The challenge of love lies in recognizing the difference between infatuation, emotion, sex, and, sometimes, the intentional deceit of the other person. Mankind, with its record of broken marriages, despair, and disillusionment, is obviously not very good at making these distinctions.

Can astrology help?

Yes. In the same way that advance knowledge can usually help in any human situation. And there is probably no situation as human, as poignant, as pathetic and universal, as the failure of man's love.

Love, of course, is not just between man and woman. It involves love of children, parents, home, and friends. But the big problems usually involve the choice of partner.

Astrology has established degrees of compatibility that exist between people born under the various signs of the Zodiac. Because people are individuals, there are numerous variations and modifications. So the astrologer, when approached on mate and marriage matters, makes allowances for them. But the fact remains that some groups of people are suited for each other and some are not, and astrology has expressed this in terms of characteristics we all can study and use as a personal guide.

No matter how much enjoyment and pleasure we find in the different aspects of each other's character, if it is not an overall compatibility, the chances of our finding fulfillment or enduring happiness in each other are pretty hopeless. And astrology can help us to find someone compatible.

Astrology and Science

Closely related to our emotions is the "other side" of our personal universe, our physical welfare. Our body, of course, is largely influenced by things around us over which we have very little control. The phone rings, we hear it. The train runs late. We snag our stocking or cut our face shaving. Our body is under a constant bombardment of events that influence our daily lives to varying degrees.

The question that arises from all this is, what makes each of us act so that we have to involve other people and keep the ball of activity and evolution rolling? This is the question that both science and astrology are involved with. The scientists have attacked it from different angles: anthropology, the study of human evolution as body, mind and response to environment; anatomy, the study of bodily structure; psychology, the science of the human mind; and so on. These studies have produced very impressive classifications and valuable information, but because the approach to the problem is fragmented, so is the result. They remain "branches" of science. Science generally studies effects. It keeps turning up wonderful answers but no lasting solutions. Astrology, on the other hand, approaches the question from the broader viewpoint. Astrology began its inquiry with the totality of human experience and saw it as an effect. It then looked to find the cause, or at least the prime movers, and during thousands of years of observation of man and his *universal* environment came up with the extraordinary principle of planetary influence—or astrology, which, from the Greek, means the science of the stars.

Modern science, as we shall see, has confirmed much of astrology's foundations—most of it unintentionally, some of it reluctantly, but still, indisputably.

It is not difficult to imagine that there must be a connection between outer space and Earth. Even today, scientists are not too sure how our Earth was created, but it is generally agreed that it is only a tiny part of the universe. And as a part of the universe, people on Earth see and feel the influence of heavenly bodies in almost every aspect of our existence. There is no doubt that the Sun has the greatest influence on life on this planet. Without it there would be no life, for without it there would be no warmth, no division into day and night, no cycles of time or season at all. This is clear and easy to see. The influence of the Moon, on the other hand, is more subtle, though no less definite.

There are many ways in which the influence of the Moon manifests itself here on Earth, both on human and animal life. It is a well-known fact, for instance, that the large movements of water on our planet—that is the ebb and flow of the tides—are caused by the Moon's gravitational pull. Since this is so, it follows that these water movements do not occur only in the oceans, but that all bodies of water are affected, even down to the tiniest puddle.

The human body, too, which consists of about 70 percent water, falls within the scope of this lunar influence. For example the menstrual cycle of most women corresponds to the 28-day lunar month; the period of pregnancy in humans is 273 days, or equal to nine lunar months. Similarly, many illnesses reach a crisis at the change of the Moon, and statistics in many countries have shown that the crime rate is highest at the time of the Full Moon. Even human sexual desire has been associated with the phases of the Moon. But it is in the movement of the tides that we get the clearest demonstration of planetary influence, which leads to the irresistible correspondence between the so-called metaphysical and the physical.

Tide tables are prepared years in advance by calculating the future positions of the Moon. Science has known for a long time that the Moon is the main cause of tidal action. But only in the last few years has it begun to realize the possible extent of this influence on mankind. To begin with, the ocean tides do not rise and fall as we might imagine from our personal observations of them. The Moon as it orbits around Earth sets up a circular wave of attraction which pulls the oceans of the world after it, broadly in an east to west direction. This influence is like a phantom wave crest, a loop of power stretching from pole to pole which passes over and around the Earth like an invisible shadow. It travels with equal effect across the land masses and, as scientists were recently amazed to observe, caused oysters placed in the dark in the middle of the United States where there is no sea to open their shells to receive the nonexistent tide. If the land-locked oysters react to this invisible signal, what effect does it have on us who not so long ago in evolutionary time came out of the sea and still have its salt in our blood and sweat?

Less well known is the fact that the Moon is also the primary force behind the circulation of blood in human beings and animals, and the movement of sap in trees and plants. Agriculturists have established that the Moon has a distinct influence on crops, which explains why for centuries people have planted according to Moon cycles. The habits of many animals, too, are directed by the movement of the Moon. Migratory birds, for instance, depart only at or near the time of the Full Moon. And certain sea creatures, eels in particular, move only in accordance with certain phases of the Moon.

Know Thyself—Why?

In today's fast-changing world, everyone still longs to know what the future holds. It is the one thing that everyone has in common: rich and poor, famous and infamous, all are deeply concerned about tomorrow.

But the key to the future, as every historian knows, lies in the past. This is as true of individual people as it is of nations. You cannot understand your future without first understanding your past, which is simply another way of saying that you must first of all know yourself.

The motto "know thyself" seems obvious enough nowadays, but it was originally put forward as the foundation of wisdom by the ancient Greek philosophers. It was then adopted by the "mystery religions" of the ancient Middle East, Greece, Rome, and is still used in all genuine schools of mind training or mystical discipline, both in those of the East, based on yoga, and those of the West. So it is universally accepted now, and has been through the ages.

But how do you go about discovering what sort of person you are? The first step is usually classification into some sort of system of types. Astrology did this long before the birth of Christ. Psychology has also done it. So has modern medicine, in its way.

One system classifies people according to the source of the impulses they respond to most readily: the muscles, leading to direct bodily action; the digestive organs, resulting in emotion; or the brain and nerves, giving rise to thinking. Another such system says that character is determined by the endocrine glands, and gives us such labels as "pituitary," "thyroid," and "hyperthyroid" types. These different systems are neither contradictory nor mutually exclusive. In fact, they are very often different ways of saying the same thing.

Very popular, useful classifications were devised by Carl Jung, the eminent disciple of Freud. Jung observed among the different faculties of the mind, four which have a predominant influence on character. These four faculties exist in all of us without exception, but not in perfect balance. So when we say, for instance, that someone is a "thinking type," it means that in any situation he or she tries to be rational. Emotion, which may be the opposite of thinking, will be his or her weakest function. This thinking type can be sensible and reasonable, or calculating and unsympathetic. The emotional type, on the other hand, can often be recognized by exaggerated language—everything is either marvelous or terrible—and in extreme cases they even invent dramas and quarrels out of nothing just to make life more interesting.

The other two faculties are intuition and physical sensation. The sensation type does not only care for food and drink, nice clothes and furniture; he or she is also interested in all forms of physical experience. Many scientists are sensation types as are athletes and nature-lovers. Like sensation, intuition is a form of perception and we all possess it. But it works through that part of the mind which is not under conscious control—consequently it sees meanings and connections which are not obvious to thought or emotion. Inventors and original thinkers are always intuitive, but so, too, are superstitious people who see meanings where none exist.

Thus, sensation tells us what is going on in the world, feeling (that is, emotion) tells us how important it is to ourselves, thinking enables us to interpret it and work out what we should do about it, and intuition tells us what it means to ourselves and others. All four faculties are essential, and all are present in every one of us. But some people are guided chiefly by one, others by another. In addition, Jung also observed a division of the human personality into the extrovert and the introvert, which cuts across these four types.

A disadvantage of all these systems of classification is that one cannot tell very easily where to place oneself. Some people are reluctant to admit that they act to please their emotions. So they deceive themselves for years by trying to belong to whichever type they think is the "best." Of course, there is no best; each has its faults and each has its good points.

The advantage of the signs of the Zodiac is that they simplify classification. Not only that, but your date of birth is personal—it is unarguably yours. What better way to know yourself than by going back as far as possible to the very moment of your birth? And this is precisely what your horoscope is all about, as we shall see in the next section.

WHAT IS A HOROSCOPE?

If you had been able to take a picture of the skies at the moment of your birth, that photograph would be your horoscope. Lacking such a snapshot, it is still possible to recreate the picture—and this is at the basis of the astrologer's art. In other words, your horoscope is a representation of the skies with the planets in the exact positions they occupied at the time you were born.

The year of birth tells an astrologer the positions of the distant, slow-moving planets Jupiter, Saturn, Uranus, Neptune, and Pluto. The month of birth indicates the Sun sign, or birth sign as it is commonly called, as well as indicating the positions of the rapidly moving planets Venus, Mercury, and Mars. The day and time of birth will locate the position of our Moon. And the moment—the exact hour and minute—of birth determines the houses through what is called the Ascendant, or Rising sign.

With this information the astrologer consults various tables to calculate the specific positions of the Sun, Moon, and other planets relative to your birthplace at the moment you were born. Then he or she locates them by means of the Zodiac.

The Zodiac

The Zodiac is a band of stars (constellations) in the skies, centered on the Sun's apparent path around the Earth, and is divided into twelve equal segments, or signs. What we are actually dividing up is the Earth's path around the Sun. But from our point of view here on Earth, it seems as if the Sun is making a great circle around our planet in the sky, so we say it is the Sun's apparent path. This twelvefold division, the Zodiac, is a reference system for the astrologer. At any given moment the planets—and in astrology both the Sun and Moon are considered to be planets—can all be located at a specific point along this path.

Now where in all this are you, the subject of the horoscope? Your character is largely determined by the sign the Sun is in. So that is where the astrologer looks first in your horoscope, at your Sun sign.

The Sun Sign and the Cusp

There are twelve signs in the Zodiac, and the Sun spends approximately one month in each sign. But because of the motion of the Earth around the Sun—the Sun's apparent motion—the dates when the Sun enters and leaves each sign may change from year to year. Some people born near the cusp, or edge, of a sign have difficulty determining which is their Sun sign. But in this book a Table of Cusps is provided for the years 1900 to 2000 (page 5) so you can find out what your true Sun sign is.

Here are the twelve signs of the Zodiac, their ancient zodiacal symbol, and the dates when the Sun enters and leaves each sign for the year 1999. Remember, these dates may change from year to year.

ARIES	Ram	March 20–April 20
TAURUS	Bull	April 20–May 21
GEMINI	Twins	May 21–June 21
CANCER	Crab	June 21–July 23
LEO	Lion	July 23–August 23
VIRGO	Virgin	August 23–September 23
LIBRA	Scales	September 23–October 23
SCORPIO	Scorpion	October 23–November 22
SAGITTARIUS	Archer	November 22–December 22
CAPRICORN	Sea Goat	December 22–January 20
AQUARIUS	Water Bearer	January 20–February 18
PISCES	Fish	February 18–March 20

It is possible to draw significant conclusions and make meaningful predictions based simply on the Sun sign of a person. There are many people who have been amazed at the accuracy of the description of their own character based only on the Sun sign. But an astrologer needs more information than just your Sun sign to interpret the photograph that is your horoscope.

The Rising Sign and the Zodiacal Houses

An astrologer needs the exact time and place of your birth in order to construct and interpret your horoscope. The illustration on the next page shows the flat chart, or natural wheel, an astrologer uses. Note the inner circle of the wheel labeled 1 through 12. These 12 divisions are known as the houses of the Zodiac.

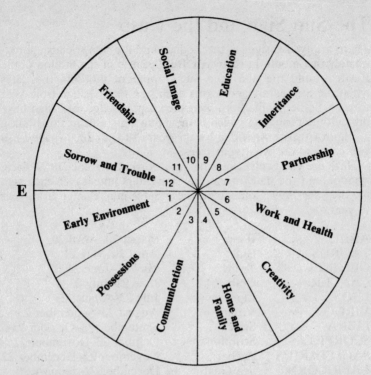

The 1st house always starts from the position marked E, which corresponds to the eastern horizon. The rest of the houses 2 through 12 follow around in a "counterclockwise" direction. The point where each house starts is known as a cusp, or edge.

The cusp, or edge, of the 1st house (point E) is where an astrologer would place your Rising sign, the Ascendant. And, as already noted, the exact time of your birth determines your Rising sign. Let's see how this works.

As the Earth rotates on its axis once every 24 hours, each one of the twelve signs of the Zodiac appears to be "rising" on the horizon, with a new one appearing about every 2 hours. Actually it is the turning of the Earth that exposes each sign to view, but in our astrological work we are discussing apparent motion. This Rising sign marks the Ascendant, and it colors the whole orientation of a horoscope. It indicates the sign governing the 1st house of the chart, and will thus determine which signs will govern all the other houses.

To visualize this idea, imagine two color wheels with twelve divisions superimposed upon each other. For just as the Zodiac is divided into twelve constellations that we identify as the signs, another twelvefold division is used to denote the houses. Now imagine one wheel (the signs) moving slowly while the other wheel (the houses) remains still. This analogy may help you see how the signs keep shifting the "color" of the houses as the Rising sign continues to change every two hours. To simplify things, a Table of Rising Signs has been provided (pages 8–9) for your specific Sun sign.

Once your Rising sign has been placed on the cusp of the 1st house, the signs that govern the rest of the 11 houses can be placed on the chart. In any individual's horoscope the signs do not necessarily correspond with the houses. For example, it could be that a sign covers part of two adjacent houses. It is the interpretation of such variations in an individual's horoscope that marks the professional astrologer.

But to gain a workable understanding of astrology, it is not necessary to go into great detail. In fact, we just need a description of the houses and their meanings, as is shown in the illustration above and in the table below.

THE 12 HOUSES OF THE ZODIAC

1st	Individuality, body appearance, general outlook on life	Personality house
2nd	Finance, possessions, ethical principles, gain or loss	Money house
3rd	Relatives, communication, short journeys, writing, education	Relatives house
4th	Family and home, parental ties, land and property, security	Home house
5th	Pleasure, children, creativity, entertainment, risk	Pleasure house
6th	Health, harvest, hygiene, work and service, employees	Health house
7th	Marriage and divorce, the law, partnerships and alliances	Marriage house
8th	Inheritance, secret deals, sex, death, regeneration	Inheritance house
9th	Travel, sports, study, philosophy and religion	Travel house
10th	Career, social standing, success and honor	Business house
11th	Friendship, social life, hopes and wishes	Friends house
12th	Troubles, illness, secret enemies, hidden agendas	Trouble house

The Planets in the Houses

An astrologer, knowing the exact time and place of your birth, will use tables of planetary motion in order to locate the planets in your horoscope chart. He or she will determine which planet or planets are in which sign and in which house. It is not uncommon, in an individual's horoscope, for there to be two or more planets in the same sign and in the same house.

The characteristics of the planets modify the influence of the Sun according to their natures and strengths.

Sun: Source of life. Basic temperament according to the Sun sign. The conscious will. Human potential.

Moon: Emotions. Moods. Customs. Habits. Changeable. Adaptive. Nurturing.

Mercury: Communication. Intellect. Reasoning power. Curiosity. Short travels.

Venus: Love. Delight. Charm. Harmony. Balance. Art. Beautiful possessions.

Mars: Energy. Initiative. War. Anger. Adventure. Courage. Daring. Impulse.

Jupiter: Luck. Optimism. Generous. Expansive. Opportunities. Protection.

Saturn: Pessimism. Privation. Obstacles. Delay. Hard work. Research. Lasting rewards after long struggle.

Uranus: Fashion. Electricity. Revolution. Independence. Freedom. Sudden changes. Modern science.

Neptune: Sensationalism. Theater. Dreams. Inspiration. Illusion. Deception.

Pluto: Creation and destruction. Total transformation. Lust for power. Strong obsessions.

Superimpose the characteristics of the planets on the functions of the house in which they appear. Express the result through the character of the Sun sign, and you will get the basic idea.

Of course, many other considerations have been taken into account in producing the carefully worked out predictions in this book: the aspects of the planets to each other; their strength according to position and sign; whether they are in a house of exaltation or decline; whether they are natural enemies or not; whether a planet occupies its own sign; the position of a planet in relation to its own house or sign; whether the sign is male or female; whether the sign is a fire, earth, water, or air sign. These are only a few of the colors on the astrologer's pallet which he or she must mix with the inspiration of the artist and the accuracy of the mathematician.

How To Use These Predictions

A person reading the predictions in this book should understand that they are produced from the daily position of the planets for a group of people and are not, of course, individually specialized. To get the full benefit of them our readers should relate the predictions to their own character and circumstances, coordinate them, and draw their own conclusions from them.

If you are a serious observer of your own life, you should find a definite pattern emerging that will be a helpful and reliable guide.

The point is that we always retain our free will. The stars indicate certain directional tendencies but we are not compelled to follow. We can do or not do, and wisdom must make the choice.

We all have our good and bad days. Sometimes they extend into cycles of weeks. It is therefore advisable to study daily predictions in a span ranging from the day before to several days ahead.

Daily predictions should be taken very generally. The word "difficult" does not necessarily indicate a whole day of obstruction or inconvenience. It is a warning to you to be cautious. Your caution will often see you around the difficulty before you are involved. This is the correct use of astrology.

In another section (pages 78–84), detailed information is given about the influence of the Moon as it passes through each of the twelve signs of the Zodiac. There are instructions on how to use the Moon Tables (pages 85–92), which provide Moon Sign Dates throughout the year as well as the Moon's role in health and daily affairs. This information should be used in conjunction with the daily forecasts to give a fuller picture of the astrological trends.

HISTORY OF ASTROLOGY

The origins of astrology have been lost far back in history, but we do know that reference is made to it as far back as the first written records of the human race. It is not hard to see why. Even in primitive times, people must have looked for an explanation for the various happenings in their lives. They must have wanted to know why people were different from one another. And in their search they turned to the regular movements of the Sun, Moon, and stars to see if they could provide an answer.

It is interesting to note that as soon as man learned to use his tools in any type of design, or his mind in any kind of calculation, he turned his attention to the heavens. Ancient cave dwellings reveal dim crescents and circles representative of the Sun and Moon, rulers of day and night. Mesopotamia and the civilization of Chaldea, in itself the foundation of those of Babylonia and Assyria, show a complete picture of astronomical observation and well-developed astrological interpretation.

Humanity has a natural instinct for order. The study of anthropology reveals that primitive people—even as far back as prehistoric times—were striving to achieve a certain order in their lives. They tried to organize the apparent chaos of the universe. They had the desire to attach meaning to things. This demand for order has persisted throughout the history of man. So that observing the regularity of the heavenly bodies made it logical that primitive peoples should turn heavenward in their search for an understanding of the world in which they found themselves so random and alone.

And they did find a significance in the movements of the stars. Shepherds tending their flocks, for instance, observed that when the cluster of stars now known as the constellation Aries was in sight, it was the time of fertility and they associated it with the Ram. And they noticed that the growth of plants and plant life corresponded with different phases of the Moon, so that certain times were favorable for the planting of crops, and other times were not. In this way, there grew up a tradition of seasons and causes connected with the passage of the Sun through the twelve signs of the Zodiac.

Astrology was valued so highly that the king was kept informed of the daily and monthly changes in the heavenly bodies, and the results of astrological studies regarding events of the future. Head astrologers were clearly men of great rank and position, and the office was said to be a hereditary one.

Omens were taken, not only from eclipses and conjunctions of the Moon or Sun with one of the planets, but also from storms and earthquakes. In the eastern civilizations, particularly, the reverence inspired by astrology appears to have remained unbroken since the very earliest days. In ancient China, astrology, astronomy, and religion went hand in hand. The astrologer, who was also an astronomer, was part of the official government service and had his own corner in the Imperial Palace. The duties of the Imperial astrologer, whose office was one of the most important in the land, were clearly defined, as this extract from early records shows:

> This exalted gentleman must concern himself with the stars in the heavens, keeping a record of the changes and movements of the Planets, the Sun and the Moon, in order to examine the movements of the terrestrial world with the object of prognosticating good and bad fortune. He divides the territories of the nine regions of the empire in accordance with their dependence on particular celestial bodies. All the fiefs and principalities are connected with the stars and from this their prosperity or misfortune should be ascertained. He makes prognostications according to the twelve years of the Jupiter cycle of good and evil of the terrestrial world. From the colors of the five kinds of clouds, he determines the coming of floods or droughts, abundance or famine. From the twelve winds, he draws conclusions about the state of harmony of heaven and earth, and takes note of good and bad signs that result from their accord or disaccord. In general, he concerns himself with five kinds of phenomena so as to warn the Emperor to come to the aid of the government and to allow for variations in the ceremonies according to their circumstances.

The Chinese were also keen observers of the fixed stars, giving them such unusual names as Ghost Vehicle, Sun of Imperial Concubine, Imperial Prince, Pivot of Heaven, Twinkling Brilliance, Weaving Girl. But, great astrologers though they may have been, the Chinese lacked one aspect of mathematics that the Greeks applied to astrology—deductive geometry. Deductive geometry was the basis of much classical astrology in and after the time of the Greeks, and this explains the different methods of prognostication used in the East and West.

Down through the ages the astrologer's art has depended, not so much on the uncovering of new facts, though this is important, as on the interpretation of the facts already known. This is the essence of the astrologer's skill.

But why should the signs of the Zodiac have any effect at all on the formation of human character? It is easy to see why people thought they did, and even now we constantly use astrological expressions in our everyday speech. The thoughts of "lucky star," "ill-fated," "star-crossed," "mooning around," are interwoven into the very structure of our language.

Wherever the concept of the Zodiac is understood and used, it could well appear to have an influence on the human character. Does this mean, then, that the human race, in whose civilization the idea of the twelve signs of the Zodiac has long been embedded, is divided into only twelve types? Can we honestly believe that it is really as simple as that? If so, there must be pretty wide ranges of variation within each type. And if, to explain the variation, we call in heredity and environment, experiences in early childhood, the thyroid and other glands, and also the four functions of the mind together with extroversion and introversion, then one begins to wonder if the original classification was worth making at all. No sensible person believes that his favorite system explains everything. But even so, he will not find the system much use at all if it does not even save him the trouble of bothering with the others.

In the same way, if we were to put every person under only one sign of the Zodiac, the system becomes too rigid and unlike life. Besides, it was never intended to be used like that. It may be convenient to have only twelve types, but we know that in practice there is every possible gradation between aggressiveness and timidity, or between conscientiousness and laziness. How, then, do we account for this?

A person born under any given Sun sign can be mainly influenced by one or two of the other signs that appear in their individual horoscope. For instance, famous persons born under the sign of Gemini include Henry VIII, whom nothing and no one could have induced to abdicate, and Edward VIII, who did just that. Obviously, then, the sign Gemini does not fully explain the complete character of either of them.

Again, under the opposite sign, Sagittarius, were both Stalin, who was totally consumed with the notion of power, and Charles V, who freely gave up an empire because he preferred to go into a monastery. And we find under Scorpio many uncompromising characters such as Luther, de Gaulle, Indira Gandhi, and Montgomery, but also Petain, a successful commander whose name later became synonymous with collaboration.

A single sign is therefore obviously inadequate to explain the differences between people; it can only explain resemblances, such as the combativeness of the Scorpio group, or the far-reaching devotion of Charles V and Stalin to their respective ideals—the Christian heaven and the Communist utopia.

But very few people have only one sign in their horoscope chart. In addition to the month of birth, the day and, even more, the hour to the nearest minute if possible, ought to be considered. Without this, it is impossible to have an actual horoscope, for the word horoscope literally means "a consideration of the hour."

The month of birth tells you only which sign of the Zodiac was occupied by the Sun. The day and hour tell you what sign was occupied by the Moon. And the minute tells you which sign was rising on the eastern horizon. This is called the Ascendant, and, as some astrologers believe, it is supposed to be the most important thing in the whole horoscope.

The Sun is said to signify one's heart, that is to say, one's deepest desires and inmost nature. This is quite different from the Moon, which signifies one's superficial way of behaving. When the ancient Romans referred to the Emperor Augustus as a Capricorn, they meant that he had the Moon in Capricorn. Or, to take another example, a modern astrologer would call Disraeli a Scorpion because he had Scorpio Rising, but most people would call him Sagittarius because he had the Sun there. The Romans would have called him Leo because his Moon was in Leo.

So if one does not seem to fit one's birth month, it is always worthwhile reading the other signs, for one may have been born at a time when any of them were rising or occupied by the Moon. It also seems to be the case that the influence of the Sun develops as life goes on, so that the month of birth is easier to guess in people over the age of forty. The young are supposed to be influenced mainly by their Ascendant, the Rising sign, which characterizes the body and physical personality as a whole.

It is nonsense to assume that all people born at a certain time will exhibit the same characteristics, or that they will even behave in the same manner. It is quite obvious that, from the very moment of its birth, a child is subject to the effects of its environment, and that this in turn will influence its character and heritage to a decisive extent. Also to be taken into account are education and economic conditions, which play a very important part in the formation of one's character as well.

People have, in general, certain character traits and qualities which, according to their environment, develop in either a positive or a negative manner. Therefore, selfishness (inherent selfishness, that is) might emerge as unselfishness; kindness and consideration as cruelty and lack of consideration toward others. In the same way, a naturally constructive person may, through frustration, become destructive, and so on. The latent characteristics with which people are born can, therefore, through environment and good or bad training, become something that would appear to be its opposite, and so give the lie to the astrologer's description of their character. But this is not the case. The true character is still there, but it is buried deep beneath these external superficialities.

Careful study of the character traits of various signs of the Zodiac are of immeasurable help, and can render beneficial service to the intelligent person. Undoubtedly, the reader will already have discovered that, while he is able to get on very well with some people, he just "cannot stand" others. The causes sometimes seem inexplicable. At times there is intense dislike, at other times immediate sympathy. And there is, too, the phenomenon of love at first sight, which is also apparently inexplicable. People appear to be either sympathetic or unsympathetic toward each other for no apparent reason.

Now if we look at this in the light of the Zodiac, we find that people born under different signs are either compatible or incompatible with each other. In other words, there are good and bad interrelating factors among the various signs. This does not, of course, mean that humanity can be divided into groups of hostile camps. It would be quite wrong to be hostile or indifferent toward people who happen to be born under an incompatible sign. There is no reason why everybody should not, or cannot, learn to control and adjust their feelings and actions, especially after they are aware of the positive qualities of other people by studying their character analyses, among other things.

Every person born under a certain sign has both positive and negative qualities, which are developed more or less according to our free will. Nobody is entirely good or entirely bad, and it is up to each of us to learn to control ourselves on the one hand and at the same time to endeavor to learn about ourselves and others.

It cannot be emphasized often enough that it is free will that determines whether we will make really good use of our talents and abilities. Using our free will, we can either overcome our failings or allow them to rule us. Our free will enables us to exert sufficient willpower to control our failings so that they do not harm ourselves or others.

Astrology can reveal our inclinations and tendencies. Astrology can tell us about ourselves so that we are able to use our free will to overcome our shortcomings. In this way astrology helps us do our best to become needed and valuable members of society as well as helpmates to our family and our friends. Astrology also can save us a great deal of unhappiness and remorse.

Yet it may seem absurd that an ancient philosophy could be a prop to modern men and women. But below the materialistic surface of modern life, there are hidden streams of feeling and thought. Symbology is reappearing as a study worthy of the scholar; the psychosomatic factor in illness has passed from the writings of the crank to those of the specialist; spiritual healing in all its forms is no longer a pious hope but an accepted phenomenon. And it is into this context that we consider astrology, in the sense that it is an analysis of human types.

Astrology and medicine had a long journey together, and only parted company a couple of centuries ago. There still remain in medical language such astrological terms as "saturnine," "choleric," and "mercurial," used in the diagnosis of physical tendencies. The herbalist, for long the handyman of the medical profession, has been dominated by astrology since the days of the Greeks. Certain herbs traditionally respond to certain planetary influences, and diseases must therefore be treated to ensure harmony between the medicine and the disease.

But the stars are expected to foretell and not only to diagnose.

Astrological forecasting has been remarkably accurate, but often it is wide of the mark. The brave person who cares to predict world events takes dangerous chances. Individual forecasting is less clear cut; it can be a help or a disillusionment. Then we come to the nagging question: if it is possible to foreknow, is it right to foretell? This is a point of ethics on which it is hard to pronounce judgment. The doctor faces the same dilemma if he finds that symptoms of a mortal disease are present in his patient and that he can only prognosticate a steady decline. How much to tell an individual in a crisis is a problem that has perplexed many distinguished scholars. Honest and conscientious astrologers in this modern world, where so many people are seeking guidance, face the same problem.

Five hundred years ago it was customary to call in a learned man who was an astrologer who was probably also a doctor and a philosopher. By his knowledge of astrology, his study of planetary influences, he felt himself qualified to guide those in distress. The world has moved forward at a fantastic rate since then, and yet people are still uncertain of themselves. At first sight it seems fantastic in the light of modern thinking that they turn to the most ancient of all studies, and get someone to calculate a horoscope for them. But is it *really* so fantastic if you take a second look? For astrology is concerned with tomorrow, with survival. And in a world such as ours, tomorrow and survival are the keywords for the twenty-first century.

ASTROLOGICAL BRIDGE TO THE 21st CENTURY

As the last decade of the twentieth century comes to a close, planetary aspects for its final years connect you with the future. Major changes completed in 1995 and 1996 give rise to new planetary cycles that form the bridge to the twenty-first century and new horizons. The years 1996 through 1999 and into the year 2000 reveal hidden paths and personal hints for achieving your potential, for making the most of your message from the planets.

All the major planets begin new cycles in the late 1990s. Jupiter, planet of good fortune, transits four zodiacal signs from 1996 through 1999 and goes through a complete cycle in each of the elements earth, air, fire, and water. Jupiter is in Capricorn, then in Aquarius, next in Pisces, and finally in Aries as the century turns. With the dawning of the twenty-first century, each new yearly Jupiter cycle follows the natural progression of the Zodiac, from Aries in 2000, then Taurus in 2001, next Gemini in 2002, and so on through Pisces in 2011. The beneficent planet Jupiter promotes your professional and educational goals while urging informed choice and deliberation. Jupiter sharpens your focus and hones your skills. And while safeguarding good luck, Jupiter can turn unusual risks into achievable aims.

Saturn, planet of reason and responsibility, has begun a new cycle in the spring of 1996 when it entered fiery Aries. Saturn in Aries through March 1999 heightens a longing for independence. Your movements are freed from everyday restrictions, allowing you to travel, to explore, to act on a variety of choices. With Saturn in Aries you get set to blaze a new trail. Saturn enters earthy Taurus in March 1999 for a three-year stay over the turn of the century into the year 2002. Saturn in Taurus inspires industry and affection. Practicality, perseverance, and planning can reverse setbacks and minimize risk. Saturn in Taurus lends beauty, order, and structure to your life. In order to take advantage of opportunity through responsibility, to persevere against adversity, look to beautiful planet Saturn.

Uranus, planet of innovation and surprise, started an important new cycle in January of 1996. At that time Uranus entered its natural home in airy Aquarius. Uranus in Aquarius into the year 2003 has a profound effect on your personality and the lens through which you see the world. A basic change in the way you project yourself is just one impact of Uranus in Aquarius. More significantly, a whole new consciousness is evolving. Winds of change blowing your way emphasize movement and freedom. Uranus in Aquarius poses involvement in the larger community beyond self, family, friends, lovers, associates. Radical ideas and progressive thought signal a journey of liberation. As the century turns, follow Uranus on the path of humanitarianism. While you carve a prestigious niche in public life, while you preach social reform and justice, you will be striving to make the world a better place for all people.

Neptune, planet of vision and mystery, is in earthy Capricorn until late 1998. Neptune in Capricorn excites creativity while restraining fanciful thinking. Wise use of resources helps you build persona and prestige. Then Neptune enters airy Aquarius during November 1998 and is there into the year 2011. Neptune in Aquarius, the sign of the Water Bearer, represents two sides of the coin of wisdom: inspiration and reason. Here Neptune stirs powerful currents bearing a rich and varied harvest, the fertile breeding ground for idealistic aims and practical considerations. Neptune's fine intuition tunes in to your dreams, your imagination, your spirituality. You can never turn your back on the mysteries of life. Uranus and Neptune, the planets of enlightenment and renewed idealism both in the sign of Aquarius, give you glimpses into the future, letting you peek through secret doorways into the twenty-first century.

Pluto, planet of beginnings and endings, has completed one cycle of growth November 1995 in the sign of Scorpio. Pluto in Scorpio marked a long period of experimentation and rejuvenation. Then Pluto entered the fiery sign of Sagittarius on November 10, 1995 and is there into the year 2007. Pluto in Sagittarius during its long stay of twelve years can create significant change. The great power of Pluto in Sagittarius may already be starting its transformation of your character and lifestyle. Pluto in Sagittarius takes you on a new journey of exploration and learning. The awakening you experience on intellectual and artistic levels heralds a new cycle of growth. Uncompromising Pluto, seeker of truth, challenges your identity, persona, and self-expression. Uncovering the real you, Pluto holds the key to understanding and meaningful communication. Pluto in Sagittarius can be the guiding light illuminating the first decade of the twenty-first century. Good luck is riding on the waves of change.

THE SIGNS OF THE ZODIAC

Dominant Characteristics

Aries: March 21–April 20

The Positive Side of Aries

The Aries has many positive points to his character. People born under this first sign of the Zodiac are often quite strong and enthusiastic. On the whole, they are forward-looking people who are not easily discouraged by temporary setbacks. They know what they want out of life and they go out after it. Their personalities are strong. Others are usually quite impressed by the Ram's way of doing things. Quite often they are sources of inspiration for others traveling the same route. Aries men and women have a special zest for life that can be contagious; for others, they are a fine example of how life should be lived.

The Aries person usually has a quick and active mind. He is imaginative and inventive. He enjoys keeping busy and active. He generally gets along well with all kinds of people. He is interested in mankind, as a whole. He likes to be challenged. Some would say he thrives on opposition, for it is when he is set against that he often does his best. Getting over or around obstacles is a challenge he generally enjoys. All in all, Aries is quite positive and young-thinking. He likes to keep abreast of new things that are happening in the world. Aries are often fond of speed. They like things to be done quickly, and this sometimes aggravates their slower colleagues and associates.

The Aries man or woman always seems to remain young. Their whole approach to life is youthful and optimistic. They never say die, no matter what the odds. They may have an occasional setback, but it is not long before they are back on their feet again.

The Negative Side of Aries

Everybody has his less positive qualities—and Aries is no exception. Sometimes the Aries man or woman is not very tactful in communicating with others; in his hurry to get things done he is apt to be a little callous or inconsiderate. Sensitive people are likely to find him somewhat sharp-tongued in some situations. Often in his eagerness to get the show on the road, he misses the mark altogether and cannot achieve his aims.

At times Aries can be too impulsive. He can occasionally be stubborn and refuse to listen to reason. If things do not move quickly enough to suit the Aries man or woman, he or she is apt to become rather nervous or irritable. The uncultivated Aries is not unfamiliar with moments of doubt and fear. He is capable of being destructive if he does not get his way. He can overcome some of his emotional problems by steadily trying to express himself as he really is, but this requires effort.

Taurus: April 21–May 20

The Positive Side of Taurus

The Taurus person is known for his ability to concentrate and for his tenacity. These are perhaps his strongest qualities. The Taurus man or woman generally has very little trouble in getting along with others; it's his nature to be helpful toward people in need. He can always be depended on by his friends, especially those in trouble.

Taurus generally achieves what he wants through his ability to persevere. He never leaves anything unfinished but works on something until it has been completed. People can usually take him at his word; he is honest and forthright in most of his dealings. The Taurus person has a good chance to make a success of his life because of his many positive qualities. The Taurus who aims high seldom falls short of his mark. He learns well by experience. He is thorough and does not believe in shortcuts of any kind. The Bull's thoroughness pays off in the end, for through his deliberateness he learns how to rely on himself and what he has learned. The Taurus person tries to get along with others, as a rule. He is not overly critical and likes people to be themselves. He is a tolerant person and enjoys peace and harmony—especially in his home life.

Taurus is usually cautious in all that he does. He is not a person who believes in taking unnecessary risks. Before adopting any one line of action, he will weigh all of the pros and cons. The Taurus person is steadfast. Once his mind is made up it seldom changes. The person born under this sign usually is a good family person—reliable and loving.

The Negative Side of Taurus

Sometimes the Taurus man or woman is a bit too stubborn. He won't listen to other points of view if his mind is set on something. To others, this can be quite annoying. Taurus also does not like to be told what to do. He becomes rather angry if others think him not too bright. He does not like to be told he is wrong, even when he is. He dislikes being contradicted.

Some people who are born under this sign are very suspicious of others—even of those persons close to them. They find it difficult to trust people fully. They are often afraid of being deceived or taken advantage of. The Bull often finds it difficult to forget or forgive. His love of material things sometimes makes him rather avaricious and petty.

Gemini: May 21–June 20

The Positive Side of Gemini

The person born under this sign of the Heavenly Twins is usually quite bright and quick-witted. Some of them are capable of doing many different things. The Gemini person very often has many different interests. He keeps an open mind and is always anxious to learn new things.

Gemini is often an analytical person. He is a person who enjoys making use of his intellect. He is governed more by his mind than by his emotions. He is a person who is not confined to one view; he can often understand both sides to a problem or question. He knows how to reason, how to make rapid decisions if need be.

He is an adaptable person and can make himself at home almost anywhere. There are all kinds of situations he can adapt to. He is a person who seldom doubts himself; he is sure of his talents and his ability to think and reason. Gemini is generally most satisfied

when he is in a situation where he can make use of his intellect. Never short of imagination, he often has strong talents for invention. He is rather a modern person when it comes to life; Gemini almost always moves along with the times—perhaps that is why he remains so youthful throughout most of his life.

Literature and art appeal to the person born under this sign. Creativity in almost any form will interest and intrigue the Gemini man or woman.

The Gemini is often quite charming. A good talker, he often is the center of attraction at any gathering. People find it easy to like a person born under this sign because he can appear easygoing and usually has a good sense of humor.

The Negative Side of Gemini

Sometimes the Gemini person tries to do too many things at one time—and as a result, winds up finishing nothing. Some Twins are easily distracted and find it rather difficult to concentrate on one thing for too long a time. Sometimes they give in to trifling fancies and find it rather boring to become too serious about any one thing. Some of them are never dependable, no matter what they promise.

Although the Gemini man or woman often appears to be well-versed on many subjects, this is sometimes just a veneer. His knowledge may be only superficial, but because he speaks so well he gives people the impression of erudition. Some Geminis are sharp-tongued and inconsiderate; they think only of themselves and their own pleasure.

Cancer: June 21–July 20

The Positive Side of Cancer

The Moon Child's most positive point is his understanding nature. On the whole, he is a loving and sympathetic person. He would never go out of his way to hurt anyone. The Cancer man or woman is often very kind and tender; they give what they can to others. They hate to see others suffering and will do what they can to help someone in less fortunate circumstances than themselves. They are often very concerned about the world. Their interest in people generally goes beyond that of just their own families and close friends; they have a deep sense of community and respect humanitarian values. The Moon Child means what he says, as a rule; he is honest about his feelings.

The Cancer man or woman is a person who knows the art of patience. When something seems difficult, he is willing to wait until the situation becomes manageable again. He is a person who knows how to bide his time. Cancer knows how to concentrate on one thing at a time. When he has made his mind up he generally sticks with what he does, seeing it through to the end.

Cancer is a person who loves his home. He enjoys being surrounded by familiar things and the people he loves. Of all the signs, Cancer is the most maternal. Even the men born under this sign often have a motherly or protective quality about them. They like to take care of people in their family—to see that they are well loved and well provided for. They are usually loyal and faithful. Family ties mean a lot to the Cancer man or woman. Parents and in-laws are respected and loved. Young Cancer responds very well to adults who show faith in him. The Moon Child has a strong sense of tradition. He is very sensitive to the moods of others.

The Negative Side of Cancer

Sometimes Cancer finds it rather hard to face life. It becomes too much for him. He can be a little timid and retiring, when things don't go too well. When unfortunate things happen, he is apt to just shrug and say, "Whatever will be will be." He can be fatalistic to a fault. The uncultivated Cancer is a bit lazy. He doesn't have very much ambition. Anything that seems a bit difficult he'll gladly leave to others. He may be lacking in initiative. Too sensitive, when he feels he's been injured, he'll crawl back into his shell and nurse his imaginary wounds. The immature Moon Child often is given to crying when the smallest thing goes wrong.

Some Cancers find it difficult to enjoy themselves in environments outside their homes. They make heavy demands on others, and need to be constantly reassured that they are loved. Lacking such reassurance, they may resort to sulking in silence.

Leo: July 21–August 21

The Positive Side of Leo

Often Leos make good leaders. They seem to be good organizers and administrators. Usually they are quite popular with others. Whatever group it is that they belong to, the Leo man or woman is almost sure to be or become the leader. Loyalty, one of the Lion's noblest traits, enables him or her to maintain this leadership position.

Leo is generous most of the time. It is his best characteristic. He or she likes to give gifts and presents. In making others happy, the Leo person becomes happy himself. He likes to splurge when spending money on others. In some instances it may seem that the Lion's generosity knows no boundaries. A hospitable person, the Leo man or woman is very fond of welcoming people to his house and entertaining them. He is never short of company.

Leo has plenty of energy and drive. He enjoys working toward some specific goal. When he applies himself correctly, he gets what he wants most often. The Leo person is almost never unsure of himself. He has plenty of confidence and aplomb. He is a person who is direct in almost everything he does. He has a quick mind and can make a decision in a very short time.

He usually sets a good example for others because of his ambitious manner and positive ways. He knows how to stick to something once he's started. Although Leo may be good at making a joke, he is not superficial or glib. He is a loving person, kind and thoughtful.

There is generally nothing small or petty about the Leo man or woman. He does what he can for those who are deserving. He is a person others can rely upon at all times. He means what he says. An honest person, generally speaking, he is a friend who is valued and sought out.

The Negative Side of Leo

Leo, however, does have his faults. At times, he can be just a bit too arrogant. He thinks that no one deserves a leadership position except him. Only he is capable of doing things well. His opinion of himself is often much too high. Because of his conceit, he is

sometimes rather unpopular with a good many people. Some Leos are too materialistic; they can only think in terms of money and profit.

Some Leos enjoy lording it over others—at home or at their place of business. What is more, they feel they have the right to. Egocentric to an impossible degree, this sort of Leo cares little about how others think or feel. He can be rude and cutting.

Virgo: August 22–September 22

The Positive Side of Virgo

The person born under the sign of Virgo is generally a busy person. He knows how to arrange and organize things. He is a good planner. Above all, he is practical and is not afraid of hard work.

Often called the sign of the Harvester, Virgo knows how to attain what he desires. He sticks with something until it is finished. He never shirks his duties, and can always be depended upon. The Virgo person can be thoroughly trusted at all times.

The man or woman born under this sign tries to do everything to perfection. He doesn't believe in doing anything halfway. He always aims for the top. He is the sort of a person who is always learning and constantly striving to better himself—not because he wants more money or glory, but because it gives him a feeling of accomplishment.

The Virgo man or woman is a very observant person. He is sensitive to how others feel, and can see things below the surface of a situation. He usually puts this talent to constructive use.

It is not difficult for the Virgo to be open and earnest. He believes in putting his cards on the table. He is never secretive or underhanded. He's as good as his word. The Virgo person is generally plainspoken and down to earth. He has no trouble in expressing himself.

The Virgo person likes to keep up to date on new developments in his particular field. Well-informed, generally, he sometimes has a keen interest in the arts or literature. What he knows, he knows well. His ability to use his critical faculties is well-developed and sometimes startles others because of its accuracy.

Virgos adhere to a moderate way of life; they avoid excesses. Virgo is a responsible person and enjoys being of service.

The Negative Side of Virgo

Sometimes a Virgo person is too critical. He thinks that only he can do something the way it should be done. Whatever anyone else does is inferior. He can be rather annoying in the way he quibbles over insignificant details. In telling others how things should be done, he can be rather tactless and mean.

Some Virgos seem rather emotionless and cool. They feel emotional involvement is beneath them. They are sometimes too tidy, too neat. With money they can be rather miserly. Some Virgos try to force their opinions and ideas on others.

Libra: September 23–October 22

The Positive Side of Libra

Libras love harmony. It is one of their most outstanding character traits. They are interested in achieving balance; they admire beauty and grace in things as well as in people. Generally speaking, they are kind and considerate people. Libras are usually very sympathetic. They go out of their way not to hurt another person's feelings. They are outgoing and do what they can to help those in need.

People born under the sign of Libra almost always make good friends. They are loyal and amiable. They enjoy the company of others. Many of them are rather moderate in their views; they believe in keeping an open mind, however, and weighing both sides of an issue fairly before making a decision.

Alert and intelligent, Libra, often known as the Lawgiver, is always fair-minded and tries to put himself in the position of the other person. They are against injustice; quite often they take up for the underdog. In most of their social dealings, they try to be tactful and kind. They dislike discord and bickering, and most Libras strive for peace and harmony in all their relationships.

The Libra man or woman has a keen sense of beauty. They appreciate handsome furnishings and clothes. Many of them are artistically inclined. Their taste is usually impeccable. They know how to use color. Their homes are almost always attractively arranged and inviting. They enjoy entertaining people and see to it that their guests always feel at home and welcome.

Libra gets along with almost everyone. He is well-liked and socially much in demand.

The Negative Side of Libra

Some people born under this sign tend to be rather insincere. So eager are they to achieve harmony in all relationships that they will even go so far as to lie. Many of them are escapists. They find facing the truth an ordeal and prefer living in a world of make-believe.

In a serious argument, some Libras give in rather easily even when they know they are right. Arguing, even about something they believe in, is too unsettling for some of them.

Libras sometimes care too much for material things. They enjoy possessions and luxuries. Some are vain and tend to be jealous.

Scorpio: October 23–November 22

The Positive Side of Scorpio

The Scorpio man or woman generally knows what he or she wants out of life. He is a determined person. He sees something through to the end. Scorpio is quite sincere, and seldom says anything he doesn't mean. When he sets a goal for himself he tries to go about achieving it in a very direct way.

The Scorpion is brave and courageous. They are not afraid of hard work. Obstacles do not frighten them. They forge ahead until they achieve what they set out for. The Scorpio man or woman has a strong will.

Although Scorpio may seem rather fixed and determined, inside he is often quite tender and loving. He can care very much for others. He believes in sincerity in all relationships. His feelings about someone tend to last; they are profound and not superficial.

The Scorpio person is someone who adheres to his principles no matter what happens. He will not be deterred from a path he believes to be right.

Because of his many positive strengths, the Scorpion can often achieve happiness for himself and for those that he loves.

He is a constructive person by nature. He often has a deep understanding of people and of life, in general. He is perceptive and unafraid. Obstacles often seem to spur him on. He is a positive person who enjoys winning. He has many strengths and resources; challenge of any sort often brings out the best in him.

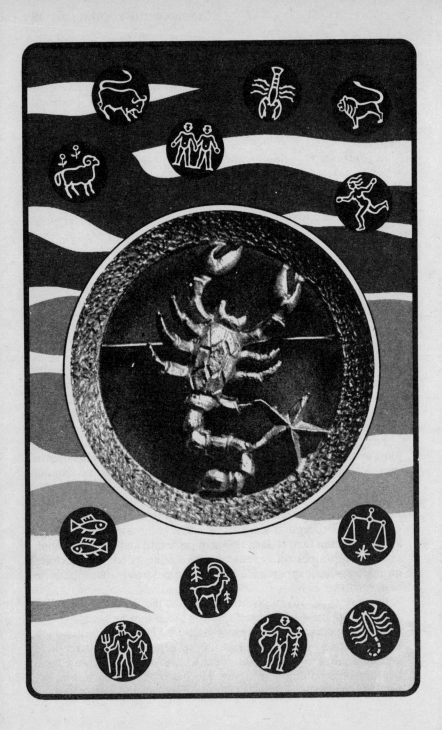

The Negative Side of Scorpio

The Scorpio person is sometimes hypersensitive. Often he imagines injury when there is none. He feels that others do not bother to recognize him for his true worth. Sometimes he is given to excessive boasting in order to compensate for what he feels is neglect.

Scorpio can be proud, arrogant, and competitive. They can be sly when they put their minds to it and they enjoy outwitting persons or institutions noted for their cleverness.

Their tactics for getting what they want are sometimes devious and ruthless. They don't care too much about what others may think. If they feel others have done them an injustice, they will do their best to seek revenge. The Scorpion often has a sudden, violent temper; and this person's interest in sex is sometimes quite unbalanced or excessive.

Sagittarius: November 23–December 20

The Positive Side of Sagittarius

People born under this sign are honest and forthright. Their approach to life is earnest and open. Sagittarius is often quite adult in his way of seeing things. They are broad-minded and tolerant people. When dealing with others the person born under the sign of the Archer is almost always open and forthright. He doesn't believe in deceit or pretension. His standards are high. People who associate with Sagittarius generally admire and respect his tolerant viewpoint.

The Archer trusts others easily and expects them to trust him. He is never suspicious or envious and almost always thinks well of others. People always enjoy his company because he is so friendly and easygoing. The Sagittarius man or woman is often good-humored. He can always be depended upon by his friends, family, and co-workers.

The person born under this sign of the Zodiac likes a good joke every now and then. Sagittarius is eager for fun and laughs, which makes him very popular with others.

A lively person, he enjoys sports and outdoor life. The Archer is fond of animals. Intelligent and interesting, he can begin an

animated conversation with ease. He likes exchanging ideas and discussing various views.

He is not selfish or proud. If someone proposes an idea or plan that is better than his, he will immediately adopt it. Imaginative yet practical, he knows how to put ideas into practice.

The Archer enjoys sport and games, and it doesn't matter if he wins or loses. He is a forgiving person, and never sulks over something that has not worked out in his favor.

He is seldom critical, and is almost always generous.

The Negative Side of Sagittarius

Some Sagittarius are restless. They take foolish risks and seldom learn from the mistakes they make. They don't have heads for money and are often mismanaging their finances. Some of them devote much of their time to gambling.

Some are too outspoken and tactless, always putting their feet in their mouths. They hurt others carelessly by being honest at the wrong time. Sometimes they make promises which they don't keep. They don't stick close enough to their plans and go from one failure to another. They are undisciplined and waste a lot of energy.

Capricorn: December 21–January 19

The Positive Side of Capricorn

The person born under the sign of Capricorn, known variously as the Mountain Goat or Sea Goat, is usually very stable and patient. He sticks to whatever tasks he has and sees them through. He can always be relied upon and he is not averse to work.

An honest person, Capricorn is generally serious about whatever he does. He does not take his duties lightly. He is a practical person and believes in keeping his feet on the ground.

Quite often the person born under this sign is ambitious and knows how to get what he wants out of life. The Goat forges ahead and never gives up his goal. When he is determined about something, he almost always wins. He is a good worker—a hard worker. Although things may not come easy to him, he will not complain, but continue working until his chores are finished.

He is usually good at business matters and knows the value of money. He is not a spendthrift and knows how to put something away for a rainy day; he dislikes waste and unnecessary loss.

Capricorn knows how to make use of his self-control. He can apply himself to almost anything once he puts his mind to it. His ability to concentrate sometimes astounds others. He is diligent and does well when involved in detail work.

The Capricorn man or woman is charitable, generally speaking, and will do what is possible to help others less fortunate. As a friend, he is loyal and trustworthy. He never shirks his duties or responsibilities. He is self-reliant and never expects too much of the other fellow. He does what he can on his own. If someone does him a good turn, then he will do his best to return the favor.

The Negative Side of Capricorn

Like everyone, Capricorn, too, has faults. At times, the Goat can be overcritical of others. He expects others to live up to his own high standards. He thinks highly of himself and tends to look down on others.

His interest in material things may be exaggerated. The Capricorn man or woman thinks too much about getting on in the world and having something to show for it. He may even be a little greedy.

He sometimes thinks he knows what's best for everyone. He is too bossy. He is always trying to organize and correct others. He may be a little narrow in his thinking.

Aquarius: January 20–February 18

The Positive Side of Aquarius

The Aquarius man or woman is usually very honest and forthright. These are his two greatest qualities. His standards for himself are generally very high. He can always be relied upon by others. His word is his bond.

Aquarius is perhaps the most tolerant of all the Zodiac personalities. He respects other people's beliefs and feels that everyone is entitled to his own approach to life.

He would never do anything to injure another's feelings. He is never unkind or cruel. Always considerate of others, the Water

Bearer is always willing to help a person in need. He feels a very strong tie between himself and all the other members of mankind.

The person born under this sign, called the Water Bearer, is almost always an individualist. He does not believe in teaming up with the masses, but prefers going his own way. His ideas about life and mankind are often quite advanced. There is a saying to the effect that the average Aquarius is fifty years ahead of his time.

Aquarius is community-minded. The problems of the world concern him greatly. He is interested in helping others no matter what part of the globe they live in. He is truly a humanitarian sort. He likes to be of service to others.

Giving, considerate, and without prejudice, Aquarius have no trouble getting along with others.

The Negative Side of Aquarius

Aquarius may be too much of a dreamer. He makes plans but seldom carries them out. He is rather unrealistic. His imagination has a tendency to run away with him. Because many of his plans are impractical, he is always in some sort of a dither.

Others may not approve of him at all times because of his unconventional behavior. He may be a bit eccentric. Sometimes he is so busy with his own thoughts that he loses touch with the realities of existence.

Some Aquarius feel they are more clever and intelligent than others. They seldom admit to their own faults, even when they are quite apparent. Some become rather fanatic in their views. Their criticism of others is sometimes destructive and negative.

Pisces: February 19–March 20

The Positive Side of Pisces

Known as the sign of the Fishes, Pisces has a sympathetic nature. Kindly, he is often dedicated in the way he goes about helping others. The sick and the troubled often turn to him for advice and assistance. Possessing keen intuition, Pisces can easily understand people's deepest problems.

He is very broad-minded and does not criticize others for their faults. He knows how to accept people for what they are. On the whole, he is a trustworthy and earnest person. He is loyal to his friends and will do what he can to help them in time of need. Generous and good-natured, he is a lover of peace; he is often willing to help others solve their differences. People who have taken a wrong turn in life often interest him and he will do what he can to persuade them to rehabilitate themselves.

He has a strong intuitive sense and most of the time he knows how to make it work for him. Pisces is unusually perceptive and often knows what is bothering someone before that person, himself, is aware of it. The Pisces man or woman is an idealistic person, basically, and is interested in making the world a better place in which to live. Pisces believes that everyone should help each other. He is willing to do more than his share in order to achieve cooperation with others.

The person born under this sign often is talented in music or art. He is a receptive person; he is able to take the ups and downs of life with philosophic calm.

The Negative Side of Pisces

Some Pisces are often depressed; their outlook on life is rather glum. They may feel that they have been given a bad deal in life and that others are always taking unfair advantage of them. Pisces sometimes feel that the world is a cold and cruel place. The Fishes can be easily discouraged. The Pisces man or woman may even withdraw from the harshness of reality into a secret shell of his own where he dreams and idles away a good deal of his time.

Pisces can be lazy. He lets things happen without giving the least bit of resistance. He drifts along, whether on the high road or on the low. He can be lacking in willpower.

Some Pisces people seek escape through drugs or alcohol. When temptation comes along they find it hard to resist. In matters of sex, they can be rather permissive.

Sun Sign Personalities

ARIES: Hans Christian Andersen, Pearl Bailey, Marlon Brando, Wernher Von Braun, Charlie Chaplin, Joan Crawford, Da Vinci, Bette Davis, Doris Day, W. C. Fields, Alec Guinness, Adolf Hitler, William Holden, Thomas Jefferson, Nikita Khrushchev, Elton John, Arturo Toscanini, J. P. Morgan, Paul Robeson, Gloria Steinem, Sarah Vaughn, Vincent van Gogh, Tennessee Williams

TAURUS: Fred Astaire, Charlotte Brontë, Carol Burnett, Irving Berlin, Bing Crosby, Salvador Dali, Tchaikovsky, Queen Elizabeth II, Duke Ellington, Ella Fitzgerald, Henry Fonda, Sigmund Freud, Orson Welles, Joe Louis, Lenin, Karl Marx, Golda Meir, Eva Peron, Bertrand Russell, Shakespeare, Kate Smith, Benjamin Spock, Barbra Streisand, Shirley Temple, Harry Truman

GEMINI: Ruth Benedict, Josephine Baker, Rachel Carson, Carlos Chavez, Walt Whitman, Bob Dylan, Ralph Waldo Emerson, Judy Garland, Paul Gauguin, Allen Ginsberg, Benny Goodman, Bob Hope, Burl Ives, John F. Kennedy, Peggy Lee, Marilyn Monroe, Joe Namath, Cole Porter, Laurence Olivier, Harriet Beecher Stowe, Queen Victoria, John Wayne, Frank Lloyd Wright

CANCER: "Dear Abby," Lizzie Borden, David Brinkley, Yul Brynner, Pearl Buck, Marc Chagall, Princess Diana, Babe Didrikson, Mary Baker Eddy, Henry VIII, John Glenn, Ernest Hemingway, Lena Horne, Oscar Hammerstein, Helen Keller, Ann Landers, George Orwell, Nancy Reagan, Rembrandt, Richard Rodgers, Ginger Rogers, Rubens, Jean-Paul Sartre, O. J. Simpson

LEO: Neil Armstrong, James Baldwin, Lucille Ball, Emily Brontë, Wilt Chamberlain, Julia Child, William J. Clinton, Cecil B. De Mille, Ogden Nash, Amelia Earhart, Edna Ferber, Arthur Goldberg, Alfred Hitchcock, Mick Jagger, George Meany, Annie Oakley, George Bernard Shaw, Napoleon, Jacqueline Onassis, Henry Ford, Francis Scott Key, Andy Warhol, Mae West, Orville Wright

VIRGO: Ingrid Bergman, Warren Burger, Maurice Chevalier, Agatha Christie, Sean Connery, Lafayette, Peter Falk, Greta Garbo, Althea Gibson, Arthur Godfrey, Goethe, Buddy Hackett, Michael Jackson, Lyndon Johnson, D. H. Lawrence, Sophia Loren, Grandma Moses, Arnold Palmer, Queen Elizabeth I, Walter Reuther, Peter Sellers, Lily Tomlin, George Wallace

LIBRA: Brigitte Bardot, Art Buchwald, Truman Capote, Dwight D. Eisenhower, William Faulkner, F. Scott Fitzgerald, Gandhi, George Gershwin, Micky Mantle, Helen Hayes, Vladimir Horowitz, Doris Lessing, Martina Navratalova, Eugene O'Neill, Luciano Pavarotti, Emily Post, Eleanor Roosevelt, Bruce Springsteen, Margaret Thatcher, Gore Vidal, Barbara Walters, Oscar Wilde

SCORPIO: Vivien Leigh, Richard Burton, Art Carney, Johnny Carson, Billy Graham, Grace Kelly, Walter Cronkite, Marie Curie, Charles de Gaulle, Linda Evans, Indira Gandhi, Theodore Roosevelt, Rock Hudson, Katherine Hepburn, Robert F. Kennedy, Billie Jean King, Martin Luther, Georgia O'Keeffe, Pablo Picasso, Jonas Salk, Alan Shepard, Robert Louis Stevenson

SAGITTARIUS: Jane Austen, Louisa May Alcott, Woody Allen, Beethoven, Willy Brandt, Mary Martin, William F. Buckley, Maria Callas, Winston Churchill, Noel Coward, Emily Dickinson, Walt Disney, Benjamin Disraeli, James Doolittle, Kirk Douglas, Chet Huntley, Jane Fonda, Chris Evert Lloyd, Margaret Mead, Charles Schulz, John Milton, Frank Sinatra, Steven Spielberg

CAPRICORN: Muhammad Ali, Isaac Asimov, Pablo Casals, Dizzy Dean, Marlene Dietrich, James Farmer, Ava Gardner, Barry Goldwater, Cary Grant, J. Edgar Hoover, Howard Hughes, Joan of Arc, Gypsy Rose Lee, Martin Luther King, Jr., Rudyard Kipling, Mao Tse-tung, Richard Nixon, Gamal Nasser, Louis Pasteur, Albert Schweitzer, Stalin, Benjamin Franklin, Elvis Presley

AQUARIUS: Marian Anderson, Susan B. Anthony, Jack Benny, John Barrymore, Mikhail Baryshnikov, Charles Darwin, Charles Dickens, Thomas Edison, Clark Gable, Jascha Heifetz, Abraham Lincoln, Yehudi Menuhin, Mozart, Jack Nicklaus, Ronald Reagan, Jackie Robinson, Norman Rockwell, Franklin D. Roosevelt, Gertrude Stein, Charles Lindbergh, Margaret Truman

PISCES: Edward Albee, Harry Belafonte, Alexander Graham Bell, Chopin, Adelle Davis, Albert Einstein, Golda Meir, Jackie Gleason, Winslow Homer, Edward M. Kennedy, Victor Hugo, Mike Mansfield, Michelangelo, Edna St. Vincent Millay, Liza Minelli, John Steinbeck, Linus Pauling, Ravel, Renoir, Diana Ross, William Shirer, Elizabeth Taylor, George Washington

The Signs and Their Key Words

		POSITIVE	NEGATIVE
ARIES	self	courage, initiative, pioneer instinct	brash rudeness, selfish impetuosity
TAURUS	money	endurance, loyalty, wealth	obstinacy, gluttony
GEMINI	mind	versatility	capriciousness, unreliability
CANCER	family	sympathy, homing instinct	clannishness, childishness
LEO	children	love, authority, integrity	egotism, force
VIRGO	work	purity, industry, analysis	faultfinding, cynicism
LIBRA	marriage	harmony, justice	vacillation, superficiality
SCORPIO	sex	survival, regeneration	vengeance, discord
SAGITTARIUS	travel	optimism, higher learning	lawlessness
CAPRICORN	career	depth	narrowness, gloom
AQUARIUS	friends	human fellowship, genius	perverse unpredictability
PISCES	confine-ment	spiritual love, universality	diffusion, escapism

The Elements and Qualities of The Signs

Every sign has both an *element* and a *quality* associated with it. The element indicates the basic makeup of the sign, and the quality describes the kind of activity associated with each.

Element	Sign	Quality	Sign
FIRE	ARIES LEO SAGITTARIUS	CARDINAL	ARIES LIBRA CANCER CAPRICORN
EARTH	TAURUS VIRGO CAPRICORN	FIXED	TAURUS LEO SCORPIO AQUARIUS
AIR.........	GEMINI LIBRA AQUARIUS	MUTABLE	GEMINI VIRGO SAGITTARIUS PISCES
WATER....	CANCER SCORPIO PISCES		

Signs can be grouped together according to their element and quality. Signs of the same element share many basic traits in common. They tend to form stable configurations and ultimately harmonious relationships. Signs of the same quality are often less harmonious, but they share many dynamic potentials for growth as well as profound fulfillment.

Further discussion of each of these sign groupings is provided on the following pages.

The Fire Signs

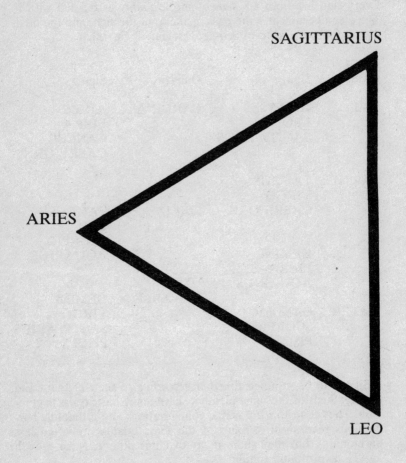

This is the fire group. On the whole these are emotional, volatile types, quick to anger, quick to forgive. They are adventurous, powerful people and act as a source of inspiration for everyone. They spark into action with immediate exuberant impulses. They are intelligent, self-involved, creative, and idealistic. They all share a certain vibrancy and glow that outwardly reflects an inner flame and passion for living.

The Earth Signs

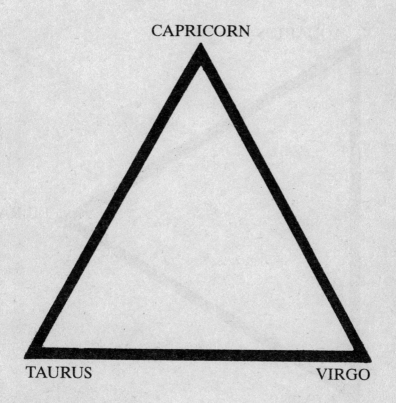

This is the earth group. They are in constant touch with the material world and tend to be conservative. Although they are all capable of spartan self-discipline, they are earthy, sensual people who are stimulated by the tangible, elegant, and luxurious. The thread of their lives is always practical, but they do fantasize and are often attracted to dark, mysterious, emotional people. They are like great cliffs overhanging the sea, forever married to the ocean but always resisting erosion from the dark, emotional forces that thunder at their feet.

The Air Signs

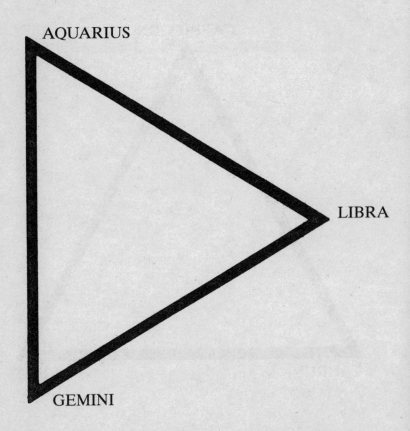

This is the air group. They are light, mental creatures desirous of contact, communication, and relationship. They are involved with people and the forming of ties on many levels. Original thinkers, they are the bearers of human news. Their language is their sense of word, color, style, and beauty. They provide an atmosphere suitable and pleasant for living. They add change and versatility to the scene, and it is through them that we can explore new territory of human intelligence and experience.

The Water Signs

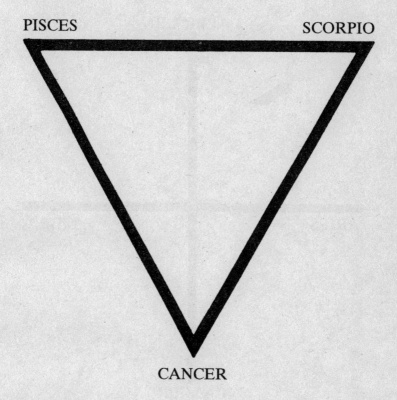

This is the water group. Through the water people, we are all joined together on emotional, nonverbal levels. They are silent, mysterious types whose magic hypnotizes even the most determined realist. They have uncanny perceptions about people and are as rich as the oceans when it comes to feeling, emotion, or imagination. They are sensitive, mystical creatures with memories that go back beyond time. Through water, life is sustained. These people have the potential for the depths of darkness or the heights of mysticism and art.

The Cardinal Signs

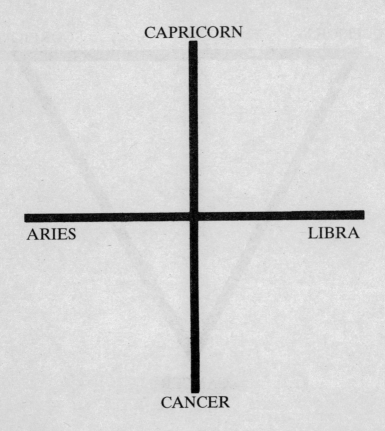

CAPRICORN

ARIES · LIBRA

CANCER

Put together, this is a clear-cut picture of dynamism, activity, tremendous stress, and remarkable achievement. These people know the meaning of great change since their lives are often characterized by significant crises and major successes. This combination is like a simultaneous storm of summer, fall, winter, and spring. The danger is chaotic diffusion of energy; the potential is irrepressible growth and victory.

The Fixed Signs

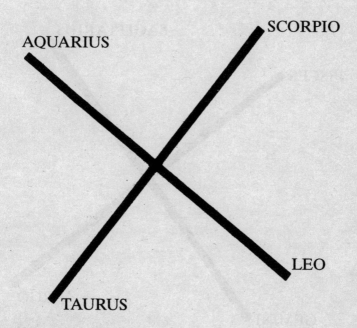

Fixed signs are always establishing themselves in a given place or area of experience. Like explorers who arrive and plant a flag, these people claim a position from which they do not enjoy being deposed. They are staunch, stalwart, upright, trusty, honorable people, although their obstinacy is well-known. Their contribution is fixity, and they are the angels who support our visible world.

The Mutable Signs

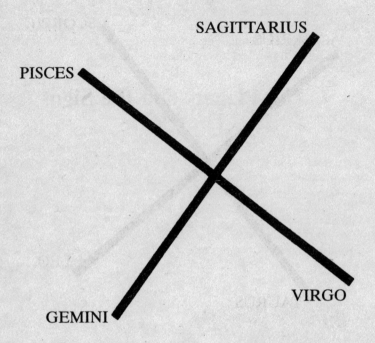

Mutable people are versatile, sensitive, intelligent, nervous, and deeply curious about life. They are the translators of all energy. They often carry out or complete tasks initiated by others. Combinations of these signs have highly developed minds; they are imaginative and jumpy and think and talk a lot. At worst their lives are a Tower of Babel. At best they are adaptable and ready creatures who can assimilate one kind of experience and enjoy it while anticipating coming changes.

THE PLANETS
OF THE SOLAR SYSTEM

This section describes the planets of the solar system. In astrology, both the Sun and the Moon are considered to be planets. Because of the Moon's influence in our day-to-day lives, the Moon is described in a separate section following this one.

The Planets and the Signs They Rule

The signs of the Zodiac are linked to the planets in the following way. Each sign is governed or ruled by one or more planets. No matter where the planets are located in the sky at any given moment, they still rule their respective signs, and when they travel through the signs they rule, they have special dignity and their effects are stronger.

Following is a list of the planets and the signs they rule. After looking at the list, read the definitions of the planets and see if you can determine how the planet ruling *your* Sun sign has affected your life.

SIGNS	RULING PLANETS
Aries	Mars, Pluto
Taurus	Venus
Gemini	Mercury
Cancer	Moon
Leo	Sun
Virgo	Mercury
Libra	Venus
Scorpio	Mars, Pluto
Sagittarius	Jupiter
Capricorn	Saturn
Aquarius	Saturn, Uranus
Pisces	Jupiter, Neptune

Characteristics of the Planets

The following pages give the meaning and characteristics of the planets of the solar system. They all travel around the Sun at different speeds and different distances. Taken with the Sun, they all distribute individual intelligence and ability throughout the entire chart.

The planets modify the influence of the Sun in a chart according to their own particular natures, strengths, and positions. Their positions must be calculated for each year and day, and their function and expression in a horoscope will change as they move from one area of the Zodiac to another.

We start with a description of the sun.

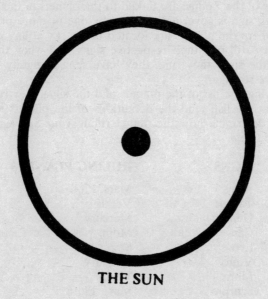

THE SUN

SUN

This is the center of existence. Around this flaming sphere all the planets revolve in endless orbits. Our star is constantly sending out its beams of light and energy without which no life on Earth would be possible. In astrology it symbolizes everything we are trying to become, the center around which all of our activity in life will always revolve. It is the symbol of our basic nature and describes the natural and constant thread that runs through everything that we do from birth to death on this planet.

To early astrologers, the Sun seemed to be another planet because it crossed the heavens every day, just like the rest of the bodies in the sky.

It is the only star near enough to be seen well—it is, in fact, a dwarf star. Approximately 860,000 miles in diameter, it is about ten times as wide as the giant planet Jupiter. The next nearest star is nearly 300,000 times as far away, and if the Sun were located as far away as most of the bright stars, it would be too faint to be seen without a telescope.

Everything in the horoscope ultimately revolves around this singular body. Although other forces may be prominent in the charts of some individuals, still the Sun is the total nucleus of being and symbolizes the complete potential of every human being alive. It is vitality and the life force. Your whole essence comes from the position of the Sun.

You are always trying to express the Sun according to its position by house and sign. Possibility for all development is found in the Sun, and it marks the fundamental character of your personal radiations all around you.

It is the symbol of strength, vigor, wisdom, dignity, ardor, and generosity, and the ability for a person to function as a mature individual. It is also a creative force in society. It is consciousness of the gift of life.

The underdeveloped solar nature is arrogant, pushy, undependable, and proud, and is constantly using force.

MERCURY

Mercury is the planet closest to the Sun. It races around our star, gathering information and translating it to the rest of the system. Mercury represents your capacity to understand the desires of your own will and to translate those desires into action.

In other words it is the planet of mind and the power of communication. Through Mercury we develop an ability to think, write, speak, and observe—to become aware of the world around us. It colors our attitudes and vision of the world, as well as our capacity to communicate our inner responses to the outside world. Some people who have serious disabilities in their power of verbal communication have often wrongly been described as people lacking intelligence.

Although this planet (and its position in the horoscope) indicates your power to communicate your thoughts and perceptions to the world, intelligence is something deeper. Intelligence is distributed throughout all the planets. It is the relationship of the planets to each other that truly describes what we call intelligence. Mercury rules speaking, language, mathematics, draft and design, students, messengers, young people, offices, teachers, and any pursuits where the mind of man has wings.

VENUS

Venus is beauty. It symbolizes the harmony and radiance of a rare and elusive quality: beauty itself. It is refinement and delicacy, softness and charm. In astrology it indicates grace, balance, and the aesthetic sense. Where Venus is we see beauty, a gentle drawing in of energy and the need for satisfaction and completion. It is a special touch that finishes off rough edges. It is sensitivity, and affection, and it is always the place for that other elusive phenomenon: love. Venus describes our sense of what is beautiful and loving. Poorly developed, it is vulgar, tasteless, and self-indulgent. But its ideal is the flame of spiritual love—Aphrodite, goddess of love, and the sweetness and power of personal beauty.

MARS

Mars is raw, crude energy. The planet next to Earth but outward from the Sun is a fiery red sphere that charges through the horoscope with force and fury. It represents the way you reach out for new adventure and new experience. It is energy and drive, initiative, courage, and daring. It is the power to start something and see it through. It can be thoughtless, cruel and wild, angry and hostile, causing cuts, burns, scalds, and wounds. It can stab its way through a chart, or it can be the symbol of healthy spirited adventure, well-channeled constructive power to begin and keep up the drive. If you have trouble starting things, if you lack the get-up-and-go to start the ball rolling, if you lack aggressiveness and self-confidence, chances are there's another planet influencing your Mars. Mars rules soldiers, butchers, surgeons, salesmen—any field that requires daring, bold skill, operational technique, or self-promotion.

JUPITER

This is the largest planet of the solar system. Scientists have recently learned that Jupiter reflects more light than it receives from the Sun. In a sense it is like a star itself. In astrology it rules good luck and good cheer, health, wealth, optimism, happiness, success, and joy. It is the symbol of opportunity and always opens the way for new possibilities in your life. It rules exuberance, enthusiasm, wisdom, knowledge, generosity, and all forms of expansion in general. It rules actors, statesmen, clerics, professional people, religion, publishing, and the distribution of many people over large areas.

Sometimes Jupiter makes you think you deserve everything, and you become sloppy, wasteful, careless and rude, prodigal and lawless, in the illusion that nothing can ever go wrong. Then there is the danger of overconfidence, exaggeration, undependability, and overindulgence.

Jupiter is the minimization of limitation and the emphasis on spirituality and potential. It is the thirst for knowledge and higher learning.

SATURN

Saturn circles our system in dark splendor with its mysterious rings, forcing us to be awakened to whatever we have neglected in the past. It will present real puzzles and problems to be solved, causing delays, obstacles, and hindrances. By doing so, Saturn stirs our own sensitivity to those areas where we are laziest.

Here we must patiently develop *method*, and only through painstaking effort can our ends be achieved. It brings order to a horoscope and imposes reason just where we are feeling least reasonable. By creating limitations and boundary, Saturn shows the consequences of being human and demands that we accept the changing cycles inevitable in human life. Saturn rules time, old age, and sobriety. It can bring depression, gloom, jealousy, and greed, or serious acceptance of responsibilities out of which success will develop. With Saturn there is nothing to do but face facts. It rules laborers, stones, granite, rocks, and crystals of all kinds.

THE OUTER PLANETS:
URANUS, NEPTUNE, PLUTO

Uranus, Neptune, Pluto are the outer planets. They liberate human beings from cultural conditioning, and in that sense are the lawbreakers. In early times it was thought that Saturn was the last planet of the system—the outer limit beyond which we could never go. The discovery of the next three planets ushered in new phases of human history, revolution, and technology.

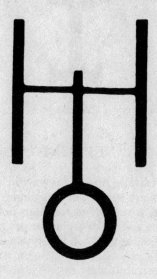

URANUS

Uranus rules unexpected change, upheaval, revolution. It is the symbol of total independence and asserts the freedom of an individual from all restriction and restraint. It is a breakthrough planet and indicates talent, originality, and genius in a horoscope. It usually causes last-minute reversals and changes of plan, unwanted separations, accidents, catastrophes, and eccentric behavior. It can add irrational rebelliousness and perverse bohemianism to a personality or a streak of unaffected brilliance in science and art. It rules technology, aviation, and all forms of electrical and electronic advancement. It governs great leaps forward and topsy-turvy situations, and *always* turns things around at the last minute. Its effects are difficult to predict, since it rules sudden last-minute decisions and events that come like lightning out of the blue.

NEPTUNE

Neptune dissolves existing reality the way the sea erodes the cliffs beside it. Its effects are subtle like the ringing of a buoy's bell in the fog. It suggests a reality higher than definition can usually describe. It awakens a sense of higher responsibility often causing guilt, worry, anxieties, or delusions. Neptune is associated with all forms of escape and can make things seem a certain way so convincingly that you are absolutely sure of something that eventually turns out to be quite different.

It is the planet of illusion and therefore governs the invisible realms that lie beyond our ordinary minds, beyond our simple factual ability to prove what is "real." Treachery, deceit, disillusionment, and disappointment are linked to Neptune. It describes a vague reality that promises eternity and the divine, yet in a manner so complex that we cannot really fathom it at all. At its worst Neptune is a cheap intoxicant; at its best it is the poetry, music, and inspiration of the higher planes of spiritual love. It has dominion over movies, photographs, and much of the arts.

PLUTO

Pluto lies at the outpost of our system and therefore rules finality in a horoscope—the final closing of chapters in your life, the passing of major milestones and points of development from which there is no return. It is a final wipeout, a closeout, an evacuation. It is a distant, subtle but powerful catalyst in all transformations that occur. It creates, destroys, then recreates. Sometimes Pluto starts its influence with a minor event or insignificant incident that might even go unnoticed. Slowly but surely, little by little, everything changes, until at last there has been a total transformation in the area of your life where Pluto has been operating. It rules mass thinking and the trends that society first rejects, then adopts, and finally outgrows.

Pluto rules the dead and the underworld—all the powerful forces of creation and destruction that go on all the time beneath, around, and above us. It can bring a lust for power with strong obsessions.

It is the planet that rules the metamorphosis of the caterpillar into a butterfly, for it symbolizes the capacity to change totally and forever a person's lifestyle, way of thought, and behavior.

THE MOON IN EACH SIGN

The Moon is the nearest planet to the Earth. It exerts more observable influence on us from day to day than any other planet. The effect is very personal, very intimate, and if we are not aware of how it works it can make us quite unstable in our ideas. And the annoying thing is that at these times we often see our own instability but can do nothing about it. A knowledge of what can be expected may help considerably. We can then be prepared to stand strong against the Moon's negative influences and use its positive ones to help us to get ahead. Who has not heard of going with the tide?

The Moon reflects, has no light of its own. It reflects the Sun—the life giver—in the form of vital movement. The Moon controls the tides, the blood rhythm, the movement of sap in trees and plants. Its nature is inconstancy and change so it signifies our moods, our superficial behavior—walking, talking, and especially thinking. Being a true reflector of other forces, the Moon is cold, watery like the surface of a still lake, brilliant and scintillating at times, but easily ruffled and disturbed by the winds of change.

The Moon takes about 27⅓ days to make a complete transit of the Zodiac. It spends just over 2¼ days in each sign. During that time it reflects the qualities, energies, and characteristics of the sign and, to a degree, the planet which rules the sign. When the Moon in its transit occupies a sign incompatible with our own birth sign, we can expect to feel a vague uneasiness, perhaps a touch of irritableness. We should not be discouraged nor let the feeling get us down, or, worse still, allow ourselves to take the discomfort out on others. Try to remember that the Moon has to change signs within 55 hours and, provided you are not physically ill, your mood will probably change with it. It is amazing how frequently depression lifts with the shift in the Moon's position. And, of course, when the Moon is transiting a sign compatible or sympathetic to yours, you will probably feel some sort of stimulation or just be plain happy to be alive.

In the horoscope, the Moon is such a powerful indicator that competent astrologers often use the sign it occupied at birth as the birth sign of the person. This is done particularly when the Sun is on the cusp, or edge, of two signs. Most experienced astrologers, however, coordinate both Sun and Moon signs by reading and confirming from one to the other and secure a far more accurate and personalized analysis.

For these reasons, the Moon tables which follow this section (see pages 86–92) are of great importance to the individual. They show the days and the exact times the Moon will enter each sign of the Zodiac for the year. Remember, you have to adjust the indicated times to local time. The corrections, already calculated for most of the main cities, are at the beginning of the tables. What follows now is a guide to the influences that will be reflected to the Earth by the Moon while it transits each of the twelve signs. The influence is at its peak about 26 hours after the Moon enters a sign. As you read the daily forecast, check the Moon sign for any given day and glance back at this guide.

MOON IN ARIES

This is a time for action, for reaching out beyond the usual self-imposed limitations and faint-hearted cautions. If you have plans in your head or on your desk, put them into practice. New ventures, applications, new jobs, new starts of any kind—all have a good chance of success. This is the period when original and dynamic impulses are being reflected onto Earth. Such energies are extremely vital and favor the pursuit of pleasure and adventure in practically every form. Sick people should feel an improvement. Those who are well will probably find themselves exuding confidence and optimism. People fond of physical exercise should find their bodies growing with tone and well-being. Boldness, strength, determination should characterize most of your activities with a readiness to face up to old challenges. Yesterday's problems may seem petty and exaggerated—so deal with them. Strike out alone. Self-reliance will attract others to you. This is a good time for making friends. Business and marriage partners are more likely to be impressed with the man and woman of action. Opposition will be overcome or thrown aside with much less effort than usual. CAUTION: Be dominant but not domineering.

MOON IN TAURUS

The spontaneous, action-packed person of yesterday gives way to the cautious, diligent, hardworking "thinker." In this period ideas will probably be concentrated on ways of improving finances. A great deal of time may be spent figuring out and going over schemes and plans. It is the right time to be careful with detail.

People will find themselves working longer than usual at their desks. Or devoting more time to serious thought about the future. A strong desire to put order into business and financial arrangements may cause extra work. Loved ones may complain of being neglected and may fail to appreciate that your efforts are for their ultimate benefit. Your desire for system may extend to criticism of arrangements in the home and lead to minor upsets. Health may be affected through overwork. Try to secure a reasonable amount of rest and relaxation, although the tendency will be to "keep going" despite good advice. Work done conscientiously in this period should result in a solid contribution to your future security. CAUTION: Try not to be as serious with people as the work you are engaged in.

MOON IN GEMINI

The humdrum of routine and too much work should suddenly end. You are likely to find yourself in an expansive, quicksilver world of change and self-expression. Urges to write, to paint, to experience the freedom of some sort of artistic outpouring, may be very strong. Take full advantage of them. You may find yourself finishing something you began and put aside long ago. Or embarking on something new which could easily be prompted by a chance meeting, a new acquaintance, or even an advertisement. There may be a yearning for a change of scenery, the feeling to visit another country (not too far away), or at least to get away for a few days. This may result in short, quick journeys. Or, if you are planning a single visit, there may be some unexpected changes or detours on the way. Familiar activities will seem to give little satisfaction unless they contain a fresh element of excitement or expectation. The inclination will be toward untried pursuits, particularly those that allow you to express your inner nature. The accent is on new faces, new places. CAUTION: Do not be too quick to commit yourself emotionally.

MOON IN CANCER

Feelings of uncertainty and vague insecurity are likely to cause problems while the Moon is in Cancer. Thoughts may turn frequently to the warmth of the home and the comfort of loved ones. Nostalgic impulses could cause you to bring out old photographs and letters and reflect on the days when your life seemed to be much more rewarding and less demanding. The love and understanding of parents and family may be important, and, if it is not forthcoming, you may have to fight against bouts of self-pity. The cordiality of friends and the thought of good times with them that are sure to be repeated will help to restore you to a happier frame of mind. The desire to be alone may follow minor setbacks or rebuffs at this time, but solitude is unlikely to help. Better to get on the telephone or visit someone. This period often causes peculiar dreams and upsurges of imaginative thinking which can be helpful to authors of occult and mystical works. Preoccupation with the personal world of simple human needs can overshadow any material strivings. CAUTION: Do not spend too much time thinking—seek the company of loved ones or close friends.

MOON IN LEO

New horizons of exciting and rather extravagant activity open up. This is the time for exhilarating entertainment, glamorous and lavish parties, and expensive shopping sprees. Any merrymaking that relies upon your generosity as a host has every chance of being a spectacular success. You should find yourself right in the center of the fun, either as the life of the party or simply as a person whom happy people like to be with. Romance thrives in this heady atmosphere and friendships are likely to explode unexpectedly into serious attachments. Children and younger people should be attracted to you and you may find yourself organizing a picnic or a visit to a fun-fair, the movies, or the beach. The sunny company and vitality of youthful companions should help you to find some unsuspected energy. In career, you could find an opening for promotion or advancement. This should be the time to make a direct approach. The period favors those engaged in original research. CAUTION: Bask in popularity, not in flattery.

MOON IN VIRGO

Off comes the party cap and out steps the busy, practical worker. He wants to get his personal affairs straight, to rearrange them, if necessary, for more efficiency, so he will have more time for more work. He clears up his correspondence, pays outstanding bills, makes numerous phone calls. He is likely to make inquiries, or sign up for some new insurance and put money into gilt-edged investment. Thoughts probably revolve around the need for future security—to tie up loose ends and clear the decks. There may be a tendency to be "finicky," to interfere in the routine of others, particularly friends and family members. The motive may be a genuine desire to help with suggestions for updating or streamlining their affairs, but these will probably not be welcomed. Sympathy may be felt for less fortunate sections of the community and a flurry of some sort of voluntary service is likely. This may be accompanied by strong feelings of responsibility on several fronts and health may suffer from extra efforts made. CAUTION: Everyone may not want your help or advice.

MOON IN LIBRA

These are days of harmony and agreement and you should find yourself at peace with most others. Relationships tend to be smooth and sweet-flowing. Friends may become closer and bonds deepen in mutual understanding. Hopes will be shared. Progress by cooperation could be the secret of success in every sphere. In business, established partnerships may flourish and new ones get off to a good start. Acquaintances could discover similar interests that lead to congenial discussions and rewarding exchanges of some sort. Love, as a unifying force, reaches its optimum. Marriage partners should find accord. Those who wed at this time face the prospect of a happy union. Cooperation and tolerance are felt to be stronger than dissension and impatience. The argumentative are not quite so loud in their bellowings, nor as inflexible in their attitudes. In the home, there should be a greater recognition of the other point of view and a readiness to put the wishes of the group before selfish insistence. This is a favorable time to join an art group. CAUTION: Do not be too independent—let others help you if they want to.

MOON IN SCORPIO

Driving impulses to make money and to economize are likely to cause upsets all around. No area of expenditure is likely to be spared the ax, including the household budget. This is a time when the desire to cut down on extravagance can become near fanatical. Care must be exercised to try to keep the aim in reasonable perspective. Others may not feel the same urgent need to save and may retaliate. There is a danger that possessions of sentimental value will be sold to realize cash for investment. Buying and selling of stock for quick profit is also likely. The attention turns to organizing, reorganizing, tidying up at home and at work. Neglected jobs could suddenly be done with great bursts of energy. The desire for solitude may intervene. Self-searching thoughts could disturb. The sense of invisible and mysterious energies in play could cause some excitability. The reassurance of loves ones may help. CAUTION: Be kind to the people you love.

MOON IN SAGITTARIUS

These are days when you are likely to be stirred and elevated by discussions and reflections of a religious and philosophical nature. Ideas of faraway places may cause unusual response and excitement. A decision may be made to visit someone overseas, perhaps a person whose influence was important to your earlier character development. There could be a strong resolution to get away from present intellectual patterns, to learn new subjects, and to meet

THE MOON IN EACH SIGN / **83**

more interesting people. The superficial may be rejected in all its forms. An impatience with old ideas and unimaginative contacts could lead to a change of companions and interests. There may be an upsurge of religious feeling and metaphysical inquiry. Even a new insight into the significance of astrology and other occult studies is likely under the curious stimulus of the Moon in Sagittarius. Physically, you may express this need for fundamental change by spending more time outdoors: sports, gardening, long walks appeal. CAUTION: Try to channel any restlessness into worthwhile study.

MOON IN CAPRICORN

Life in these hours may seem to pivot around the importance of gaining prestige and honor in the career, as well as maintaining a spotless reputation. Ambitious urges may be excessive and could be accompanied by quite acquisitive drives for money. Effort should be directed along strictly ethical lines where there is no possibility of reproach or scandal. All endeavors are likely to be characterized by great earnestness, and an air of authority and purpose which should impress those who are looking for leadership or reliability. The desire to conform to accepted standards may extend to sharp criticism of family members. Frivolity and unconventional actions are unlikely to amuse while the Moon is in Capricorn. Moderation and seriousness are the orders of the day. Achievement and recognition in this period could come through community work or organizing for the benefit of some amateur group. CAUTION: Dignity and esteem are not always self-awarded.

MOON IN AQUARIUS

Moon in Aquarius is in the second last sign of the Zodiac where ideas can become disturbingly fine and subtle. The result is often a mental "no-man's land" where imagination cannot be trusted with the same certitude as other times. The dangers for the individual are the extremes of optimism and pessimism. Unless the imagination is held in check, situations are likely to be misread, and rosy conclusions drawn where they do not exist. Consequences for the unwary can be costly in career and business. Best to think twice and not speak or act until you think again. Pessimism can be a cruel self-inflicted penalty for delusion at this time. Between the two extremes are strange areas of self-deception which, for example, can make the selfish person think he is actually being generous. Eerie dreams which resemble the reality and even seem to continue into the waking state are also possible. CAUTION: Look for the fact and not just for the image in your mind.

MOON IN PISCES

Everything seems to come to the surface now. Memory may be crystal clear, throwing up long-forgotten information which could be valuable in the career or business. Flashes of clairvoyance and intuition are possible along with sudden realizations of one's own nature, which may be used for self-improvement. A talent, never before suspected, may be discovered. Qualities not evident before in friends and marriage partners are likely to be noticed. As this is a period in which the truth seems to emerge, the discovery of false characteristics is likely to lead to disenchantment or a shift in attachments. However, when qualities are accepted, it should lead to happiness and deeper feeling. Surprise solutions could bob up for old problems. There may be a public announcement of the solving of a crime or mystery. People with secrets may find someone has "guessed" correctly. The secrets of the soul or the inner self also tend to reveal themselves. Religious and philosophical groups may make some interesting discoveries. CAUTION: Not a time for activities that depend on secrecy.

NOTE: When you read your daily forecasts, use the Moon Sign Dates that are provided in the following section of Moon Tables. Then you may want to glance back here for the Moon's influence in a given sign.

MOON TABLES

Atlanta, Boston, Detroit, Miami, Washington, Montreal,
  Ottawa, Quebec, Bogota, Havana, Lima, Santiago..Same time

Chicago, New Orleans, Houston, Winnipeg, Churchill,
  Mexico City....................................... Deduct 1 hour

Albuquerque, Denver, Phoenix, El Paso, Edmonton,
  Helena .... Deduct 2 hours

Los Angeles, San Francisco, Reno, Portland,
  Seattle, Vancouver .... Deduct 3 hours

Honolulu, Anchorage, Fairbanks, Kodiak .... Deduct 5 hours

Nome, Samoa, Tonga, Midway.................... Deduct 6 hours

Halifax, Bermuda, San Juan, Caracas, La Paz,
  Barbados..Add 1 hour

St. John's, Brasilia, Rio de Janeiro, Sao Paulo,
  Buenos Aires, Montevideo..........................Add 2 hours

Azores, Cape Verde Islands...........................Add 3 hours

Canary Islands, Madeira, Reykjavik ....Add 4 hours

London, Paris, Amsterdam, Madrid, Lisbon,
  Gibraltar, Belfast, Rabat ....Add 5 hours

Frankfurt, Rome, Oslo, Stockholm, Prague,
  Belgrade..Add 6 hours

Bucharest, Beirut, Tel Aviv, Athens, Istanbul, Cairo,
  Alexandria, Cape Town, Johannesburg ....Add 7 hours

Moscow, Leningrad, Baghdad, Dhahran,
  Addis Ababa, Nairobi, Teheran, Zanzibar.........Add 8 hours

Bombay, Calcutta, Sri Lanka.................... Add 10 ½ hours

Hong Kong, Shanghai, Manila, Peking, Perth...... Add 13 hours

Tokyo, Okinawa, Darwin, Pusan.................... Add 14 hours

Sydney, Melbourne, Port Moresby, Guam.......... Add 15 hours

Auckland, Wellington, Suva, Wake................. Add 17 hours

1999 MOON SIGN DATES—
NEW YORK TIME

JANUARY			FEBRUARY			MARCH		
Day Moon Enters			**Day Moon Enters**			**Day Moon Enters**		
1.	Cancer	3:16 am	1.	Virgo	8:38 pm	1.	Virgo	5:06 am
2.	Cancer		2.	Virgo		2.	Virgo	
3.	Leo	5:32 am	3.	Virgo		3.	Libra	1:35 pm
4.	Leo		4.	Libra	4:57 am	4.	Libra	
5.	Virgo	10:50 am	5.	Libra		5.	Libra	
6.	Virgo		6.	Scorp.	4:07 pm	6.	Scorp.	0:23 am
7.	Libra	7:54 pm	7.	Scorp.		7.	Scorp.	
8.	Libra		8.	Scorp.		8.	Sagitt.	0:47 pm
9.	Libra		9.	Sagitt.	4:39 am	9.	Sagitt.	
10.	Scorp.	7:50 am	10.	Sagitt.		10.	Sagitt.	
11.	Scorp.		11.	Capric.	4:11 pm	11.	Capric.	0:55 am
12.	Sagitt.	8:24 pm	12.	Capric.		12.	Capric.	
13.	Sagitt.		13.	Capric.		13.	Aquar.	10:33 am
14.	Sagitt.		14.	Aquar.	0:58 am	14.	Aquar.	
15.	Capric.	7:30 am	15.	Aquar.		15.	Pisces	4:31 pm
16.	Capric.		16.	Pisces	6:41 am	16.	Pisces	
17.	Aquar.	4:12 pm	17.	Pisces		17.	Aries	7:14 pm
18.	Aquar.		18.	Aries	10:07 am	18.	Aries	
19.	Pisces	10:41 pm	19.	Aries		19.	Taurus	8:10 pm
20.	Pisces		20.	Taurus	0:30 pm	20.	Taurus	
21.	Pisces		21.	Taurus		21.	Gemini	9:06 pm
22.	Aries	3:26 am	22.	Gemini	2:55 pm	22.	Gemini	
23.	Aries		23.	Gemini		23.	Cancer	11:34 pm
24.	Taurus	6:53 am	24.	Cancer	6:10 pm	24.	Cancer	
25.	Taurus		25.	Cancer		25.	Cancer	
26.	Gemini	9:30 am	26.	Leo	10:45 pm	26.	Leo	4:23 am
27.	Gemini		27.	Leo		27.	Leo	
28.	Cancer	11:58 am	28.	Leo		28.	Virgo	11:35 am
29.	Cancer					29.	Virgo	
30.	Leo	3:17 pm				30.	Libra	8:50 pm
31.	Leo					31.	Libra	

Summer time to be considered where applicable.

1999 MOON SIGN DATES—
NEW YORK TIME

APRIL		MAY		JUNE	
Day Moon Enters		**Day Moon Enters**		**Day Moon Enters**	
1. Libra		1. Scorp.		1. Capric.	
2. Scorp.	7:50 am	2. Sagitt.	2:37 am	2. Capric.	
3. Scorp.		3. Sagitt.		3. Aquar.	8:38 am
4. Sagitt.	8:08 pm	4. Capric.	3:13 pm	4. Aquar.	
5. Sagitt.		5. Capric.		5. Pisces	6:02 pm
6. Sagitt.		6. Capric.		6. Pisces	
7. Capric.	8:40 am	7. Aquar.	2:41 am	7. Pisces	
8. Capric.		8. Aquar.		8. Aries	0:09 am
9. Aquar.	7:25 pm	9. Pisces	11:17 am	9. Aries	
10. Aquar.		10. Pisces		10. Taurus	2:44 am
11. Aquar.		11. Aries	3:54 pm	11. Taurus	
12. Pisces	2:36 am	12. Aries		12. Gemini	2:49 am
13. Pisces		13. Taurus	4:57 pm	13. Gemini	
14. Aries	5:47 am	14. Taurus		14. Cancer	2:15 am
15. Aries		15. Gemini	4:08 pm	15. Cancer	
16. Taurus	6:08 am	16. Gemini		16. Leo	3:08 am
17. Taurus		17. Cancer	3:40 pm	17. Leo	
18. Gemini	5:40 am	18. Cancer		18. Virgo	7:13 am
19. Gemini		19. Leo	5:38 pm	19. Virgo	
20. Cancer	6:28 am	20. Leo		20. Libra	3:11 pm
21. Cancer		21. Virgo	11:16 pm	21. Libra	
22. Leo	10:07 am	22. Virgo		22. Libra	
23. Leo		23. Virgo		23. Scorp.	2:19 am
24. Virgo	5:05 pm	24. Libra	8:30 am	24. Scorp.	
25. Virgo		25. Libra		25. Sagitt.	2:52 pm
26. Virgo		26. Scorp.	8:06 pm	26. Sagitt.	
27. Libra	2:47 am	27. Scorp.		27. Sagitt.	
28. Libra		28. Scorp.		28. Capric.	3:13 am
29. Scorp.	2:14 pm	29. Sagitt.	8:38 am	29. Capric.	
30. Scorp.		30. Sagitt.		30. Aquar.	2:20 pm
		31. Capric.	9:07 pm		

Summer time to be considered where applicable.

1999 MOON SIGN DATES— NEW YORK TIME

JULY		AUGUST		SEPTEMBER	
Day Moon Enters		**Day Moon Enters**		**Day Moon Enters**	
1. Aquar.		1. Aries	11:48 am	1. Taurus	
2. Pisces	11:35 pm	2. Aries		2. Gemini	0:26 am
3. Pisces		3. Taurus	4:10 pm	3. Gemini	
4. Pisces		4. Taurus		4. Cancer	3:11 am
5. Aries	6:22 am	5. Gemini	6:58 pm	5. Cancer	
6. Aries		6. Gemini		6. Leo	6:30 am
7. Taurus	10:23 am	7. Cancer	8:54 pm	7. Leo	
8. Taurus		8. Cancer		8. Virgo	10:58 am
9. Gemini	0:01 pm	9. Leo	10:57 pm	9. Virgo	
10. Gemini		10. Leo		10. Libra	5:17 pm
11. Cancer	0:28 pm	11. Leo		11. Libra	
12. Cancer		12. Virgo	2:23 am	12. Libra	
13. Leo	1:27 pm	13. Virgo		13. Scorp.	2:09 am
14. Leo		14. Libra	8:25 am	14. Scorp.	
15. Virgo	4:40 pm	15. Libra		15. Sagitt.	1:36 pm
16. Virgo		16. Scorp.	5:41 pm	16. Sagitt.	
17. Libra	11:20 pm	17. Scorp.		17. Sagitt.	
18. Libra		18. Scorp.		18. Capric.	2:14 am
19. Libra		19. Sagitt.	5:33 am	19. Capric.	
20. Scorp.	9:31 am	20. Sagitt.		20. Aquar.	1:39 pm
21. Scorp.		21. Capric.	6:00 pm	21. Aquar.	
22. Sagitt.	9:49 pm	22. Capric.		22. Pisces	9:52 pm
23. Sagitt.		23. Capric.		23. Pisces	
24. Sagitt.		24. Aquar.	4:50 am	24. Pisces	
25. Capric.	10:09 am	25. Aquar.		25. Aries	2:35 am
26. Capric.		26. Pisces	0:51 pm	26. Aries	
27. Aquar.	8:55 pm	27. Pisces		27. Taurus	4:52 am
28. Aquar.		28. Aries	6:10 pm	28. Taurus	
29. Aquar.		29. Aries		29. Gemini	6:22 am
30. Pisces	5:28 am	30. Taurus	9:42 pm	30. Gemini	
31. Pisces		31. Taurus			

Summer time to be considered where applicable.

1999 MOON SIGN DATES—
NEW YORK TIME

OCTOBER		NOVEMBER		DECEMBER	
Day Moon Enters		**Day Moon Enters**		**Day Moon Enters**	
1. Cancer	8:32 am	1. Virgo	11:08 pm	1. Libra	0:30 pm
2. Cancer		2. Virgo		2. Libra	
3. Leo	0:14 pm	3. Virgo		3. Scorp.	10:36 pm
4. Leo		4. Libra	6:58 am	4. Scorp.	
5. Virgo	5:41 pm	5. Libra		5. Scorp.	
6. Virgo		6. Scorp.	4:47 pm	6. Sagitt.	10:28 am
7. Virgo		7. Scorp.		7. Sagitt.	
8. Libra	0:53 am	8. Scorp.		8. Capric.	11:15 pm
9. Libra		9. Sagitt.	4:16 am	9. Capric.	
10. Scorp.	10:02 am	10. Sagitt.		10. Capric.	
11. Scorp.		11. Capric.	5:01 pm	11. Aquar.	12:00 pm
12. Sagitt.	9:20 pm	12. Capric.		12. Aquar.	
13. Sagitt.		13. Capric.		13. Pisces	11:19 pm
14. Sagitt.		14. Aquar.	5:47 am	14. Pisces	
15. Capric.	10:05 am	15. Aquar.		15. Pisces	
16. Capric.		16. Pisces	4:22 pm	16. Aries	7:31 am
17. Aquar.	10:18 pm	17. Pisces		17. Aries	
18. Aquar.		18. Aries	10:58 pm	18. Taurus	11:46 am
19. Aquar.		19. Aries		19. Taurus	
20. Pisces	7:34 am	20. Aries		20. Gemini	0:40 pm
21. Pisces		21. Taurus	1:27 am	21. Gemini	
22. Aries	0:42 pm	22. Taurus		22. Cancer	11:53 am
23. Aries		23. Gemini	1:15 am	23. Cancer	
24. Taurus	2:26 pm	24. Gemini		24. Leo	11:33 am
25. Taurus		25. Cancer	0:30 am	25. Leo	
26. Gemini	2:34 pm	26. Cancer		26. Virgo	1:35 pm
27. Gemini		27. Leo	1:20 am	27. Virgo	
28. Cancer	3:10 pm	28. Leo		28. Libra	7:15 pm
29. Cancer		29. Virgo	5:12 am	29. Libra	
30. Leo	5:48 pm	30. Virgo		30. Libra	
31. Leo				31. Scorp.	4:37 am

Summer time to be considered where applicable.

1999 PHASES OF THE MOON—
NEW YORK TIME

New Moon	First Quarter	Full Moon	Last Quarter
Dec. 18 ('98)	Dec. 26 ('98)	Jan. 1	Jan. 9
Jan. 17	Jan. 24	Jan. 31	Feb. 8
Feb. 16	Feb. 22	March 2	March 10
March 17	March 24	March 31	April 8
April 15	April 22	April 30	May 8
May 15	May 22	May 30	June 6
June 13	June 20	June 28	July 6
July 12	July 20	July 28	Aug. 4
Aug. 11	Aug. 18	Aug. 26	Sept. 2
Sept. 9	Sept. 17	Sept. 25	Oct. 1
Oct. 9	Oct. 17	Oct. 24	Oct. 31
Nov. 7	Nov. 16	Nov. 23	Nov. 29
Dec. 7	Dec. 15	Dec. 22	Dec. 29

Each phase of the Moon lasts approximately seven to eight days, during which the Moon's shape gradually changes as it comes out of one phase and goes into the next.

There will be a partial solar eclipse during the New Moon phase on February 16 and August 11.

There will be a lunar eclipse during the Full Moon phase on July 28.

1999 FISHING GUIDE

	Good	Best
January	3-4-5-17-24-28-30-31	1-2-9-29
February	1-2-3-16-23-27-28	8
March	1-2-3-10-28-29-30	4-5-17-24-31
April	16-22	1-2-3-9-27-28-29-30
May	2-3-8-15-22-29-30-31	1-27-28
June	13-20-25-26-27-30	1-2-7-28-29
July	1-6-13-25-28-29-30	20-26-27-31
August	11-19-23-24-25-26-29	4-27-28
September	2-9-17-22-25-26	23-24-27-28
October	22-23-24-26-27-31	2-9-17-21-25
November	16-20-23-24-29	8-21-22-25-26
December	7-16-20-21-22-24-25	19-23

1999 PLANTING GUIDE

	Aboveground Crops	Root Crops
January	1-20-21-25-29	2-8-9-10-11-12-16
February	17-21-25-26	4-5-6-7-8-12-13
March	20-21-24-25-31	4-5-6-7-11-12-16
April	17-21-27-28-29	1-2-3-4-8-9-12-13
May	18-19-25-26-27-28	1-5-6-10-14
June	14-15-21-22-23-24	1-2-6-7-10-11-29
July	18-19-20-21-22-26-27	3-4-8-12-31
August	15-16-17-18-22-23	4-5-8-9-27-28-31
September	11-12-13-14-18-19-23-24	1-4-5-27-28
October	10-11-12-16-17-21	2-8-25-29-30
November	8-12-13-17-18-21-22	5-6-7-25-26
December	9-10-14-15-19	2-3-4-5-23-29-30-31

	Pruning	Weeds and Pests
January	2-11-12	4-5-6-7-13-14
February	7-8	1-2-3-9-10-14-15
March	6-7-16	2-9-10-14
April	3-4-12-13	5-6-10-11-15
May	1-10	2-3-7-8-12-30-31
June	6-7	4-5-8-9-12
July	3-4-12-31	1-2-6-10-29
August	8-9-27-28	2-6-7-10-29-30
September	4-5	2-3-7-8-9-26-30
October	2-29-30	4-5-6-7-27-31
November	7-25-26	1-2-3-23-24-27-28-29-30
December	4-5-23-31	7-25-26-27-28

MOON'S INFLUENCE OVER PLANTS

Centuries ago it was established that seeds planted when the Moon is in signs and phases called Fruitful will produce more growth than seeds planted when the Moon is in a Barren sign.

Fruitful Signs: Taurus, Cancer, Libra, Scorpio, Capricorn, Pisces
Barren Signs: Aries, Gemini, Leo, Virgo, Sagittarius, Aquarius
Dry Signs: Aries, Gemini, Sagittarius, Aquarius

Activity	Moon In
Mow lawn, trim plants	**Fruitful sign:** 1st & 2nd quarter
Plant flowers	**Fruitful sign:** 2nd quarter; best in Cancer and Libra
Prune	**Fruitful sign:** 3rd & 4th quarter
Destroy pests; spray	**Barren sign:** 4th quarter
Harvest potatoes, root crops	**Dry sign:** 3rd & 4th quarter; Taurus, Leo, and Aquarius

MOON'S INFLUENCE OVER YOUR HEALTH

ARIES	Head, brain, face, upper jaw
TAURUS	Throat, neck, lower jaw
GEMINI	Hands, arms, lungs, shoulders, nervous system
CANCER	Esophagus, stomach, breasts, womb, liver
LEO	Heart, spine
VIRGO	Intestines, liver
LIBRA	Kidneys, lower back
SCORPIO	Sex and eliminative organs
SAGITTARIUS	Hips, thighs, liver
CAPRICORN	Skin, bones, teeth, knees
AQUARIUS	Circulatory system, lower legs
PISCES	Feet, tone of being

Try to avoid work being done on that part of the body when the
Moon is in the sign governing that part.

MOON'S INFLUENCE OVER DAILY AFFAIRS

The Moon makes a complete transit of the Zodiac every 27 days
7 hours and 43 minutes. In making this transit the Moon forms
different aspects with the planets and consequently has favorable
or unfavorable bearings on affairs and events for persons according to the sign of the Zodiac under which they were born.

When the Moon is in conjunction with the Sun it is called a
New Moon; when the Moon and Sun are in opposition it is called
a Full Moon. From New Moon to Full Moon, first and second
quarter—which takes about two weeks—the Moon is increasing
or waxing. From Full Moon to New Moon, third and fourth quarter, the Moon is decreasing or waning.

Activity	Moon In
Business: buying and selling new, requiring public support	Sagittarius, Aries, Gemini, Virgo 1st and 2nd quarter
meant to be kept quiet	3rd and 4th quarter
Investigation	3rd and 4th quarter
Signing documents	1st & 2nd quarter, Cancer, Scorpio, Pisces
Advertising	2nd quarter, Sagittarius
Journeys and trips	1st & 2nd quarter, Gemini, Virgo
Renting offices, etc.	Taurus, Leo, Scorpio, Aquarius
Painting of house/apartment	3rd & 4th quarter, Taurus, Scorpio, Aquarius
Decorating	Gemini, Libra, Aquarius
Buying clothes and accessories	Taurus, Virgo
Beauty salon or barber shop visit	1st & 2nd quarter, Taurus, Leo, Libra, Scorpio, Aquarius
Weddings	1st & 2nd quarter

VIRGO

VIRGO

Character Analysis

People born under the sign of Virgo are generally practical. They believe in doing things thoroughly; there is nothing slipshod or haphazard about the way they do things. They are precise and methodical. The man or woman born under this sixth sign of the Zodiac respects common sense and tries to be rational in his or her approach to tasks or problems.

Virgo is the sign of work and service. It is the symbol of the farmer at harvest time, and so the man or woman born under this sign is sometimes called the Harvester. These people's tireless efforts to bring the fruits of the Earth to the table of humanity create great joy and beneficence. Celebration through work and harvest is the characteristic of the sign of Virgo.

Sincerity, zeal, and devotion mark the working methods of the Virgo man and woman. They have excellent critical abilities; they know how to analyze a problem and come up with a solution. Virgo is seldom fooled by superficialities, and can go straight to the heart of the matter.

Virgo knows how to break things down to the minutest detail; he or she prefers to work on things piece by piece. Inwardly, he is afraid of being overwhelmed by things that seem larger than life. For this reason, one often finds the Virgo occupied with details. His powers of concentration are greatest when he can concentrate on small, manageable things.

The Virgo person believes in doing things correctly; he's thorough and precise. He's seldom carried away by fantasy; he believes in keeping his feet firmly on the ground. People who seem a bit flighty or impractical sometimes irritate him.

Virgo knows how to criticize other people. It is very easy for him to point out another's weaknesses or faults; he is seldom wrong. However, Virgo is sometimes a bit sharp in making criticisms and often offends a good friend or acquaintance. The cultivated Virgo, however, knows how to apply criticism tactfully. He or she is considerate of another's feelings.

The Virgo person believes in applying himself in a positive manner to whatever task is set before him. He is a person full of purpose and goodwill. He is diligent and methodical. He is seldom given to impulse, but works along steadily and constructively.

Anything that is scientific, technological, and practical arouses Virgo's interest. The technical and craft aspects of the arts impress these people, and many Virgos become expert designers, graphic artists, and handicrafters. The precision so important to these disciplines is a quality Virgo possesses in abundance. Combined with imagination and flair, the attention to detail often makes Virgos first-rate artists.

Whether or not individual Virgos are talented in artistic areas, most of these people are usually very interested in anything of an artistic nature. Virgos also are great readers. They have a deep appreciation for the way the intricacies of life weave together, then unravel, and finally are rewoven into a new fabric or design.

Virgos also possess an innate verbal ability that is especially suited to the study of a language, whether the language is a machine language such as in computers or a tongue spoken by other people. Virgo has no trouble applying his or her native intelligence and skill either in a learning or teaching capacity. Virgos enjoy school. They often study a wide range of subjects, but not in great depth, in order to have a well-rounded education. Virgos like friends and colleagues to be as well-informed as they are if not more so. Virgo has a deep respect for culture, education, and intellect.

Usually, Virgo takes in stride whatever comes into his or her life. Basically, he is an uncomplicated person, who views things clearly and sharply. He has a way of getting right down to the meat of the matter. Generally a serious-minded person, he believes in being reliable. He is not one who will take great risks in life as he has no interest in playing the hero or the idealist. Virgo believes in doing what he can, but without flourishes.

Quite often he is a quiet, modest person. He believes that appearance is important and thus does his best to look well-groomed. He feels that being neat is important and dislikes untidiness in anything.

The Virgo man or woman likes to deal with life on a practical level and they usually look for the uncomplicated answer or solution to any problem or dilemma. Even if Virgos are urged to look into the mystical side of existence, they may dismiss it as being either unfounded or irrelevant.

On the whole, the Virgo person is even-tempered. He or she does not allow himself to become angry easily. He knows how to take the bitter with the sweet. But if someone does him a wrong turn, he is not likely to forget it. His good nature is not to be abused.

Health

Many persons born under this sign are amazingly healthy. They frequently live to see a ripe old age. This longevity is generally due to the fact that people born under this sign take all things in moderation. Virgo is not the type of person who burns the candle at both ends. They acknowledge their limits and avoid excess.

Frequently Virgos are small and neat-featured. Virgo women are sometimes quite attractive in a sort of dry way. Both men and women of this sign have a youthful appearance throughout life. When young, Virgos are generally very active. However, as they reach middle age and beyond they have a tendency to put on a bit of weight.

The Virgo person usually enjoys good health, although some have a tendency to be overly concerned about it. They imagine ailments they do not really have. Still, they do manage to stay fit. Other Virgos see themselves as being rather strong and resourceful, even when they are ill. For that reason they seldom feel moved to feel sorry for another ailing Virgo. Actually, serious illnesses frighten Virgos. They will do all they can to remain in good health.

The medicine cabinet of someone born under this sign is often filled with all sorts of pills, tablets, and ointments. Most of them will never be used.

As a rule, Virgo watches his diet. He stays away from foods that won't agree with him. He keeps a balanced diet and is moderate in his drinking habits. Virgos need plenty of exercise to keep the body fit. Most Virgos do not have a particular liking for strenuous sport. But the wise Virgo always will get some kind of energetic exercise, preferably a brisk and long walk, or a daily workout. Another thing that Virgos need is rest. They should get at least eight hours sleep per day.

On the whole, Virgo is a sensitive person. His nerves may be easily affected if he finds himself in a disagreeable situation. The stomach is another area of concern. When a Virgo becomes sick, this area is usually affected. Digestion complaints are not rare among persons born under this sign. Regular meals are important for the Virgo. Quick snacks and fast food may play havoc with his digestive system. In spite of this particular weakness, Virgos manage to lead normal, healthy lives. They should try to avoid becoming too concerned with ups and downs. Many of their illnesses may turn out to be imaginary.

Occupation

Virgos delight in keeping busy. They are not afraid of hard work. By nature, they are ambitious people and are happiest when they are putting their talents and abilities to good use. They can best be described as goal-directed; they never lose sight of their objective once committed. They are very thorough in whatever they undertake. Even routine work is something that they can do without finding fault. In fact, work that is scheduled—or that follows a definite pattern—is well suited to their steady natures. Virgos will put aside other things, if necessary, in order to attain a goal. They prefer to work under peaceful conditions, and will seldom do anything to irritate their superiors.

They learn well and are not afraid to undertake any kind of work—even the most menial—if it is necessary. Sometimes, however, they neglect their own conditions because they are so involved in their work. For this reason, Virgos occasionally fall ill or become a bit nervous. Any kind of work that allows them to make use of their talent for criticism will please them.

Virgo men and women usually shine as bookkeepers, accountants, teachers, and pharmacists. The cultivated Virgo person often turns to the world of science where they are likely to do well. Some great writers and poets have been born under this sixth sign of the Zodiac.

It is very important that Virgo has the kind of work that is suited to his personality. It may take a while before he actually finds his niche in life, and he may have to struggle at times in order to make ends meet. But because he is not afraid of work, he manages to come out on top.

Virgo is a perfectionist. He or she is always looking for ways to improve the work scheme or technique. He is never satisfied until things are working smoothly. He will even do more than his share in order to secure regularity and precision in a job he is doing. It is not unusual for the average Virgo to have various ideas about how to better the job they are doing, how to streamline things. They are extremely resourceful people as far as energy is concerned. In most cases, they can work longer than others, without letting it show. Because Virgo is so concerned with detail, they may seem obsessive or compulsive to co-workers.

The enterprising Virgo can go far in business if a partner is somewhat adventurous and enthusiastic, qualities which tend to balance those of the Virgo person. At times, Virgo can be quite a worrier. Battling problems large and small may prevent him from making the headway he feels is necessary in his work. A partner who knows how to cut the work and worries in half by taking advantage of shortcuts is someone the average Virgo businessperson could learn to value. People enjoying working with Virgo men and women, because they are so reliable and honest. They usually set a good example for others on the job.

If not careful, the ambitious Virgo can become the type of person who thinks about nothing else but the job. They are not afraid of taking on more than the average worker. But they can make the mistake of expecting the same of others. This attitude can lead to conflict and unpleasantness. Generally, Virgo does achieve what he sets out for, because he knows how to apply himself. He is seldom the envy of others because he is not the type of person who is easily noticed or recognized.

Virgo is a quiet person. He or she enjoys working in peaceful and harmonious surroundings. Conflict at work is bound to upset him and affect his nerves. He works well under people. He is not against taking orders from those who prove themselves his superiors. On the whole, the man or woman born under this sign does not like to be delegated with the full responsibility of a task or project. He or she would rather have a supporting or a subordinate role.

Virgo men and women frequently excel in a trade. They often make good metalsmiths and carpenters, jewelers and wood carvers. They can work in miniature, creating a variety of pleasing items.

The Virgo person is one who is very concerned about security. Now and again he may have cause to worry about his financial position. On the whole, he is conscious of the value of money. He or she is a person who will never risk security by going out on a limb. He knows how to put money away for a rainy day. Many times he will scout about for new ways of increasing his savings. Bettering his financial situation is something that constantly concerns him. When he does invest, it usually turns out to his advantage. He generally makes sure that the investment he makes is a sure thing. He does not believe in gambling or taking big risks.

Sometimes the Virgo, because of his keen interest in money and profit, is the victim of a fraud. Dishonest people may try to take advantage of his interest in monetary gain. The well-off Virgo is extremely generous and enjoys looking after the needs of others. He sees to it that those he cares for live in comfort.

Not all Virgos are fortunate enough to become extremely wealthy, but all of them work hard for what they achieve.

Home and Family

People born under this sign are generally homebodies. They like to spend as much time as possible surrounded by the things and the people they enjoy. They make excellent hosts and enjoy entertaining guests and visitors. It is important to Virgos that the people around them be happy and content. Virgo is most at ease when companions behave correctly, that is, if they are respectful of individuals' needs and property. Virgos do not like people to take advantage of their hospitality or to abuse what they consider a privilege. But on the whole Virgos are easygoing. The demands they may make of guests and family are reasonable.

A harmonious atmosphere at home is important to the person

born under this sign. As long as this can be guaranteed, Virgo remains in good humor. They are likely to have a number of insurance policies on the home, family, and possessions. They believe that you can never be safe enough.

In spite of their love of home, Virgo is likely to have an avid interest in travel. If they cannot make many changes in their environment, they are bound to make them in their home. The Virgo homemaker never tires of rearranging things. Generally, Virgos have a good sense of beauty and harmony. They know how to make a room inviting and comfortable. Change is always of interest to the person born under this sign. They like to read of faraway places, even if they never get a chance to visit them. A new job or a new home address from time to time can brighten Virgo's spirits immeasurably.

The Virgo woman is as neat as a pin. Usually she is an excellent cook, and takes care that her kitchen never gets out of order or becomes untidy even while she is working in it. She believes that everything has its proper place and should be kept there. Because she is so careful with her possessions, they often appear brand new.

Others may feel that the Virgo man or woman, because of his or her cool, calm ways, is not especially cut out to be a good parent. But the opposite is true. Virgo people know how to bring up their youngsters correctly. They generally pass on their positive qualities to their children without any trouble. They teach them that honesty and diligence are important. They instill them with an appreciation for common sense in all matters.

Although the Virgo father or mother may deeply love their children, they have a tendency to be rather strict. They are always concerned that their children turn out well. Sometimes they expect too much of them. Some of them can be old-fashioned and believe that a child belongs in a child's place. They expect this not only of their own youngsters but also of other people's children.

Social Relationships

The Virgo man or woman is particular about the friends he makes. He is fond of people who have a particular direction in life. He is inclined to avoid drifters or irresolute people. Those who have made their mark win his admiration. Virgo likes intelligent people, those who are somewhat cultured in their interests.

As a good friend, Virgo is invaluable; there is nothing he or she would not do to help someone in need. Virgo stands by friends even in their most difficult moments. The only demand he makes is that his interest in another's affairs be valued. He does not like to feel that his help is not appreciated. It is important that Virgo be thanked for even the slightest favor.

Quite often people born under this sign are rather timid or at least retiring; they have to be drawn out by others. After Virgos get to know someone well, however, they bloom. In spite of their initial shyness, they do not enjoy being alone. They like company; they like to be reassured by people. They prefer intelligent, informed people as companions. Virgo can overlook negative qualities in someone if they feel that person is basically sincere toward others. The Virgo person needs friends. In solitude, the average Virgo is apt to feel stranded or deserted. They enjoy having someone around who will make a fuss over them, no matter how small.

Virgo is a perfectionist. Sometimes they criticize others too strongly for their faults, and as a result, they may not have as many friends as they would like.

Virgo can be cliquey, enjoying a fairly closed circle of friends and acquaintances. Gossip and intrigue might be a mainstay of such a clique. The smaller the circle, the more comfortable Virgo will feel and the more chances there will be for Virgo to orchestrate the social and recreational activities. In an intimate group setting Virgo's shyness disappears, giving way to the delicious wit and clever turn of phrase basic to this verbal, mental sign.

Gala parties with lots of hangers-on and freeloaders are not Virgo's style. A typical noisy blast can be a turn-off to one who is finicky and fastidious. The mere sight of overindulgence and overfamiliarity can make Virgo long for the glamour of posh surroundings accompanied only by a lover or close friend.

Frequent home entertaining also can be a problem. The fussy Virgo will fret about all the details that must be arranged to host a successful social. Then the neat, tidy Virgo will worry about the mess created in the house after a perfect get-together. On the whole, Virgo men and women prefer socializing in a few select places known for gracious service and fine food.

Of all the signs in the Zodiac, Virgo is most drawn to human welfare issues, a fact that leads these men and women into groups whose goal is to improve people's lot in life. The Virgo dedication to a cause is remarkable. Their example is an inspiration for everyone to follow. Doing someone a good turn comes naturally to Virgo. Their qualities of service and kindness are genuine, as friends who admire and respect them will testify.

Love and Marriage

In love and romance, the person born under the sign of Virgo is not inclined to be overly romantic. To a partner, they may seem reserved and inhibited. Their practical nature prevails even in affairs of the heart. They are least likely to be swept off their feet when in love. Chances are they may flirt a bit in the beginning of a relationship, but soon thereafter they settle down to the serious side of love. Virgo standards are very high, and it may be some time before they find someone who can measure up to them. As a consequence, Virgo frequently marries rather late in life.

It is important for the Virgo man or woman to find the right person because they are easily influenced by someone they love. On the other hand, Virgo has a protective side to their nature. When in love they will try to shield the object of their affection from the unpleasant things in life.

The person born under the sign of Virgo may be disappointed in love more than once. People whom they set great store in may prove to be unsuitable. Sometimes it is Virgo's own fault. They may be too critical of small weaknesses that a partner or lover has.

Some Virgos seem prim and proper when it comes to romance. They would prefer to think that it is not absolutely necessary and that intellect is everything. It may take some doing to get such a Virgo to change this attitude. At any rate, they are not fond of being demonstrative as far as affection goes. They do not like to make a show of love in front of others.

If their lover is too demanding or forceful in the relationship, they may feel inclined to break off the affair. Virgo appreciates gentleness and consideration in love life. On the whole, they are not easy to approach. The person who finds him or her interesting will have to be very tactful and patient when trying to convince Virgo of their love.

In married life, Virgo is apt to be very practical. They are interested in preserving the happiness they have found and will do everything in their power to keep the relationship alive. It is quite important that the Virgo man or woman marry someone with a similar outlook. Someone quite opposite may misinterpret Virgo's calm and cool manner as being unfeeling. Virgo makes a faithful mate. He or she can always be depended upon. They know how to keep things in the home running smoothly. They will do what they can to preserve harmony because they dislike discord and unpleasantness. A cooperative person, Virgo is willing to make concessions if they seem necessary. In short, the Virgo man or woman can make a success of marriage if they have had the good fortune to choose the right person.

Romance and the Virgo Woman

The Virgo woman is often a serious person. She knows what she wants out of life and what to expect from people. She is discriminating in her choice of men. It may take considerable time before she will admit to herself that she is in love. She is not afraid to wait in matters of romance; it is important to her that she select the right person. She may be more easily attracted to an intelligent man than to a handsome one. She values intellect more than physical attributes.

It is important for the Virgo woman to trust someone before she falls in love with him. She will allow a relationship to develop into a love affair only after she has gotten to know the man well on strictly a companionship basis at first.

The Virgo woman is reputed to be prim and proper about sex. But this description does not tell the whole story, or even the right story. In fact, Virgo can exhibit extremes in sexual attitudes and behavior. It is an age-old dilemma, contrast, contradiction—call it what you will—between the madonna and the hooker. There is Virgo the Virgin, whose purity is renowned and whose frigidity is assumed. Then there is Virgo the Harvester, whose promiscuity is whispered and whose fruitfulness is celebrated.

Indeed, the difference between an old-fashioned Virgo and a liberated Virgo are remarkable but very hard to discern in the beginning of an affair. One thing is sure, though. Cheat on your Virgo woman, and you can kiss the relationship good-bye. That is, unless you have discussed the possibility of having an open relationship—on both sides and managed in good taste. Remember, no matter what her sexual proclivities are, the Virgo woman cannot stand vulgarity in any form.

The Virgo woman generally makes a good wife. She knows how to keep the household shipshape. She likes looking after people she loves. She is efficient and industrious. There is almost nothing she will not do for the man she loves. She is capable of deep affection and love, but must be allowed to express herself in her own way.

As a mother, she is ideal. She teaches all her youngsters to be polite and well-mannered, and constantly worries about their health and welfare. Fearing all manner of mishaps, injuries, illnesses, and minor ailments, the Virgo mother may tend to restrict the kids' freedom at play and in school. However, she always has the children's best interests at heart.

Romance and the Virgo Man

The Virgo man, practical and analytical as he is in most matters, is rather cautious when it comes to love and romance. He is not what one would call romantic. He may be shy and hesitant. It may be up to the female to begin the relationship. He may prefer not to start an affair until he has dated for a while.

Virgo is particular. If his love partner makes one false move, he is likely to dissolve the relationship. An understanding and patient woman can help him to be a little more realistic and open in his approach to love. But first she must know what kind of man she is dealing with.

The witty, talkative Virgo man enjoys flirting. But he will never press his luck nor take advantage of a compromising situation. He won't accuse you of stringing him along. It may seem as if he is waiting for you to make the next move. And you probably have to be the aggressor if the dating relationship is to get beyond the holding-hands stage and into serious lovemaking. Make sure, though, you don't go overboard with physical demonstrations of affection—especially in public places. Virgo is easily embarrassed by touching and kissing in front of other people. Any degree of sexual intimacy is strictly reserved for the bedroom.

The strong, silent Virgo type usually appeals to women who like the challenge of overcoming his apparent resistance to her feminine charms. Little does she know that he might be scared silly of making a fool of himself or of being criticized. Virgo projects his own personality traits onto people who get close to him. So he naturally believes that a woman who approaches is just as critical and faultfinding as he is. Fortunately, though, he doesn't project the egotism and chauvinism that could turn many a woman off. So if you want to play the seduction game, you will thrill to the ultimate conquest of winning this hard-to-get, nearly perfect guy.

The Virgo man enjoys family life and does everything he can to keep his wife and children happy and secure. He may want to have a hand in running the household because he feels he is more efficient than his mate. He is a calm, steady, and faithful person.

As a father he could be a bit of a fussbudget. He may not know how to communicate with his children effectively in some matters. However, he is loving and responsible. He does what he can to see that they have a proper upbringing.

Woman—Man

VIRGO WOMAN
ARIES MAN

Although it's possible that you could find happiness with a man born under the sign of the Ram, it's uncertain as to how long that happiness would last.

An Aries who has made his mark in the world and is somewhat steadfast in his outlooks and attitudes could be quite a catch for you. On the other hand, men under this sign are often swift-footed and quick-minded. Their industrious mannerisms may fail to impress you, especially if you feel that much of their get-up-and-go often leads nowhere.

When it comes to a fine romance, you want someone with a nice, broad shoulder to lean on. You are likely to find a relationship with someone who doesn't stay put for too long somewhat upsetting.

Aries may have a little trouble in understanding you, too, at least in the beginning of the relationship. He may find you a bit too shy and moody. An Aries tends to speak his mind; he's likely to criticize you at the drop of a hat.

You may find a man born under this sign too demanding. He may give you the impression that he expects you to be at his constant beck and call. You have a lot of patience at your disposal, and he may try every last bit of it. He may not be as thorough as you in everything he does. In order to achieve success or a goal quickly, he may overlook small but important details, then regret the oversight when it is far too late.

Being married to an Aries does not mean that you'll have a secure and safe life as far as finances are concerned. Not all Aries are rash with cash, but they lack the sound head you perhaps have for putting away something for that inevitable rainy day. He'll do his best, however, to see that you're adequately provided for, even though his efforts may leave something to be desired as far as you're concerned.

With an Aries man for a mate, you'll find yourself constantly among people. An Aries generally has many friends—and you may not heartily approve of them all. People born under the sign of the Ram are often more interested in interesting people than they are in influential ones. Although there may be a family squabble from time to time, you are stable enough to take it in your stride.

Aries men love children. They make wonderful fathers. Kids take to them like ducks to water. The Ram's quick mind and behavior appeal to the young. Aries ability to jump from one activity to another will suit and delight a child's attention span.

VIRGO WOMAN
TAURUS MAN

Some Taurus men are strong and silent. They do all they can to protect and provide for the women they love. In general, the Taurus man will never let you down. He's steady, sturdy, and reliable. He's pretty honest and practical, too. He says what he means and means what he says. He never indulges in deceit and will always put his cards on the table.

The Taurus man is very affectionate. Being loved, appreciated, and understood is very important for his well-being. Like you, he is also looking for peace and security in his life. If you both work toward these goals together, you'll find that they are easily attained.

If you should marry a Taurus man, you can be sure that the wolf will never darken your door. He is a notoriously good provider and will do everything he can to make his family comfortable and happy.

He'll appreciate the way you have of making a home warm and inviting. A comfortable couch and the evening papers are essential ingredients in making your Taurus husband happy at the end of the workday. Although he may be a big lug of a guy, you'll find that he's fond of gentleness and soft things. If you puff up his pillow and tuck him in at night, he won't complain.

You probably will like his friends. Taurus tends to seek out individuals who are successful or prominent. You also admire people who work hard and achieve their goals.

The Taurus man doesn't care too much for change. He's a stay-at-home of the first order. Chances are that the house you move into after you're married will be the house you'll live in for the rest of your life.

You'll find that the man born under the sign of the Bull is easy to get along with. It's unlikely that you'll have many quarrels or arguments.

Although he'll be gentle and tender with you, your Taurus man is far from being a sensitive type. He's a man's man. More than likely, he loves such sports as fishing and football. He can be earthy as well as down to earth.

The Taurus father loves the children, but he will do everything he can not to spoil them. He believes that children should stay in their place and, in adult company, should be seen but not heard. The Taurus father is an excellent disciplinarian. Your youngsters will be polite and respectful.

VIRGO WOMAN
GEMINI MAN
The Gemini man is a good catch. Many a woman has set her cap for him and failed to bag him. Generally, Gemini men are intelligent, witty, and outgoing. Many of them tend to be versatile.

On the other hand, some of them seem to lack that sort of common sense that you set so much store in. Their tendency to start a half-dozen projects, then toss them up in the air out of boredom may do nothing more than exasperate you.

One thing that causes a Twin's mind and affection to wander is a bore. But it is unlikely that an active woman like you would ever allow herself to be accused of being one. The Gemini man who has caught your heart will admire you for your ideas and intellect, perhaps even more than for your homemaking talents and good looks.

A strong-willed woman could easily fill the role of rudder for her Gemini's ship-without-a-sail. The intelligent Gemini is often aware of his shortcomings and doesn't mind if someone with better bearings gives him a shove in the right direction—when it's needed. The average Gemini doesn't have serious ego hang-ups and will even gracefully accept a well-deserved chewing out from his mate or lover or girl friend.

A successful and serious-minded Gemini could make you a very happy woman, perhaps, if you gave him half a chance. Although he may create the impression that he has a hole in his head, the Gemini man generally has a good head on his shoulders. Some Geminis, who have learned the art of being steadfast, have risen to great heights in their professions.

Once you convince yourself that not all people born under the sign of the Twins are witless grasshoppers, you won't mind dating a few to test your newborn conviction. If you do wind up walking down the aisle with one, accept the fact that married life with him will mean your taking the bitter with the sweet.

Life with a Gemini man can be more fun than a barrel of clowns. You'll never be allowed to experience a dull moment. Don't leave money matters to him, or you'll both wind up behind the eight ball.

Gemini men are always attractive to the opposite sex. You'll perhaps have to allow him a chance to flirt harmlessly. The occasion will seldom amount to more than that if you're his ideal mate.

The Gemini father is a pushover for children. See that you keep the young ones in line, otherwise they'll be running the house. He loves them so much, he generally lets them do what they want. Gemini's sense of humor is infectious, so the children will naturally come to see the fun and funny sides of life.

VIRGO WOMAN
CANCER MAN

The man born under the sign of Cancer may very well be the man after your own heart. Generally, Cancers are steady people. They are interested in security and practicality. Despite their seemingly grouchy exterior at times, men born under the sign of the Crab are sensitive and kind individuals.

Cancers are almost always hard workers and are very interested in making successes of themselves economically as well as socially. You'll find that their conservative outlook on many things often agrees with yours. They will be men on whom you can depend come rain or come shine. They will never shirk their responsibilities as providers. They will always see that their family never wants.

Your patience will come in handy if you decide it's a Cancer you want for a mate. He isn't the type that rushes headlong into romance. He wants to be sure about love as you do. If, after the first couple of months of dating, he suggests that you take a walk with him down lovers' lane, don't jump to the conclusion that he's about to make his great play. Chances are he'll only hold your hand and seriously observe the stars.

Don't let his coolness fool you, though. Beneath his starched reserve lies a very warm heart. He's just not interested in showing off as far as affection is concerned. Don't think his interest is wandering if he doesn't kiss you goodnight at the front door; that just isn't his style. For him, affection should only be displayed for two sets of eyes—yours and his. He's passionate only in private, which is something Virgo can understand and appreciate.

He will never step out of line. He's too much of a gentleman for that. When you're alone with him and there's no chance of being disturbed or spied upon, he'll pull out an engagement ring (the one that belonged to his grandmother) and slip it on your trembling finger.

Speaking of relatives, you'll have to get used to the fact that Cancer is overly fond of his mother. When he says his mother's the most wonderful woman in the world, you'd better agree with him, that is, if you want to become his wife.

He'll always be a faithful husband. A Cancer never pussyfoots around after he has taken that marriage vow. He doesn't take marriage responsibilities lightly. He'll see that everything in the house runs smoothly and that bills are paid promptly. He'll take out all kinds of insurance policies on his family and property. He'll arrange it so that when retirement time rolls around, you'll both be very well off.

Cancers make proud, patient, and protective fathers. But they can be a little too protective. Their sheltering instincts can interfere with a youngster's natural inclination toward independence. Still, the Cancer father doesn't want to see his kids learning about life the hard way from the streets.

VIRGO WOMAN
LEO MAN

To know a man born under the sign of the Lion is not necessarily to love him, even though the temptation may be great. When he fixes most girls with his leonine double-whammy, it causes their hearts to pitter-patter and their minds to cloud over.

You are a little too sensible to allow yourself to be bowled over by a regal strut and a roar. Still, there's no denying that Leo has a way with women, even sensible women like yourself. Once he's swept a girl off her feet, it may be hard for her to scramble upright again. Still, you are no pushover for romantic charm, especially if you feel it's all show.

He'll wine you and dine you in the fanciest places. He'll croon to you under the moon and shower you with diamonds if he can get ahold of them. Still, it would be wise to find out just how long that shower is going to last before consenting to be his wife.

Lions in love are hard to ignore, let alone brush off. Your resistance will have a way of nudging him on until he feels he has you completely under his spell. Once mesmerized by this romantic powerhouse, you will probably find yourself doing things of which you never dreamed. Leos can be vain pussycats when involved romantically. They like to be babied and pampered. This may not be your cup of tea exactly. Still when you're romantically dealing with a man born under the sign of Leo, you'll think up ways to make him purr.

Although he may be magnificent and magnanimous while trying to win you, he'll yowl or mew if he thinks he's not quite getting the tender love and care he feels is his due. If you keep him well supplied with affection, you can be sure his eyes will never gaze on someone else and his heart will never wander.

A Leo man often tends to be authoritarian. He can be depended upon to lord it over others in one way or another. If he is the top honcho at his firm, he'll most likely do everything he can to stay on top. If he's not number one, he's probably working on it and will be sitting on the throne before long.

You'll have more security than you can use if he is in a position to support you in the manner to which he feels you should be accustomed. He is inclined to be too lavish, though, at least by your standards.

You'll always have plenty of friends when you have a Leo for a mate. He's a natural-born wheeler-dealer and entertainer. He loves to let his hair down at parties.

As fathers, Leos tend to spoil their children. But they can also be strict when they think that the rules of the royal kingdom are being broken. You'll have to do your best to smooth over the children's roughed-up feelings.

VIRGO WOMAN
VIRGO MAN

The Virgo man is all business or so he may seem to you. He is usually very cool, calm, and collected. He's perhaps too much of a fussbudget to arouse deep romantic interests in a woman like you. Torrid romancing to him is just so much sentimental mush. He can do without it and can make that quite evident in short order. He's keen on chastity and, if necessary, he can lead a sedentary, sexless life without caring very much about the fun others think he's missing. In short, you may find him a first-class dud.

The Virgo man doesn't have much of an imagination; flights of fancy don't interest him. He is always correct and likes to be handled properly. Almost everything about him is orderly. There's a place for everything and everything in its place is an adage he'll fall upon quite regularly.

He does have an honest-to-goodness heart, believe it or not. The woman who finds herself strangely attracted to his cool, feet-flat-on-the-ground ways will discover that his is a constant heart, not one that goes in for flings or sordid affairs. A practical man, even in matters of the heart, he wants to know just what kind of person you are before he takes a chance on you.

The impulsive woman had better not make the mistake of kissing her Virgo friend on the street, even if it's only a peck on the cheek. He's not at all demonstrative and hates public displays of affection. Love, according to him, should be kept within the confines of one's home with the curtains drawn. Once he believes that you are on the level with him as far as your love is concerned, you'll see how fast he can lose his cool. Virgos are considerate, gentle lovers. He'll spend a long time, though, getting to know you. He'll like you before he loves you.

A romance with a Virgo man can be a sometime or, rather, a one-time thing. If the bottom ever falls out, don't bother reaching for the adhesive tape. Nine times out of ten he won't care about patching up. He's a once-burnt-twice-shy guy. When he crosses your telephone number out of his address book, he's crossing you out of his life for good.

Neat as a pin, he's thumbs-down on what he considers sloppy housekeeping. An ashtray with just one stubbed out cigarette in it can annoy him even if it's only two seconds old. Glassware should always sparkle and shine if you want to keep him happy. If you marry him, keep your sunny side up.

If you marry a Virgo man, instill a sense of order in the kids, or at least have them behaving by the time he gets home. The Virgo father wants his children to be kind and courteous and always helpful to the neighbors. The children should be kept as spotless as your house. Kids with dirty faces and hands displease him.

VIRGO WOMAN
LIBRA MAN
Men born under the sign of Libra are frequently too wrapped up in their own private dreams to be really interesting as far as love

and romance are concerned. Many times, the Libra man is a difficult person to bring back down to earth. It is hard for him to face reality. Although he may be very cautious about weighing both sides of an argument, he may never really come to a reasonable decision about anything. Decision making is something that often makes the Libra man uncomfortable. He'd rather leave that job to someone else. Don't ask him why, he probably doesn't know himself.

Qualities such as permanence and constancy are important to you in a love relationship. The Libra man may be an enigma to you. One moment he comes on hard and strong with declarations of his love; the next moment you find he's left you like yesterday's mashed potatoes. It does no good to wonder what went wrong. Chances are it was nothing on which you can put your finger. It's just one of Libra's strange ways.

He is not exactly what you would term an ambitious person. You are perhaps looking for a mate or friend with more drive and fidelity. You are the type of person who is interested in making some headway in the areas that interest you. Libra is often content just to drift along. He does have drive, however, but it's not the long-range kind.

It's not that Libra is shiftless or lazy. He's interested in material things and he appreciates luxuries, but he may not be willing to work hard enough to obtain them. Beauty and harmony interest him. He'll dedicate a lot of time to arranging things so that they are aesthetically pleasing. It would be difficult to call the Libra man practical; nine times out of ten, he isn't.

If you do begin a relationship with a man born under this sign, you will have to coax him now and again to face various situations in a realistic manner. You'll have your hands full, that's for sure. But if you love him, you'll undoubtedly do your best to understand him, no matter how difficult this may be.

If you become involved with a Libra man, either temporarily or permanently, you'd better take over the task of managing his money. Often he has little understanding of financial matters. He tends to spend without thinking, following his whims.

The Libra father is gentle and patient. He can be firm without exercising undue strictness or discipline. Although he can be a harsh judge at times, with the kids he will radiate sweetness and light in the hope that will grow up imitating his gracious manner.

VIRGO WOMAN
SCORPIO MAN
Some people have a hard time understanding the man born under the sign of Scorpio. Few, however, are able to resist his fiery

charm. When angered, he can act like the scorpion he is, ready to strike out and defend himself. His sting can leave an almost permanent mark. If you find yourself interested in the Scorpio man, you'd better learn how to keep on his good side.

The Scorpio man can be rather blunt when he chooses. At times, he may seem hard-hearted. He can be touchy every now and then, and this sensitiveness may get on your nerves after a while. When you feel as though you can't take it anymore, you'd better tiptoe away from the scene rather than chance an explosive confrontation. He's capable of giving you a sounding-out that will make you pack your bags and go back to Mother—for good.

If he finds fault with you, he'll let you know. He might misinterpret your patience and think it a sign of indifference. But you are the type of woman who can adapt to almost any sort of relationship or circumstance if you put your heart and mind to it.

Scorpio men are very perceptive and intelligent. In some respects, they know how to use their brains more effectively than most. They believe in winning, in whatever they do. Second place holds no interest for them. In business, they usually achieve the position they want through a combination of drive and intellect.

Your interest in home life probably won't be shared by him. No matter how comfortable you've managed to make the house, it will have very little influence on him with regard to making him aware of his family responsibilities. He does not like to be tied down, generally, and would rather be out on the battlefield of life, belting away at what he feels to be a just and worthy cause. Don't try to keep the home fires burning too brightly while you wait for him to come home from work; you might run out of firewood.

The Scorpio man is passionate in all things, including love. Most women are easily attracted to him and you are perhaps no exception. Those who allow themselves to be swept off their feet by a Scorpio man soon find that they're dealing with a carton of romantic fireworks. The Scorpio man is passionate with a capital P, make no mistake about that.

Scorpio men are straight to the point. They can be as sharp as a razor blade and just as cutting to anyone who crosses them.

Scorpio fathers like large families, generally. In spite of the extremes in his personality, the Scorpio man is able to transform conflicting characteristics when he becomes a father. He is adept with difficult youngsters because he knows how to tap the best in a child. He believes in preparing his children for the hard knocks life sometimes delivers.

VIRGO WOMAN
SAGITTARIUS MAN

The woman who has set her cap for a man born under the sign of Sagittarius may have to use a great deal of strategy before she can get him to drop down on bended knee. Although some Sagittarius may be marriage-shy, they're not ones to skitter away from romance. A high-spirited woman may find a relationship with a Sagittarius, whether a fling or the real thing, a very enjoyable experience.

As a rule, Sagittarius people are bright, happy, and healthy people. They have a strong sense of fair play. Often they're a source of inspiration to others. They're full of ideas and drive.

You'll be taken by the Archer's infectious grin and his light-hearted friendly nature. If you do wind up being the woman in his life, you'll find that he will treat you more like a buddy than the love of his life. It's his way.

You'll admire his broad-mindedness in most matters, including that of the heart. If, while dating you, he claims that he still wants to play the field, he'll expect you to enjoy the same liberty. Once he's promised to love, honor, and obey, however, he does just that.

A woman who has a keen imagination and a great love of freedom will not be disappointed if she does marry an Archer. The Sagittarius man likes to share his many interests, and he has a genuine belief in equality.

If he does insist on a night out with the boys once a week, he won't scowl if you decide to let him shift for himself in the kitchen while you pursue some of your own interests. He believes in fairness, and he is no male chauvinist.

The Sagittarius is not much of a homebody. Many times he's occupied with faraway places either in his dreams or in reality. He enjoys—just as you do—being on the go. A humdrum existence, especially at home, bores him. At the drop of a hat, he may ask you to take off with him into the wild blue yonder—his idea of a break from routine.

Sagittarius likes surprising people. He'll take great pride in showing you off to his friends. He'll always be a considerate mate; he will never embarrass or disappoint you intentionally. He's very tolerant when it comes to friends; you'll probably spend a lot of time entertaining people.

The Sagittarius father will dote on any son or daughter, but he may be bewildered by the newborn. The Archer usually becomes comfortable with youngsters once they have passed through the baby stage. As soon as the children are old enough to walk and talk, the Sagittarius dad encourages each and every visible sign of talent and skill.

VIRGO WOMAN
CAPRICORN MAN

The Capricorn man is frequently not the romantic lover that attracts most women. Still, with his reserve and calm, he is capable of giving his heart completely once he has found the right woman. The Capricorn man is thorough and deliberate in all that he does. His slow, steady approach is sure to win the one he loves.

He doesn't believe in flirting and would never lead a heart on a merry chase just for the game of it. If you win his trust, he'll give you his heart on a platter. Many times, it is the woman who has to take the lead when romance is in the air. As long as he knows you're making the advances in earnest, he won't mind—in fact, he'll probably be grateful.

But don't start thinking he's a cold fish; he isn't. Although some Capricorns are indeed very capable of expressing passion, others often have difficulty in trying to display affection. He should have no trouble in this area, however, once he has found a patient and understanding lover.

The Capricorn man is very interested in getting ahead. He's quite ambitious and usually knows how to apply himself well to whatever task he undertakes. He certainly isn't a spendthrift. Like you, he knows how to handle money with extreme care. You, with your knack for putting away pennies for that rainy day, should have no difficulty understanding his way with money.

The Capricorn man thinks in terms of future security. He wants to make sure that he and his wife have something to fall back on when they reach retirement age. There's nothing wrong with that; in fact, it's a plus quality.

The Capricorn man will want you to handle household matters efficiently. The fastidious Virgo woman will have no trouble doing so. If he should check up on you from time to time, don't let it irritate you. Once you assure him that you can handle everything to his liking, he'll leave you alone.

Although he's a hard man to catch when it comes to marriage, once he's made that serious step, he's inclined to become possessive. The Capricorn man needs to know that he has the support of his wife in whatever he does, every step of the way.

The Capricorn man wants to be liked. He may seem dull to some, but underneath his reserve there is sometimes an adventurous streak that has never had a chance to express itself. He may be a real daredevil in his heart of hearts. The right woman, the affectionate, adoring woman can bring out that hidden zest in his nature.

Capricorn makes a loving, dutiful father, even though he may not understand his children completely. The Goat believes that there are goals to be achieved, and that there is the right way to achieve them. The Capricorn father can be quite a scold when it comes to disciplining the youngsters. You'll have to step in and bend the rules sometimes.

VIRGO WOMAN
AQUARIUS MAN

You might find the Aquarius man the most broad-minded man you have ever met. On the other hand, you might find him the most impractical. Many times, he's more of a dreamer than a doer. If you don't mind putting up with a man whose heart and mind are as wide as the sky and whose head is almost always in the clouds, then start dating that Aquarius who has somehow captured your fancy. Maybe you, with your good sense, can bring him back down to earth when he gets too starry-eyed.

He's no dumbbell, make no mistake about that. He can be busy making some very complicated and idealistic plans when he's got that out-to-lunch look in his eyes. But more than likely, he'll never execute them. After he's shared one or two of his progressive ideas with you, you may think he's a nut. But don't go jumping to conclusions. There's a saying that Aquarius is a half-century ahead of everybody else in the thinking department.

If you decide to marry him, you'll find out how right his zany whims are on or about your 50th anniversary. Maybe the waiting will be worth it. Could be that you have an Einstein on your hands and heart.

Life with an Aquarius won't be one of total despair if you can learn to temper his airiness with your down-to-earth Virgo practicality. He won't gripe if you do. Aquarius always maintains an open mind. He'll entertain the ideas and opinions of everybody. But he may not agree with all of them.

Don't go tearing your hair out when you find that it's almost impossible to hold a normal conversation with your Aquarius friend at times. Usually chasing the big idea, he can overlook the vital details. Always try to keep in mind that he means well.

His broad-mindedness doesn't stop when it comes to you and your personal freedom. You won't have to give up any of your hobbies or projects after you're married. He will encourage you to continue them and to be as independent as he is.

He'll be a kind and generous husband. He'll never quibble over petty things. Keep track of the money you both spend. He can't. Money burns a hole in his pocket.

At times, you may feel like calling it quits. Chances are, though, that you'll always give him another chance.

The Aquarius is a good family man. He can be a shining example for the children because he sees them as individuals in their own right, not as extensions of himself. Kids love him and vice versa. He'll be tolerant with them as he is with adults.

VIRGO WOMAN
PISCES MAN

The man born under Pisces is quite a dreamer. Sometimes he's so wrapped up in his dreams that he's difficult to reach. To the average, active woman, he may seem a little passive.

He's easygoing most of the time. He seems to take things in his stride. He'll entertain all kinds of views and opinions from just about everyone, nodding or smiling vaguely, giving the impression that he's with them one hundred percent while that may not be the case at all. His attitude may be why bother when he's confronted with someone who is wrong but thinks he's right. The Pisces man will seldom speak his mind if he thinks he'll be rigidly opposed.

The Pisces man is oversensitive at times. He's afraid of getting his feelings hurt. He'll sometimes imagine a personal affront when none's been made. More than likely, you'll find this complex of his maddening. At times you may feel like giving him a swift kick where it hurts the most. It won't do any good, though.

One thing you'll admire about this man is his concern for people who are sickly or troubled. He'll make his shoulder available to anyone in the mood for a good cry. He can listen to one hard-luck story after another without seeming to tire. When his advice is asked, he can be depended upon to offer some wise counsel. He often knows what is upsetting someone before that person is aware of it himself.

Still, at the end of the day, the Pisces man will want some peace and quiet. If you've got a problem when he comes home, don't unload it in his lap. If you do, you might find him short-tempered. He's a good listener, but he can only take so much turmoil.

Pisces are not aimless although they may seem so at times. The positive sort of Pisces man is often successful in his profession and is likely to become rich and influential. Material gain, however, is never a direct goal for a man born under the sign of the Fishes.

The weaker Pisces is usually content to stay on the level where he finds himself.

Because of their seemingly laissez-faire manner, people under the sign of Pisces are immensely popular with children. For tots, the Pisces father plays the double role of confidant and playmate. It will never enter his mind to discipline a child, no matter how spoiled or incorrigible that child becomes.

Man—Woman

VIRGO MAN
ARIES WOMAN

The Aries woman may be a little too bossy and busy for you. Generally, Aries is an ambitious creature. She can become a little impatient with a Virgo who by nature is more thorough and deliberate than she is, especially if she feels you're taking too much time.

The Aries woman is a fast worker. Sometimes she's so fast she forgets to look where she's going. When she stumbles or falls, it would be nice if you were there to catch her. But Aries is a proud woman. She doesn't like to be criticized when she errs. The Virgo tongue lashings can turn her into a block of ice.

Don't begin to think that the Aries woman frequently gets tripped up in her plans. Many times she is capable of taking aim and hitting the bull's-eye. You'll be flabbergasted by her accuracy as well as by her ambition. On the other hand, you're apt to spot a flaw in her plans before she does.

You are perhaps somewhat slower than Aries in attaining your goals. Still, you are not inclined to make mistakes along the way. You're almost always well prepared.

The Aries woman can be sensitive at times. She likes to be handled with gentleness and respect. Let her know that you love her for her brains as well as for her good looks. Never give her cause to become jealous. When your Aries date sees green, you'd better forget about sharing a rosy future together. Handle her with tender love and care and she's yours.

The Aries woman can be giving if she feels her partner is deserving. She is no iceberg; she responds to the proper masculine flame. She needs a man she can admire and of whom she can feel proud. She can cause you plenty of heartache if you've made up your mind about her but she hasn't made up hers about you. The Aries woman is very demanding at times. Some tend to be highstrung. They can be difficult if they feel their independence is being hampered.

The cultivated Aries woman makes a wonderful homemaker and hostess. You'll find she's very clever in decorating and using color. Your house will be tastefully furnished; she'll make sure that it radiates harmony. The Aries wife knows how to make guests feel at home.

Although the Aries woman may not be keen on burdensome responsibilities, she is fond of children and the joy they bring. She is skilled at juggling both career and motherhood, so her kids will never feel that she is an absentee parent. In fact, as the youngsters grow older, they might want a little more of the liberation that is so important to her.

VIRGO MAN
TAURUS WOMAN

A Taurus woman could perhaps understand you better than most women. She is very considerate and loving. She is thorough and methodical in whatever she does. She is anxious to avoid mistakes.

Home is very important to the Taurus woman. She is an excellent homemaker. Although your home may not be a palace, it will become, under her care, a comfortable and happy abode. She'll love it when friends drop by for the evening. She is a good cook and enjoys feeding people well.

The Taurus woman is serious about love and affection. When she has taken a tumble for someone, she'll stay by him forever, if possible. She will try to be practical in romance, to some extent. When she decides she wants a certain man, she keeps after him until he's won her. Generally, the Taurus woman is a passionate lover, even though she may appear staid at first glance. She is on the lookout for someone who can return her affection fully. Taurus women are sometimes given to fits of jealousy and possessiveness. They expect fair play in the area of marriage. When it doesn't come about, they can be bitingly sarcastic and mean.

The Taurus woman is usually an easygoing person intent on keeping the peace. She won't argue unless she must. She'll do her best to keep your love relationship on an even keel.

Marriage is generally a one-time thing for Taurus. Once they've taken the serious step, they seldom try to back out of it. Taurus women need love and warmth. With the right man, they become ideal wives.

The Taurus woman will respect you for your steady ways. She'll have confidence in your common sense. She'll share with you all the joys and burdens of parenthood.

Taurus women seldom put up with nonsense from their children. It is not that they are strict, but rather that they are concerned. They like their children to be well behaved and dutiful. Nothing pleases a Taurus mother more than a compliment from a neighbor or teacher about her child's behavior.

Although some children may inwardly resent the iron hand of a Taurus mother, in later life they are often thankful that they were brought up in such an orderly and conscientious way.

VIRGO MAN
GEMINI WOMAN

You may find a romance with a woman born under the sign of the Twins a many-splendored thing. She will provide the intellectual companionship you often look for in a friend or mate. A Gemini partner can appreciate your aims and desires because she travels pretty much the same road as you do intellectually, that is, at least part of the way. She may share your interests but she will lack your tenacity.

She suffers from itchy feet. She can be here, there, all over the place. Her eagerness to be on the move may make you dizzy. Still, you'll enjoy and appreciate her liveliness and mental agility.

The Gemini woman often has a sparkling personality. You'll be attracted to her warmth and grace. While she's on your arm you'll probably notice that many male eyes are drawn to her. She may even return a gaze or two, but don't let that worry you. All women born under this sign have nothing against a harmless flirtation once in a while. But if she feels she is already spoken for, she will never let it get out of hand.

Although she may not be as handy as you'd like in the kitchen, you'll never go without a tasty meal. The Gemini woman is always in a rush. She won't feel she's cheating by breaking out the instant mashed potatoes or the frozen peas. She may not be a good cook but she is clever. With a dash of this and a suggestion of that, she can make an uninteresting TV dinner taste like a gourmet meal. Then, again, maybe you've struck it rich and have a Gemini lover who finds complicated recipes a challenge to her intellect. If so, you'll find every meal a tantalizing and mouth-watering surprise.

When you're beating your brains out over the Sunday cross-word puzzle and find yourself stuck, just ask your Gemini woman. She'll give you all the right answers without batting an eyelash.

Just like you, she loves all kinds of people. You may even find that you're a bit more discriminating than she. Often all that a Gemini requires is that her friends be interesting and stay inter-esting. But one thing she's not able to abide is a dullard.

Leave the party organizing to your Gemini sweetheart or mate, and you'll never have a chance to know what a dull moment is. She'll bring out the swinger in you if you give her half the chance.

A Gemini mother enjoys her children, which can be the truest form of love. Like them, she's often restless, adventurous, and easily bored. She will never complain about their fleeting interests because she understands the changes they will go through as they mature.

VIRGO MAN
CANCER WOMAN
The Cancer woman needs to be protected from the cold, cruel world. She'll love you for your masculine yet gentle manner; you make her feel safe and secure. You don't have to pull any he-man or heroic stunts to win her heart; that's not what interests her.

She's more likely to be impressed by your sure, steady ways—

that way you have of putting your arm around her and making her feel she's the only girl in the world. When she's feeling glum and tears begin to well up in her eyes, you have that knack of saying just the right thing. You know how to calm her fears, no matter how silly some of them may seem.

The woman born under the sign ruled by the Moon is inclined to have her ups and downs. You have that talent for smoothing out the ruffles in her sea of life. She'll probably worship the ground you walk on or put you on a very high pedestal. Don't disappoint her if you can help it. She'll never disappoint you.

The Cancer woman will take great pleasure in devoting the rest of her natural life to you. She'll darn your socks, mend your overalls, scrub floors, wash windows, shop, cook, and do just about anything in order to please you and let you know that she loves you. Sounds like that legendary good old-fashioned girl, doesn't it? Contrary to popular belief, there are still some around, and many of them are Cancers.

Of all the signs of the Zodiac, the Cancer-born are the most maternal. In caring for and bringing up children, Cancer women know just how to combine the right amount of tenderness with the proper dash of discipline. A child couldn't ask for a better mother. Cancer women are sympathetic, affectionate, and patient with their children.

While we're on the subject of motherhood, there's one thing you should be warned about: never be unkind to your mother-in-law. It will be the only golden rule your Cancer wife will probably expect you to follow. No mother-in-law jokes in the presence of your mate, please. They'll go over like a lead balloon. Mother is something pretty special for her. She may be the crankiest, nosiest old bat. But she's your wife's mother. You'd better treat her like she's one of the landed gentry. Sometimes this may be difficult to swallow. But if you want to keep your home together and your wife happy, learn to grin and bear it.

Treat your Cancer wife like a queen, and she'll treat you royally.

VIRGO MAN
LEO WOMAN

The Leo woman can make most men roar like lions. If any woman in the Zodiac has that indefinable something that can make men lose their heads and find their hearts, it's the Leo woman.

She's got more than a fair share of charm and glamour. She knows how to make the most of her assets, especially when she's in the company of the opposite sex. Jealous men are apt to lose their cool or their sanity when trying to woo a woman born under the sign of the Lion. The Lioness likes to kick up her heels quite often and doesn't care who knows it. She frequently makes heads turn and tongues wag. You don't necessarily have to believe any of what you hear—it's probably jealous gossip or wishful thinking. Still, other women in her vicinity turn green with envy and will try anything to put her out of the running.

Although this vamp makes the blood rush to your head and makes you momentarily forget all the things you thought were important and necessary in your life, you may feel differently when you come back down to earth and the stars are out of your eyes. You may feel that she isn't the type of girl you planned to bring home to Mother. Not that your mother might disapprove of your choice, but you might after the shoes and rice are a thing of the past. Although the Leo woman may do her best to be a good wife for you, chances are she'll fall short of your idea of what a good wife should be like.

If you're planning on not going as far as the altar with the Leo woman, you'd better be financially equipped for some very expensive dating. Be prepared to shower her with expensive gifts and to take her dining and dancing to the smartest spots in town. Promise her the moon if you're in a position to go that far. Luxury and glamour are two things that are bound to lower a Leo's resistance. She's got expensive tastes, and you'll have to cater to them if you expect to get to first base with her.

If you've got an important business deal to clinch and you have doubts as to whether you can swing it or not, bring your Leo woman along to the business luncheon. More than likely, with her on your arm, you'll be able to win any business battle with both hands tied. She won't have to say or do anything, just be there at your side. The grouchiest oil magnate can be transformed into a gushing, obedient schoolboy if there's a charming Leo woman in the room.

Leo mothers are sometimes blind to the faults of their children. On the other hand, the Leo mother can be strict when she wants them to learn something. She expects her youngsters to follow the rules, and she is a patient teacher. Being easygoing and friendly, she loves to pal around with the kids while proudly showing them off on every occasion.

VIRGO MAN
VIRGO WOMAN

The Virgo woman may be even too difficult for the Virgo man to understand at first. Her waters run deep. Even when you think you know her, don't take any bets on it. She's capable of keeping things hidden in the deep recesses of her womanly soul—things she'll only release when she's sure that you're the man she wants. But it may take her some time to come around to this decision. Virgos are finicky about almost everything. Many of them have the idea that the only people who can do things correctly are Virgos.

Nothing offends a Virgo woman more than slovenly dress, sloppy character, or a careless display of affection. Make sure your tie is not crooked and your shoes sport a bright shine before you go calling on this lady. Keep your off-color jokes for the locker room; she'll have none of that.

Take her arm when crossing the street, but don't rush the romance. Trying to corner her in the back of a cab may be one way of striking out. Never criticize the way she looks. In fact, the best policy is to agree with her as much as possible.

Still, there's just so much a man can take. All those dos and don'ts you have to observe if you want to get to first base with a Virgo may be just a little too much to ask of you. After a few dates, you may decide that she just isn't worth all that trouble. However, the Virgo woman is usually mysterious enough to keep her men running back for more. Chances are you'll be intrigued by her airs and graces.

If lovemaking means a great deal to you, you'll be disappointed at first in the cool ways of your Virgo woman. However, under her glacial facade there lies a hot cauldron of seething excitement. If you're patient and artful in your romantic approach, you'll find that all the caution was well worth the trouble. When Virgos love, it's all or nothing as far as they're concerned.

One thing a Virgo woman can't stand in love is hypocrisy. She doesn't care what the neighbors say. If her heart tells her to go ahead, she does. She is very concerned with human truths. If her heart stumbles upon another fancy, she will be true to that new heartthrob and leave you standing in the rain.

She's honest to her heart and will be as true to you as you are with her. Do her wrong once, however, and it's farewell.

The Virgo mother has high expectations for her children, and she will strive to bring out the very best in them. She is more tender than strict, though, and will nag rather than discipline. But youngsters sense her unconditional love for them, and usually turn out just as she hoped they would.

VIRGO MAN
LIBRA WOMAN
Libra invented the notion that it's a woman's prerogative to change her mind. Her changeability, in spite of its undeniable charm, could actually drive even a man of your patience up the wall. She's capable of smothering you with love and kisses one day, and on the next avoid you like the plague.

If you think you're a man of steel nerves then perhaps you can tolerate these sudden changes without suffering too much. However, if you admit that you're only a mere mortal who can take so much, then you'd better fasten your attention on a partner who's somewhat more constant.

But don't get the wrong idea. A love affair with a Libra can have a lot of pluses to it. The Libra woman is soft, very feminine, and warm. She doesn't have to vamp all over the place in order to gain a man's attention. Her delicate presence is enough to warm the cockles of any man's heart. One smile, and you're a piece of putty in the palm of her hand.

She can be fluffy and affectionate, which you will like. On the other hand, her indecision about which dress to wear, what to cook for dinner, or whether to redecorate could make you tear your hair out. What will perhaps be more exasperating is her flat denial of the accusation that she cannot make even the simplest decision. The trouble is that she wants to be fair or just in all matters. She'll spend hours weighing pros and cons. Don't make her rush into a decision; that will only irritate her.

The Libra woman likes to be surrounded by beautiful things. Money is no object when beauty is concerned. There will always be plenty of flowers in the house. She'll know how to arrange them tastefully, too. Women under this sign are fond of beautiful clothes and furnishings. They will run up bills without batting an eyelash, if given the chance.

Once she's involved with you, the Libra woman will do everything in her power to make you happy. She'll wait on you hand and foot when you're sick and bring you breakfast in bed Sundays. She'll be very thoughtful and devoted. If anyone dares suggest you're not the grandest man in the world, your Libra wife will give that person a good sounding-out.

The Libra mother works wonders with children. Gentle persuasion and affection are all she uses in bringing them up. It works. She is sensitive and sensible, with an intuitive understanding of what a child needs. Her youngsters will never lack for anything that could make their lives easier and richer. Still, you will always come before the children.

VIRGO MAN
SCORPIO WOMAN

When the Scorpio woman chooses to be sweet, she's apt to give the impression that butter wouldn't melt in her mouth but, of course, it would. When her temper flies, so will everything else that isn't bolted down. She can be as hot as a tamale or as cool as a cucumber when she wants. Whatever mood she's in, you can be sure it's for real. She doesn't believe in poses or hypocrisy.

The Scorpio woman is often seductive and sultry. Her femme fatale charm can pierce through the hardest of hearts. The Scorpio woman can be a whirlwind of passion. But life with her will not be all smiles and smooth sailing. If you think you can handle a woman who is quick to retaliate and hold a grudge, then try your luck. Your stable and steady nature will probably have a calming effect on her. You're the kind of man she can trust and rely on. But never cross her, even on the smallest thing, or she'll make you pay for it.

Generally, the Scorpio woman will keep family battles within the walls of your home. When company visits, she can be depended upon to give the impression that married life with you is one big joyride. It's just her way of expressing her loyalty to you, at least in front of others. The Scorpio woman will certainly see that others have a high opinion of you both. She'll support you in whatever it is you want to do.

Although she's an individualist, after she has married, she'll put her own interests aside for those of the man she loves. With a woman like this behind you, you can't help but go far. She'll never try to take over your role as boss of the family and she'll give you all the support you need in order to fulfill that role. She won't complain if the going gets rough, for she is a courageous woman. She's as anxious as you to find that place in the sun for you both. She is as determined a person as you are.

Although the Scorpio mother loves her children, she will not put them on a pedestal. She is devoted to developing her youngsters' talents. The Scorpio mother is protective yet encouraging. The opposites within her nature mirror the contradictions within life itself. Under her skillful guidance, the children will learn how to cope with extremes and will grow up to become well-rounded individuals. She will teach her young ones to be courageous and steadfast.

VIRGO MAN
SAGITTARIUS WOMAN

You'll most likely never meet a more good-natured woman than the one under the sign of Sagittarius. Generally, she is full of bounce and good cheer. Her sunny disposition seems almost permanent and can be relied upon even on the rainiest of days.

The woman born under the sign of the Archer is rarely malicious. But she is often a little short on tact and says literally anything that comes into her head, regardless of the occasion. Sometimes the words that tumble out of her mouth are downright cutting and cruel. But no matter what she says, she means well.

Unfortunately, the Sagittarius woman is capable of losing some of her friends—and perhaps even some of yours—through such carelessness.

On the other hand, you will appreciate her honesty and good intentions. To you, these qualities play an important part in life. With a little patience and practice, you can probably help cure your Sagittarius of her loose tongue. In most cases, she'll give in to your better judgment and try to follow your advice.

Chances are, she'll be the outdoors type and sportswoman. Long hikes, fishing trips, and white-water canoeing will probably appeal to her. She's a busy person, one who sets great store in mobility. She won't sit still for one minute if it's not necessary.

She is very friendly and likes lots of company. When your buddies drop by for poker and beer, she won't have any trouble fitting in.

On the whole, she is a very kind and sympathetic woman. If she feels she's made a mistake, she'll be the first to call your attention to it. She's not afraid to own up to her own faults and shortcomings.

You might lose your patience with her once or twice. After she's seen how upset her shortsightedness and careless comments have made you, she'll do her best to please you.

The Sagittarius woman is not the kind who will pry into your business affairs. But she'll always be there, ready to offer advice if you need it.

The Sagittarius woman is seldom suspicious. Your word will almost always be good enough for her.

The Sagittarius mother is a wonderful and loving friend to her children. She is not afraid if a youngster learns some street smarts along the way. To bolster such knowledge, or to counteract it, she may preach a bit too much for the kids. Then you can switch the focus to the practical. But you will appreciate how she encourages the children to study in order for them to get a well-rounded and broad education.

VIRGO MAN
CAPRICORN WOMAN

The Capricorn may not be the most romantic woman of the Zodiac, but she's certainly not frigid when she meets the right man. She believes in true love. She doesn't appreciate flings. To her, they're just a waste of time. She's looking for a man who means business—in life as well as in love. Although she can be very affectionate with her lover or mate, she tends to let her head govern her heart. That is not to say she is a cool, calculating cucumber. On the contrary, she just feels she can be more honest about love if she consults her brains first.

The Capricorn woman is faithful, dependable, and systematic in just about everything she undertakes. She is very concerned with security and makes sure that every penny she spends is spent wisely. She is very economical about using her time, too. She does not believe in whittling away her energy on a scheme that is bound not to pay off.

Ambitious herself, she is often attracted to the ambitious man—one who is interested in getting somewhere in life. If a man with this temperament wins her heart, she'll stick by him and do all she can to help him get to the top.

The Capricorn woman is almost always diplomatic. She makes an excellent hostess. She can be very influential when your business acquaintances come to dinner.

The Capricorn woman is likely to be very concerned, if not extremely proud, of her family tree. Relatives are very important to her, particularly if they're socially prominent. Never say a cross word about her family members. She is likely to punish you by not talking to you for days.

As a rule, she's thorough in whatever she does. The Capricorn woman is well-mannered, well-groomed, and gracious, no matter what her background.

If you should marry a woman born under this sign, you need never worry about her going on a wild shopping spree. She understands the value of money better than most women. If you turn over your paycheck to her at the end of the week, you can be sure that a good hunk of it will wind up in the bank.

The Capricorn mother is very ambitious for her children. She wants them to have every advantage and to benefit from things she perhaps lacked as a child. She will train the youngsters to be polite and kind, and to honor traditional codes of conduct. She can be correct to a fault. But the meticulous Virgo mate will not find fault with the Capricorn mother's careful ways.

VIRGO MAN
AQUARIUS WOMAN

If you find that you've fallen head over heels for a woman born under the sign of the Water Bearer, you'd better fasten your safety belt. It may take you quite a while to actually discover what she is like. Even then, you may have nothing to go on but a series of vague hunches. The Aquarius woman is like a rainbow, full of bright and shining hues. She's like no one you've ever known. There is something elusive about her.

The Aquarius woman can be pretty odd and eccentric at times. Some say this is the source of her mysterious charm. You might think she's just a screwball, and you may be 50 percent right. The

Aquarius woman often has her head full of dreams. By nature, she is often unconventional; she has her own thoughts about how the world should be run. Sometimes her ideas may seem weird, but chances are they're just a little too progressive. Keep in mind the saying: The way the Aquarius thinks, so will the world in 50 years.

She'll probably be the most tolerant and open-minded woman you've ever encountered.

If you find that she's too much mystery and charm for you to handle, tell her so and say that you think it would be best to call it quits. She'll probably agree without making a scene yet still want to remain friends. The Aquarius woman is like that. Perhaps you'll both find it easier to get along in a friendship than in a romance.

The Aquarius woman is not a jealous person and, while you're romancing her, she won't expect you to be, either. You'll find her a free spirit most of the time. Just when you think you know her inside out, you'll discover that you don't really know her at all.

She's a very sympathetic and warm person. She is always helpful to those in need of assistance and advice.

She'll seldom be suspicious even when she has every right to be. If the man she loves makes a little slip, she's inclined to forgive and forget it.

The Aquarius mother is bighearted and seldom refuses her children anything. Her open-minded attitude is easily transmitted to her youngsters. They have every change of growing up as respectful and tolerant individuals who feel at ease anywhere.

VIRGO MAN
PISCES WOMAN
Many a man dreams of an alluring Pisces woman. You're perhaps no exception. She's soft and cuddly and very domestic. She'll let you be the brains of the family; she's contented to play a behind-the-scenes role in order to help you achieve your goals. The illusion that you are the master of the household is the kind of magic that the Pisces woman is adept at creating.

She can be very ladylike and proper. Your business associates and friends will be dazzled by her warmth and femininity. Although she's a charmer, there is a lot more to her than just a pretty exterior. There is a brain ticking away behind that soft, womanly facade. You may never become aware of it—that is, until you're married to her. It's no cause for alarm, however; she'll most likely never use it against you, only to help you and possibly set you on a more successful path.

If she feels you're botching up your married life through careless behavior or if she feels you could be earning more money than you do, she'll tell you about it. But any wife would, really.

She will never try to usurp your position as head and breadwinner of the family.

No one had better dare say one uncomplimentary word about you in her presence. It's likely to cause her to break into tears. Pisces women are usually very sensitive beings. Their reaction to adversity, frustration, or anger is just a plain, good, old-fashioned cry. They can weep buckets when inclined.

She can do wonders with a house. She is very fond of dramatic and beautiful things. There will always be plenty of fresh-cut flowers around the house. She will choose charming artwork and antiques, if they are affordable. She'll see to it that the house is decorated in a dazzling yet welcoming style.

She'll have an extra special dinner prepared for you when you come home from an important business meeting. Don't dwell on the boring details of the meeting, though. But if you need that grand vision, the big idea, to seal a contract or make a conquest, your Pisces woman is sure to confide a secret that will guarantee your success. She is canny and shrewd with money, and once you are on her wavelength you can manage the intricacies on your own.

Treat her with tenderness and generosity and your relationship will be an enjoyable one. She's most likely fond of chocolates. A bunch of beautiful flowers will never fail to make her eyes light up. See to it that you never forget her birthday or your anniversary. These things are very important to her. If you let them slip your mind, you'll send her into a crying fit that could last a considerable length of time.

If you are patient and kind, you can keep a Pisces woman happy for a lifetime. She, however, is not without her faults. Her sensitivity may get on your nerves after a while. You may find her lacking in practicality and good old-fashioned stoicism. You may even feel that she uses her tears as a method of getting her own way.

The Pisces mother totally believes in her children, and that faith never wavers. Her unconditional love for them makes her a strong, self-sacrificing mother. That means she can deny herself in order to fulfill their needs. She will teach her youngsters the value of service to the community while not letting them lose their individuality.

VIRGO
LUCKY NUMBERS 1999

Lucky numbers and astrology can be linked through the movements of the Moon. Each phase of the thirteen Moon cycles vibrates with a sequence of numbers for your Sign of the Zodiac over the course of the year. Using your lucky numbers is a fun system that connects you with tradition.

New Moon	First Quarter	Full Moon	Last Quarter
Dec. 18 ('98)	Dec. 26 ('98)	Jan. 1	Jan. 9
5 7 7 5	8 6 9 4	5 3 0 8	2 6 1 3
Jan. 17	Jan. 24	Jan. 31	Feb. 8
3 7 0 4	4 2 5 9	4 0 7 2	2 6 8 3
Feb. 16	Feb. 22	March 2	March 10
3 1 7 5	8 3 2 0	0 1 5 9	9 2 6 4
March 17	March 24	March 31	April 8
4 7 7 1	5 4 0 3	3 7 2 4	4 8 6 9
April 15	April 22	April 30	May 8
9 7 1 2	1 0 6 9	7 8 0 5	5 3 6 4
May 15	May 22	May 30	June 6
4 7 2 9	0 8 3 7	2 9 4 2	2 5 3 6
June 13	June 20	June 28	July 6
6 0 9 5	8 5 9 4	4 1 8 2	2 9 3 7
July 12	July 20	July 28	August 4
7 6 2 5	5 9 3 5	8 7 1 0	8 2 6 5
August 11	August 18	August 26	Sept. 2
5 0 1 4	8 3 9 4	6 2 5 3	6 0 9 5
Sept. 9	Sept. 17	Sept. 25	Oct. 1
0 8 3 7	9 4 2 3	9 4 7 2	2 1 0 6
Oct. 9	Oct. 17	Oct. 24	Oct. 31
9 4 8 1	0 5 3 9	7 1 5 4	4 0 5 3
Nov. 7	Nov. 16	Nov. 23	Nov. 29
7 2 4 8	8 6 9 0	1 8 7 0	3 6 1 5
Dec. 7	Dec. 15	Dec. 22	Dec. 29
5 7 2 9	9 3 1 9	5 3 8 2	2 6 1 0

VIRGO
YEARLY FORECAST 1999

*Forecast for 1999 Concerning Business
and Financial Affairs, Job Prospects,
Travel, Health, Romance and Marriage
for Those Born with the Sun
in the Zodiacal Sign of Virgo.
August 22–September 22*

For those born under the influence of the Sun in the zodiacal sign of Virgo, ruled by Mercury, planet of communication and diplomacy, this is a year of change and adjustment. Your routine is seldom likely to be entirely settled, partly due to changes going on in your working life. There will be greater emphasis on developing partnership interests and collaborations. Joint financial and property undertakings figure strongly in your activities. While you should benefit from such ventures, each involvement needs to be carefully mapped out, ensuring that is both legal and in your best interests. Where business matters are concerned, much is likely to be gained through greater involvement in shared enterprises. The drying up of one area of revenue may seem like a natural result stemming from what has gone before. With the slate wiped clean, there should be plenty of room for expansion into new fields. Money demands careful handling again this year. Periods of heavy spending may be followed by more spartan living. However, there is opportunity for you to create more security for the future through joint contracts and investments. Routine occupational affairs are prone to flux and change. You may need to adapt to working with different media or newer technology. Changes taking place should seem refreshing rather than daunting, despite feeling disorganized without a fixed routine in place. Travel opportunities are greater this year than last, but long-distance trips must be tightly sandwiched between obligations based closer to your home ground. Much of your travel this year relates to work commitments and career expansion. Your health and general well-being will tend to fluctuate, with extra care and rest necessary at times. Ill health can probably be avoided or at least significantly reduced if you instigate regular eating, sleeping, and exercise regimes. Romance is sure to be fulfilling this year. Single Virgos can look forward to several opportunities to enter into an uplifting and rewarding relationship. For married Virgo men and women, the emphasis this year is on expanding mutual interests.

This is a year of mixed blessings for professional Virgo people. You are coming to the end of an era in one particular field of interest. This area may have served you well in the past, but this year you have to move on and find new opportunities to take up the slack. Opportunities abroad may start to open up for you. Various contacts from the past may also be instrumental in helping you get new business interests off the ground. It is important to plan expansion moves very carefully. Ideally, you must avoid depleting resources which, in the long term, you will need to fall back on for other purposes. Working with a group should be of significant benefit. This may include joining a business club or attending regular business conferences and seminars. Burdens generally are likely to seem less if they are spread out and undertaken collectively. An unusual opportunity may arise to develop a business interest relating to highly aggressive or competitive activity. This could turn out to be quite lucrative initially, but look at the longer term implications as well. Debts from the past may be a burden this year. It is in your best interests to stay on good terms with bank managers and tax officials. If you offer a clearly defined plan and concrete funds, even if only for short periods, you are likely to be better able to maintain the other person's confidence. Avoid speculating with certainty about what revenue you may have at your disposal in the future. Potential financial backers will be more easily persuaded by tangible results, such as meeting a profit goal or cutting costs over a specific period. If you need funding for a new project, you probably will need to find an investor. Financial officials are unlikely to approve a loan until and unless you have some solid backing behind you. The period between November 27 and December 31 may yield a surprising number of innovative opportunities which relate primarily to the fields of technology and science.

Financially, it is important to budget carefully this year. It may be tempting to spend a lot early in the year, especially if you trying to furnish or redecorate your home. Think about the future. If you use credit cards for payment, the sum you expend must be repaid at some point. And if you are prone to make impulse purchases, bills can really mount up. There will be opportunities to get more involved in joint investments. Your mate or partner may be in a position to invest on behalf of both of you without incurring extra costs for you personally. If you are considering a joint property investment, look carefully into the legal implications. If you are carrying a large debt currently, joint ownership may be less advisable because of your credit rating or the fear of foreclosure. Alternatives should be available, such as a silent partnership. Allocating property to you in a will is another possibility. You are apt to benefit this year from a family legacy. However, plan your budget according to money you know will definitely be coming in. Avoid leaving too much to chance. The periods between January 1 and 26 and again from June 4 to July 5 are times to be especially careful with your spending.

In routine occupational affairs you cannot count on a static situation this year. Changes going on within your work environment mean that you have to be adaptable. Fortunately, flexibility is a great strength of Virgo people. The introduction of a better computer system or other advanced technology is likely to make for a more efficient setup. This should appeal to your desire for order and overall competence. Everyday life is also likely to contain a great deal of change. Buildings in your local environment may be taken down, with new structures replacing them. You may have to get used to shopping in new stores. Roads and highways may be realigned. Becoming involved in such changes as a worker or an overall contractor can be very lucrative for you. If you decide to do some sort of volunteer work to help out your local community, working with children or the elderly is ideal. Go out of your way to help those who are less fortunate than you. Although you expect nothing in return, rewards are foreseen.

Travel opportunities are likely to increase this year. You may need to frequently travel a long distance, possibly abroad in relation to work. There may be sufficient time to do some sightseeing as well as carry out your business. However, there may be little breathing space between trips. The intensity of such travel could therefore be quite taxing. Employers are likely to be accommodating within their budgets. For example, if you have to fly frequently, it is unlikely that you will be expected to travel at off-peak hours in order to get a cut-rate fare. If you are required to undertake specialized training for which you have to travel a long distance, expect the company to provide reasonable local accommodations. In fact, some such trips could turn out to be quite luxurious in many respects. Pleasure trips may have to wait until quite late in the year before you find time to get away. The periods between June 29 and August 24 and from October 18 to November 26 are the most ideal times for personal travel, especially if you are accompanied by your mate or partner.

Minor health problems may plague you intermittently. Virgo people tend to have a lot of nervous energy. With your regular routine undergoing frequent upheaval this year, there may be a tendency to get stressed out all too often. It is important to try to structure life as consistently as you can. Avoid skipping meals and eating junk food instead. If you find it difficult to make time to exercise, try to find an activity that you can do close to home. Aerobic videos could be one answer. For health problems that are not too serious, such as insomnia, it is likely to be worthwhile looking into natural herbal remedies.

This year is rewarding and satisfying for love and romance. In a fairly new relationship there is a likelihood of a strong commitment being made. The decision to marry could follow naturally from discussions concerning a property move. Single Virgos are highly likely to link up with someone special this year, possibly while traveling. For married Virgo men and women, there is more opportunity to spend time sharing and enjoying mutual interests and also to develop activities that you can enjoy together.

VIRGO
DAILY FORECAST

January–December 1999

JANUARY

1. FRIDAY. Mixed. Because you are likely to be in a career-oriented frame of mind as the new year begins, this is a key day for plotting and planning. A sound business proposition could come your way. Make a point of looking into it in depth in order to discover what is really involved. An important informal agreement may be hammered out or a contract signed. Squabbles at home are possible throughout the day. It is probably best not to spend too much time cooped up with loved ones. Opt for a change of scene, which should clear the air at home or at the very least, give you a new and better perspective.

2. SATURDAY. Stressful. There may be a lot of tension in a close friendship, perhaps due to romantic interest being directed at you which is not altogether welcome. You are apt to feel that the other person is overstepping the boundaries. Be straightforward about the situation, and make your position clear. If you are harboring romantic notions, be certain to look before you leap. You could be in for disappointment if you do not check out the status of the other person before you make a move. A secret desire is unlikely to be fulfilled, but this is no reason to lose sight of your special dreams. By being more flexible than usual you can eventually get what you want.

3. SUNDAY. Frustrating. This is another day when you are apt to have your moves thwarted when it comes to romance. It is a time for being realistic and facing the music. The sooner you accept what cannot be, the easier it will be to move on to new plans. Money matters, especially personal expenses, require more care than usual. Someone in your social circle may try to take advantage of your good nature. You could end up stuck with the entire bill for a restaurant meal if you are not vigilant. Do not allow others to run roughshod over you; stick up for your rights. A true friend will respect your wishes without questioning your motivation.

4. MONDAY. Rewarding. Virgos can look forward to a positive development regarding a matter that has been worrisome lately. In dealing with any kind of anxiety or uneasiness, it is best to investigate the matter further. You should get positive results and reassuring responses. A business deal that has been in the works can now lead to a satisfactory agreement. Do not hesitate to sign a contract. Where routine work is concerned, there may be a disruption to your schedule, with unexpected tasks being heaped on you at the eleventh hour. Greater ease and a more peaceful life is indicated in relation to home matters.

5. TUESDAY. Confusing. You should be able to make very good progress with any behind-the-scenes efforts. Research, in particular, should produce the results you are looking for. Make extra time for your loved ones. This is a day when important discussions can take place. Family plans and arrangements can be made successfully. On the other hand, work relationships may be an area of confusion. There could be a misunderstanding about who is supposed to handle a particular task. It is best to double-check with the boss if you are at all uncertain about your responsibility. A minor health problem could resurface. It is probably best to take life at your own pace in order to avoid increased stress.

6. WEDNESDAY. Rewarding. You will tend to be happier focusing on your own plans. Family obligations and domestic demands could force you to split your attention two ways. Be wary of getting too involved in other people's problems. You are not apt to be in the mood for a long counseling session and could later feel resentful if all your time gets taken up in this way. Aim to get to the heart of a problem quickly. With care and advance preparations, this should turn out to be quite a rewarding day. Some entertainment this evening is likely to lift your spirits. Children are sure to be uplifting company as their natural enthusiasm rubs off on you.

7. THURSDAY. Cautious. There is a strong need to again concentrate primarily on your own world at the moment. Partners can tend to be quite demanding. It is in your own best interests to say no when you feel that too much is being asked of you. Make time for a project which is important to you at a personal creative level. Other people may think that you are idling away your time, but it is important for you to do as you please for a portion of the day. A generous offer from someone you have not previously considered to be an ally should be treated with healthy suspicion. Even the kindest folk are usually looking for some kind of reward or recognition, now or in the future.

8. FRIDAY. Favorable. Financial matters play a dominant role in a Virgo's everyday life. If you have been short of cash lately, a solution to the problem could suddenly appear. There may be an offer of extra work which can be done in your spare time to earn some extra money. If you are trying to think of a profitable sideline which you could develop, consider domestic tasks for older busy people who cannot get around or do not have much time to spare. If you are planning on buying a gift for someone you know, keep your price limit in mind. Ambitious salespeople may try to talk you into something which is far too expensive.

9. SATURDAY. Disquieting. A strong focus remains on financial matters. This is not the best time to be looking for bargains. You are likely to get exactly what you pay for, and potentially may not even get good value for your money. Put off a spending spree until another time. Sports activities may not seem all that rewarding or appealing. This is one of those days when it is not worth going all out to try to prove yourself. Any anger left over from a recent upset is likely to have a negative effect on your current performance. Seek an outlet for the anger which will not be destructive, or simply resolve to drop it.

10. SUNDAY. Disconcerting. You could find it hard to meet some of your bills if you have been a bit free and easy with your money lately. Take time to sit down and refigure your budget. If you have to cut back for a short while, make the cuts on items that you will not miss too much. Do not bank on being able to borrow from a family member if you run short of cash. If you have made an arrangement for an evening meeting or entertainment, check the details carefully. This is not the day for leaving too much to chance. Someone at a distance is hoping to hear from you; call or write today to ease their mind.

11. MONDAY. Variable. This is an excellent day for local trips and communications of all kinds. Go out of your way to visit and contact people you have not seen in a while. You may receive a romantic letter or telephone call. If you are unattached, be open to invitations from neighbors and relatives. One particular get-together could lead to meeting someone new with whom you strike up a strong rapport. For Virgo parents, this is a favorable time for introducing new ideas to children so that they know your expectations. There may be some tension with people in your working life. Try to keep an open mind, and do not expect everything to go according to plan.

12. TUESDAY. Fortunate. A social get-together with neighbors, relatives, or colleagues is likely to be especially fortunate for single Virgos. The same opportunities to meet someone which existed yesterday extend into today. A letter or phone call later in the day should lift your spirits. Good news is especially likely through the mail. Work matters are improving, with more opportunity to get to the heart of a problem. Meetings can be arranged and schedules set. One particularly laborious job which has been trying your patience can be completed if you put your mind to it. Opt for an early night if you have been feeling a little under par.

13. WEDNESDAY. Manageable. You are likely to be in the mood to do something artistic or creative around the home. This is an ideal time to plan a dinner party particularly if you want to get in a certain person's good graces or want to ask for a favor. Even though you could end up talking shop all evening, your time spent together is likely to be productive and enjoyable. More practically, current conditions favor tackling intricate tasks which require patience and concentration. Attend to whatever you have been putting off. Your regular schedule may be thrown out of kilter; this is another day to prepare for the unexpected.

14. THURSDAY. Excellent. All personal relationships should be easygoing and enjoyable. Being around those most familiar to you is likely to do much to lift your spirits. A surprise party organized on your behalf is possible if there is something special to celebrate. An unexpected gift could be coming your way. If you have been thinking about redecorating your home, this is a favorable time for picking out materials and choosing a color scheme. Romance is in the air this evening. Single Virgo people are unlikely to be short of invitations to go out and socialize. A confident sparkle should make you the center of attention and could draw someone special to your side.

15. FRIDAY. Quiet. Opt for a quiet day. Beware of plans that will leave you and your partner feeling cooped up. Arrange something specific to do rather than simply watching television; you could end up squabbling about which programs you both want to see. A discussion regarding money matters should prove profitable. This is a propitious time for working out a new budget, particularly if you are planning an important purchase and need to start saving for it. A mystery in connection with your family or with a colleague is likely to be solved. You should feel reassured that all is well by the end of the day.

16. SATURDAY. Cautious. Take to heart good advice given to you, particularly by a female relative or associate. This is especially useful in regard to romantic matters. It is likely that this person has some valuable insight to share. Trouble with your car or other vehicle should be given prompt attention before it gets any worse. If you have children, take time to really listen to what they tell you. A teenager, in particular, may need to talk but feel embarrassed, which may lead them to communicate in a kind of code. Although this is one of those days when you may feel like spoiling yourself, beware of making too many impulse buys all at once.

17. SUNDAY. Difficult. Entertainment is likely to be more enjoyable if you have a companion to share the good times with. Single Virgo people should not hesitate to accept a house or dinner party invitation. In this type of context you could pair up with an interesting new partner. Money may be tight at the moment, but if you are thinking about opting out of social affairs altogether, think again. Instead, look for ways to economize, for example by borrowing a special outfit rather than purchasing something new. If you are deciding where to go out, urge others to accept a place you can afford. The company you keep is more important than the background atmosphere.

18. MONDAY. Deceptive. Expect to get off to rather a shaky start at work this week. Messages may be confusing. Double-check instructions before launching into action. There is a good chance that you will end up completing a difficult project by the end of the day despite earlier complications. Thorough groundwork is the key to success. Tying colleagues down to specific plans, actions, or arrangements may not be as simple as it should be. Make a point of overseeing people you cannot really rely upon to get the job done. Helpers may have a tendency to disappear from the scene, forcing you to work longer and harder to meet a deadline.

19. TUESDAY. Satisfactory. Charm is your key to success today, especially where work and professional matters are concerned. Discretion is also very important. If you want to get tasks completed in double-quick time, team up with other people. Make the most of resources which you sometimes forget are available. There should be an opportunity to settle a worrisome joint financial matter, but nothing needs to be rushed in this respect. Serious, long-term matters deserve considered thought and as much debate as it takes to arrive at an amicable decision. You may need to cut personal spending and give the overall family budget first priority.

20. WEDNESDAY. Disconcerting. If you are going on a date with someone new, do not expect to find out a great deal about the other person without considerable effort. Be very careful not to seem prying, which could make the person clam up. In an ongoing relationship, try not to spend too much time cooped up together at home; you are apt to get on each other's nerves. While getting to the root of your mate or partner's problem should be helpful, you need to summon up a high degree of determination in order to succeed. If you are willing to put up with frayed tempers, much can be achieved. Strive to keep a sense of humor through it all.

21. THURSDAY. Useful. Both work and personal partnerships should be much more mellow and peaceful today than yesterday, even if you are involved in lively debate. This is one of those days when it is easier to reach agreements and see eye-to-eye, even if your opinions have previously been at loggerheads. For single Virgo men and women, a true meeting of minds is likely with someone you are introduced to by a mutual friend. This could potentially lead to love in the future. If you are involved in any type of legal matters, discussions and developments which take place now are likely to work in your favor. A neutral go-between can prove very helpful in reaching an amicable solution.

22. FRIDAY. Buoyant. Get an early start. Partnerships should be especially happy and fulfilling. You can achieve the most by working as part of a team. Virgo singles looking for a new partner should not be short of offers. However, you may need to fully utilize your innate Virgo discrimination. Not everyone you meet is going to be your idea of the perfect lifetime partner. You can sort out confusion over a joint financial matter if you make an effort to search for the missing piece of the puzzle. Double billing might be the problem. Be careful not to take on so much at work that it becomes difficult to do anything well.

23. SATURDAY. Changeable. Thoroughly investigating new financial offerings should be well worth the time and effort. If you are being forced to move, consider sharing new accommodations. In this way it is possible that you will both be able to save considerably on costs. If your energy has been sluggish, a new sport or exercise regimen could be useful. A romantic conversation can lead to a closer relationship. Someone you come into contact with, possibly a child, may inspire you to see life in a different way. Whether or not you are consciously aware of it, changes going on in every aspect of your life can be stressing you out.

24. SUNDAY. Productive. If you are planning to go shopping with your mate or partner, decide beforehand exactly what you want to buy. It is a good idea to pick out decorating materials and paint together, so that you agree on everything right from the start. Children may be awkwardly inquisitive. It can be helpful to take them aside and spend some time explaining the essence of a complicated relationship or other matter in order to avoid further embarrassment. Sound decisions need to be made and actions taken regarding your joint financial situation. Be careful not to overcommit personal finances because of a temporary need or want.

25. MONDAY. Frustrating. Although you may long to get away from the usual scene to somewhere that will excite and stimulate you, such disruptions to your routine may not provide quite what you are looking for. You need to be more thoughtful in seeking out what you really want. If you are thinking about taking an educational course of some kind, stick with tried-and-tested learning centers. A new subject may sound appealing, but look into the long-range value of the knowledge you will gain. If you are involved in any legal dealings, be prepared for a change in the situation. Guard against reading more into a statement than is actually intended.

26. TUESDAY. Fair. This is another day when routine matters can seem very dull, causing you to yearn for something totally different. A close friend or partner may provide your ticket to an exciting event, whether literally or figuratively speaking. For single Virgos, there is a chance of meeting someone particularly stimulating through mutual academic interests. A change of scene socially could also bring someone new and interesting into your life. A mild flirtation while you are commuting or traveling could lead to something much more substantial later. For married Virgos, your spouse could have a significant impact on the future. An inheritance or other financial windfall is foreseen.

27. WEDNESDAY. Lucky. Focus on career matters. This is an excellent day for pushing ahead with efforts that you know will be appreciated by people in high places. If influential higher-ups are visiting your work location, make an extra effort to be noticed for the best possible reasons. First impressions count for a lot. Avoid getting bogged down with work which takes you behind the scenes and out of the limelight. Other people can handle those tasks instead of you, and just as effectively. Unexpected new work is likely to come your way. This should make Virgo people who have been out of work especially happy. A well-calculated gamble is likely to pay off.

28. THURSDAY. Sensitive. Partnership interests have to come before work and career matters. However, it is not always easy or advisable to mix business with pleasure. Be careful that you are not doing anything which could create a bad impression and potentially injure your reputation. A joint business or financial deal which has been in the works can now be brought to fruition. Solid offers are coming your way where there have been only vague hopes, ideas, and suggestions. For single Virgo people, friendship can lead to romance, either directly or indirectly. A close associate may introduce you to someone very attractive and compatible.

29. FRIDAY. Happy. Excellent rapport exists between you and your mate or partner, leading to a very loving day. You can achieve a lot together because you are on such good terms, with the energy flowing freely between you. The same is true of a key business partnership. Intimate conversations are likely to lead to a passionate encounter. Attached as well as single Virgo men and women have much to look forward to in the romance stakes. You may also be surprised by a kind gesture from an old enemy. This is likely to be a genuine offer and could lead to giving up bad feelings and moving onto another level.

30. SATURDAY. Changeable. Hopes and wishes which have so far been private to you can now be shared with a close friend or partner. It is quite possible that this person can help you fulfill a special dream. If the person is part of your secret desire, be bold in expressing your feelings. You are likely to receive a highly positive response. Be careful to avoid mixing business with pleasure, which can lead to overspending or unwise decisions. Confused communications are possible in the middle of the day. Avoid making arrangements in a hurry and most problems can be avoided. Enjoy a night on the town with friends.

31. SUNDAY. Disquieting. You are likely to feel a little under par. Although health conscious, you have a natural Virgo tendency to overwork. It would be wise to take stock of your current situation and start to offload some of your responsibilities. If you do not want to relinquish particular tasks, at least consider postponing them. The more you are treat this as the day of rest that it traditionally is, the better. Stay home, away from the hustle and bustle of life on the outside. Rest up and get your bearings. A problem from the past needs to be solved sooner or later, but do not pressure yourself to come up with the ultimate solution today.

FEBRUARY

1. MONDAY. Fair. This should be a steady start to the new month. Your energy level should stay fairly even if you work at a consistent pace. For Virgo people worried about money, it is likely that a solution will come to light. You may be able to earn some overtime pay this week, or a loan opportunity may arise which is both helpful and affordable. Double-check any new information which comes your way. People you work with may not mean to be misleading, but their messages could be confusing. It is in your best interests to be extra thorough in everything you do. You should be able to tie up a few outstanding matters by the end of the day.

2. TUESDAY. Unsettling. If you have been thinking about going on a diet, this is the perfect day to begin. Working out an exercise program which will support your efforts can help you achieve good results more quickly. There may be a temptation to compare yourself too much with others, which could undermine your self-confidence. It is best to concentrate fully on your own ambitions. Focus on what will please and satisfy you personally. Family members could be a drain on your emotions and probably your wallet as well. Be firm about your plans and stick up for yourself without backing down.

3. WEDNESDAY. Confusing. This is not a day for being complacent in any area of your life. A part of your normal routine may be missing today, replaced by some unexpected and unusual tasks. If you start out with an open mind, the day should turn out to be exciting rather than daunting. You may hear from a colleague you knew when you worked at another job. This is apt to be the last person you expect to hear from, but be friendly. While this person may want something from you, they may also have something to offer in return. There is little that you cannot cope with if you take things in stride and avoid making any hasty decisions.

4. THURSDAY. Variable. Do not expect an easy time where partnerships are concerned. If you have to work closely with a colleague, there are likely to be arguments. While you probably have definite ideas about what you want to achieve and how you want to proceed, try to be a little flexible. You both need to compromise if you are to achieve anything of significance. The same applies in a close love relationship. Your partner may be seeing the world from a very different perspective than yours. Adjust your focus and you should find it much easier to get along. Mutual understanding is the key along with open, frank discussion.

5. FRIDAY. Mixed. There may be an unexpected financial bonus for you or for your mate or partner. If you have been putting in extra effort at work, it could pay off now even if you do not expect it. There should also be an opportunity to put a joint business or financial situation on a more stable footing. If you are in the mood to spend on your home, look for bargains in used furniture or new artwork. A rocky romantic relationship is likely to continue to be volatile. You may get to the point where you feel it is not really worth the intense emotional investment required. Do not be afraid to try a trial separation if this is something you have been contemplating.

6. SATURDAY. Tedious. Virgo people in the process of trying to find property to buy need to look systematically. Then, although you may find the ideal property, it may not be available at the ideal price. If you are about to make a major purchase, be prepared for a delay. Surveys may reveal serious flaws of which you were not aware. Renegotiating the price may be necessary as a result. If you are intent on going out shopping, you may end up having to go to more stores than you anticipate in order to obtain exactly what you want. Be generous with your time estimates so that you are not under any pressure.

7. SUNDAY. Deceptive. This is not the best day for serious future planning, even if you feel so inclined. It is all too easy to overlook details which, in retrospect, turn out to be quite major. Concentrate on being more physically active than usual. If you have not been exercising very much lately, you might benefit from joining a gym or health club. Relations with your loved ones should be especially good. You should have an opportunity to talk over things that really matter. For single Virgo men and women, there should be an opportunity to meet someone new, probably close to home. Get to bed earlier than usual tonight.

8. MONDAY. Frustrating. Virgos who commute to work could be in for a frustrating start to the day. There is a risk of detours which lengthen your journey. If you have to drive, try to avoid routes where road repairs are in progress. If traveling by train or plane, be prepared to have to wait more than usual. At work, colleagues are apt to be argumentative. It is best to act with utmost diplomacy in making suggestions or issuing orders. Much can be achieved if you go out of your way to negotiate and to understand the other person's point of view. A heavy-handed approach is unlikely to produce the results you want.

9. TUESDAY. Rewarding. Today should be more productive at work than yesterday. Co-workers and higher-ups have a more generous attitude. There is sufficient time to bring up ideas which you have been waiting to discuss in depth. This should be a helpful day for expanding relationship interests generally. You and your mate or partner may need to discuss and plan a weekend break for the near future. An authority figure who has been cool lately is likely to adopt a friendlier approach. Something of importance may be told to you in confidence; keep it a secret. This is a favorable day for future planning.

10. WEDNESDAY. Disquieting. Conditions favor getting projects finished at work. You are surprised by some of your inspirations. Be on the lookout for a shortcut which can drastically reduce the effort you have to put into one particular task. On the domestic scene there may be disagreements with your mate or partner. You are apt to be eager to get on with household chores while your loved one prefers to socialize or to watch TV. Try to find time for both practical tasks and some extra togetherness. Doing some chores together is apt to be more conducive to maintaining harmony between you.

11. THURSDAY. Satisfactory. Spend most of this day tying up loose ends at home and at work. You should be able to pin other people down to arrangements without a hitch. It can be a particularly pleasant day if you hear from distant friends and contacts by telephone or letter. Make more of an effort to stay in touch with people who live far away. Save on your telephone bill by writing if you have a lot to say. Where joint business and financial transactions are concerned, final agreements can be ironed out. Read over the small print of any contract so that you are aware of all the details and will not be taken by surprise in the future.

12. FRIDAY. Useful. If you rely on creative skills in your work, this should be an especially productive day. Your imagination is active and your thinking incisive. Demands should be fewer than usual, giving you more time to think inventively. Virgo parents may want to devote more time and energy to children. They are likely to appreciate it if you are direct with them. Talking about your own childhood as a guide for their future will probably not be helpful. If you are single, this evening may bring a passionate encounter. If you have played the role of matchmaker, the meeting should be dynamic.

13. SATURDAY. Happy. This promises to be a happy start to the weekend. Since you should not have too many demands on your time, immerse yourself in creative activities and artistic hobbies. You are likely to find it easy to make progress with painting, writing, and similar interests. Activities shared with others are also sure to be enjoyable; do not confine yourself to activities which isolate you. Virgo singles involved in a new romance can look forward to a highly charged atmosphere with a new or longtime partner. This evening should prove much more romantically rewarding than you dare to expect.

14. SUNDAY. Confusing. Children are likely to be harder work than usual, being in the mood to break rules and test limits. Put some time aside to discuss current problems. There may be a logical reason behind their negative behavior. A project or hobby that you are working on could turn out to be quite draining physically or financially. Limit the amount of time and money you spend on it. Make do with materials already on hand. Your energy should pick up again by evening, giving you more enthusiasm for household chores which have been piling up. Do not worry if you cannot make firm future arrangements. The people you contact may need more time to plan or to rearrange their schedule.

15. MONDAY. Variable. This promises to be a productive day. With intense work you should be able to finish up one particular task which has been dragging on. An important business deal can be concluded today. You are likely to be pleasantly surprised by the speed with which a complicated transaction is finalized. Colleagues should be cooperative. A team you are part of probably feels like a happy family. This is the perfect day for laying the groundwork for new projects or initiatives. Allow sufficient time to investigate new ideas in depth; what you discover should be encouraging.

16. TUESDAY. Challenging. A promising new start is likely in work matters. You may be offered new responsibility. Changes in your basic schedule and routine are also likely, which should be pleasantly refreshing. It is important to do thorough research in order to get a new project successfully off the ground. In this way you should be able to lay a firm foundation which is a major key to success. Partnership affairs are apt to be spirited. Focus on physical activities, such as sports, which you can share in your leisure hours together. Consider joining a bowling team with your mate or partner or learning a winter sport such as skiing.

17. WEDNESDAY. Mixed. Work matters are likely to be full of dynamism. Working as part of a team should bring especially rewarding results, a case of two heads being better than one. Where your personal relationships are concerned, you and your mate or partner may disagree over domestic or property matters. If you feel that your loved one is shirking domestic tasks, say so. However, try to understand if pressure from work is the reason. You may need to be especially supportive temporarily without complaining or making unfavorable comparisons.

18. THURSDAY. Fair. A love relationship should be especially happy and warm. For single Virgo men and women, there is a likelihood of meeting someone with whom you feel special rapport. Accept social invitations; these are likely to lead to meeting the right person. Joint finances or business interests are likely to receive a boost. You may receive more interest on a loan or investment than you expected. Bank extra money instead of going on a spending spree. If there are household chores to be done, blitz through them this evening. You are likely to feel more comfortable if mess and clutter are cleared out of the way.

19. FRIDAY. Exciting. A financial dispute can be amicably resolved. Financial transactions generally should go in your favor. Virgo business professionals can look forward to an interesting new proposition. Once you have done your homework, you may be convinced that the investment is more sound than it first appeared to be. Surprises are in store for you at work. Any unexpected change in routine should be refreshing rather than upsetting. If there has been any bad feeling between you and your mate or partner over money matters, you can clear the air by having a calm discussion.

20. SATURDAY. Tricky. Getting away from routine and regularity should appeal. It may not be easy, however, to find the time to indulge in a change of scene and also attend to urgent home or work responsibilities. Get whatever cannot wait out of the way early this morning, leaving the afternoon and evening free to do as you please. An escape to somewhere of historical interest could be fascinating. It is important to avoid a destination that holds bad memories for you, however. If you have been having disturbing dreams, do not attribute too much importance to them; the real meaning may be quite subtle.

21. SUNDAY. Stressful. You are likely to feel extremely restless. However, this is one of those days when you may find it hard to make up your mind about what to do. If local activities seem more inviting than an arrangement which entails traveling quite a distance, come up with an excuse to cancel out of the latter. As a Virgo you like to please others, but there is little point in doing so if your heart is not in it. Although speaking your mind may lead to arguments, you will probably respect yourself more for having stood your ground. You may be surprised by how much you achieve once you set your sights on a specific goal.

22. MONDAY. Successful. This should be a productive start to the working week. Relations with authority figures are likely to be harmonious. If you want to ask for a favor, such as extra leave, now is a good time to approach the boss. You should be able to expand new interests to a significant degree. For Virgo people who have recently been offered a promotion at work, ensuing financial negotiations should work out. It is worth pushing for that little extra increase if you can justify it with a comparison of other people's salaries and perks.

23. TUESDAY. Exciting. Professional relationships are apt to be a source of inspiration. If you and an expert collaborate on plans for a new project, you should come up with better ideas than either of you would alone. It is important, nonetheless, to respect the established hierarchy and not overstep your designated responsibilities. Allow the initiative to come from others and all should be well. Do not expect to be able to complete all that you schedule for yourself. Some tasks are bound to take longer than you think once you examine precisely what is involved.

24. WEDNESDAY. Sensitive. Virgo commuters could end up with insufficient information. Be careful about scheduling your day too tightly. If you unwittingly park somewhere illegal, ignorance will probably be no excuse if you receive a ticket. If you are making an important journey by public transportation, be sure to refer to an up-to-date timetable. If your printed information is out of date, check by telephone before starting out. On the work scene, the boss may take you to task about details you overlooked or ignored. It is best to admit to an error on your part and do all that you can to rectify the matter. You may have no option but to put in some overtime hours tonight.

25. THURSDAY. Changeable. A friend you usually feel comfortable with may ask some difficult probing questions. Be prepared to think on your feet in order to come up with a suitable response without having to reveal whatever you do not wish to discuss openly. In the workplace, group efforts are not very likely to be productive. Lack of mutual goals and interests may reflect an imbalance of commitment. If you want to launch a new project which you are personally enthusiastic about, it is important to work with people who share your same degree of eagerness and enthusiasm. Otherwise you will be better off working alone.

26. FRIDAY. Useful. Working with others is likely to prove much more productive today than yesterday. You should be able to negotiate any differences of opinion quite amicably. This is a favorable day for getting back together with a friend with whom you had a falling out; a reconciliation is foreseen. Tact and diplomacy are the keys to long-term success. You should be in the frame of mind to talk your way through problems or difficulties. As a Virgo you sometimes lack the confidence to attempt to negotiate a better deal, but this tendency does not prevail today. You should be feeling more certain of your ability to express your thoughts and to hold out for what you want.

27. SATURDAY. Easygoing. Somebody you have been able to rely on as a trustworthy, dependable friend in the past may let you down today. While it could be tempting to keep quiet and feel bitter, it is better to speak your mind. Think back to time in the past when you let a similar matter go, perhaps with someone else, and the dissatisfaction you felt as a result. This should help give you the courage to express current anger and disappointment. The day should improve if you take time out for yourself. Rest and relaxation can be a real cure in overcoming any minor setback and restoring your good humor.

28. SUNDAY. Disconcerting. You need to take life easy. Arrange to have some time alone in order to collect your thoughts; you should feel better for having done so. There is a chance, however, that you will be unexpectedly asked to help a neighbor or friend. If you do not feel up to the task, do not feel obliged to offer your services. An intimate get-together is likely to be more enjoyable than a large social gathering this evening. If a family member changes plans at the last moment, consider staying in and resting rather than scrambling to find an entertainment alternative.

MARCH

1. MONDAY. Productive. This is a starred day for putting together long-term plans with a view to broadening your horizons. In work matters you may be called upon to use your leadership qualities more. Although as a Virgo you sometimes shy away from taking the lead, be more confident about doing so today. While you may be getting into fresh territory, some of your past experience relates helpfully to the new task. Family members are likely to be demanding. Your loved one may show signs of jealousy if you are spending more time away from home than usual. Be cautious in what you say; extra tact is necessary in order to avoid hurt feelings.

2. TUESDAY. Challenging. Too much mess and clutter at home can start to get on your nerves. You may even feel that you cannot think straight or plan properly because of it. Take the time to straighten it and you should feel a lot better. If you are going to eat out, be careful what you choose on the menu. Spicy food could be more risky for you than usual. Stick with something safe which you know will not upset your sensitive digestive system. At work, this is the perfect day for taking the initiative in trying new methods. Be prepared for others to balk temporarily until the new ideas are proven to be effective.

3. WEDNESDAY. Unsettling. Advice regarding financial matters may not be as helpful as you hope. Be especially leery of a commission-making salesperson who is out to make a sale. Your partner may admit having spent money from your mutual account without having mentioned doing so. While an apology may be in order, being critical is not the best way to keep this from happening in the future. Try to agree on a workable budget. If you intend to go out shopping, make a point of keeping the receipts for what you purchase. This should save any later hassle if the item needs to be exchanged or returned for a refund.

4. THURSDAY. Variable. You may be offered cash-in-hand work which will boost your income. If you have been out of work, this is a very favorable day for resuming your job search. It may be worth writing to companies who are not advertising positions; you could get an interview due to fortunate timing. Avoid speculating and any type of gambling. Although you may be tempted to take more financial risks than usual, it is unlikely that these will pay off. If you have been waiting for money due you, there should be good news in the mail. A valuable item which you feared was lost may be found in a most unlikely place. Protect your wallet when you are in a crowd.

4. FRIDAY. Exciting. The work scene is likely to be more exciting than you anticipate. There may be an unexpected visitor or event, which should lead to a stimulating interlude. If you are currently seeking work, now is the time to brainstorm possible openings. Follow your good Virgo intuition. Contact companies that are currently expanding or have recently merged. It is quite possible that you will stumble upon a golden opportunity by chance. For Virgo business people, an unusual but potentially quite lucrative proposition is likely. Do not postpone your decision if this looks like a genuinely good deal. Independent action is favored over teamwork.

6. SATURDAY. Unsettling. If you are planning to travel locally, expect traffic delays. Even routine shopping may take extra time due to road detours or problems with finding a place to park. The less you try to cram into your schedule, the better. If you are going somewhere special this evening, you may feel a lot less stressed about the whole affair if you do not have to rush to get ready. If you need to write an important letter, it may be difficult to find exactly the right words to express what you want to say. It could be helpful to consult a friend who is gifted at putting thoughts in words.

7. SUNDAY. Sensitive. Take special care if you are driving. If you are in a bad temper, there is a risk that you will get involved in a minor accident due to a lack of concentration. Unexpected and perhaps unwelcome responsibilities are likely to be heaped on you in regard to your neighbors or relatives. Even on such short notice, if you think on your feet you can probably find an excuse which gets you off the hook. Partnerships should run smoothly. If you have been hoping to hear from someone special, it is likely that they will get in touch later today. However, do not sit by the phone waiting.

8. MONDAY. Quiet. This should be a peaceful start to the working week. As a Virgo you are generally happier when your life is well organized. Today you are likely to have some spare time on your hands. Use this opportunity to sort through accumulated paperwork. Correspondence pertaining to a recently completed project should be put in order and stored away. Attend to your filing so that you are prepared for any potential background request in the future. Virgo people who work from home may be able to save on the telephone bill by sending out letters instead of telephoning people at a distance. This also gives you a record of what you said and what you are promising.

9. TUESDAY. Fair. This should be a good day for completing minor matters at work and at home. If you have not done any spring cleaning, now is the ideal time to leap into action. Make routine checks around your property, inside and out. This is a good time to take care of any repairs, either personally or by calling on the services of a professional. Financial or property negotiations may come to a temporary halt, but do not worry. This is just a pause in the proceedings. A change of schedule at work should prove refreshing. You could have a surprise visitor to your home this evening.

10. WEDNESDAY. Mixed. If you and your partner are spending the day at home, do not expect a totally harmonious atmosphere. You are apt to have different ideas about what to do and when to do it. You may want to get on with chores around the house while your mate or partner chooses to focus less on the domestic side of life. A change of scene should be good for both of you. If you have been waiting for an agreement in regard to a property transaction, good news should arrive today. This is the perfect time for bartering for a good deal on repairs or gardening to improve your current property. A family member is likely to have some financial good fortune, giving you part of the windfall.

11. THURSDAY. Slow. There is strong emphasis today on creativity and leisure. You could be in the mood to do something you have never tried before. If someone close to you has an important occasion coming up, you may decide to make a gift that is unique and personalized. Children are likely to be good fun. They will probably appreciate a trip to an unusual location; such a journey would be an enjoyable break for you, too. Hitches are possible in ongoing property negotiations despite thinking that all has been settled. Keep in mind that minor matters really are just minor; you will not even remember them in a month.

12. FRIDAY. Lucky. If you are in the mood, go shopping for clothes or for a special item for your home. If you are thinking of redecorating a room in your house, this is an ideal day for picking out a color scheme. Be upfront with your mate or partner about how much you intend to spend. You should be able to make good progress with work efforts. If you are involved in research, be prepared to go into the latest project in more detail than usual. You are apt to make an illuminating discovery once you get into the specifics. This is a favorable time for taking more initiative in a romance. Do not wait for a phone call; let your feelings be known.

13. SATURDAY. Disquieting. Virgos are seldom happy when surrounded by mess and clutter. Children, in particular, could get on your nerves because of their tendency to be untidy and noisy. No matter how many warnings you issue, it may seem as though nothing changes for the better. Try locking yourself away in a quiet part of the house and letting them get on with their fun. For young children, bringing in a babysitter for a while might be the answer. Any work you want to complete today is likely to take longer than you expect. Keep an eye on the time, especially if you are going out this evening. You need a little extra time to change emotional gears.

14. SUNDAY. Manageable. If you need to get household chores out of the way, you should make good progress. A request from a local group looking for donations of secondhand goods may prompt you to clean out a closet or the basement. Short trips could turn out to be more stressful than you expect. Once you get into the flow of an activity, try not to break the mood; it could be difficult to get back into it later. Social arrangements are prone to change. If you intend to meet someone who can be quite unreliable, be sure to double-check details with them in advance.

15. MONDAY. Excellent. This is a particularly productive start to the workweek. You should find it easy to get into a new work project and to make progress with ongoing ones. Sharing the load with others can make routine chores more pleasant. The various demands being made on you at the moment should not cause stress or strain. If you need to negotiate financial matters, turn on the charm. New propositions require a firm plan and ongoing strategy. However, you can use your Virgo powers of persuasion to your advantage, allowing you to get your way in almost all situations.

16. TUESDAY. Rewarding. Virgo men and women who recently began a new romance should see some promising signs today. It may be possible to put the relationship on a more stable or permanent footing. This is a favorable day for teamwork and joint undertakings. You can get much more done by sharing the load. If you and your mate or partner have the opportunity to get away from your normal environment, do not hesitate. An important commitment is apt to be made in unusual surroundings. Family members may be quite demanding, but you need to stand your ground and not give in on matters of principle.

17. WEDNESDAY. Challenging. You are at an important turning point. If you have been avoiding close involvement and commitment in a certain one-to-one relationship, your emotions will probably change now. You should feel more inclined to work cooperatively, preparing for that all-important person to enter fully into your life. For Virgo men and women already involved with a romantic or business partner, your relationship is about to move one step further. The beginning of an important new phase is imminent. With new projects, it is important to set down firm guidelines right at the start and stick to them without deviating.

18. THURSDAY. Sensitive. You may be asked to sign an important document. If it is any kind of a contract or agreement, be sure to read the document thoroughly. If you are not clear about any of the terms, clarify exactly what is meant and have it put in writing. Additional work offered to you now could boost your income. It may be necessary to keep quiet about the job, especially if you are being paid in cash. An amicable resolution is likely to negotiations concerning a recent accident. Try to avoid becoming involved in a lawsuit by settling out of court if possible.

19. FRIDAY. Profitable. There is likely to be an unusual earning or investment opportunity for you to consider. Look into the matter thoroughly as soon as you can, since there may well be a time limit attached to it. Partnerships of all kinds should be productive and harmonious. If you have recently argued with someone, this is the perfect day to attempt to patch things up. There is not much which cannot be righted with a few carefully chosen words. A pleasant social invitation is likely. If it is from someone of the opposite sex, there may be romantic connotations which bode well for your future happiness.

20. SATURDAY. Demanding. You are apt to feel restless and in need of a change of scene. However, first there is a lot to get done in terms of work or domestic priorities. Time is not your ally. You need to stick to a very tight schedule in order to fit in everything that you wish to do. It is important to set strict limits for yourself. You may feel the urge to gamble, but it is not advisable because you may not be able to recognize when it is time to stop. Concentrate more on areas of life where you are better able to exert control. Friends make the best companions tonight.

21. SUNDAY. Productive. Unexpected problems are likely to keep you busy. It may seem that life is all work and no play. While urgent matters cannot be ignored, also try to find time for yourself. You can probably make better progress with routine tasks if you have something exciting to look forward to. Do not cancel a social arrangement unless you are convinced that you cannot afford the time. A complete change of scene could do much to lift your spirits and rejuvenate you. Contact with people from a different country or culture should also be highly stimulating.

22. MONDAY. Fair. You should be able to make good progress in the business world. As a Virgo you are usually good at handling detailed work, although sometimes you can get lost in detail and waste a lot of time. Today you can instinctively find just the right balance. Understanding all that is involved in a contract or move should provide you with a winning hand. One difficulty may be that you cannot complete a specific deal or project as quickly as you would like. Other people may not be available to do their part, or they could be stalling for time. Try not to worry; trust that things will work out as they should, all in their own good time.

23. TUESDAY. Variable. You may be introduced to an important influential figure. Do not be intimidated by this person's position or power. It is not in your interests to give in too much to please others. They are apt to be looking for courage and initiative, not hoping you fit into what has already been established. Work matters should progress smoothly when you are dealing with others within a hierarchy. Surprisingly, problems could occur with someone who works at your same level. This may be due to some competition between you which has not been openly expressed. Do not bend over backwards to be accommodating; hold your ground.

24. WEDNESDAY. Useful. Team efforts should produce the most satisfactory results. Getting together with others at the planning stage of a new project is likely to yield a number of excellent, unexpected ideas. A well-thought-out strategy is your key to successfully influencing people. It is best to avoid borrowing from friends and acquaintances or loaning anything of value to them. As much as you may want to help somebody, arrangements set up now could become very complex and create friction between you later on. An opportunity to socialize with people you do not know could be exciting.

25. THURSDAY. Profitable. On this socially oriented day the success of a business deal is likely to depend on good communication between all individuals involved. Do not make the mistake of keeping people in the dark or assuming a letter will be sufficient. If you feel that you are not being kept fully informed, ask questions until you get answers. Do not put your own needs aside in favor of the interests of others. You must find out all that you need to know in order to get a job done properly. Ignorance will not be an acceptable excuse. Discussions with your mate or partner concerning mutual interests should go very well.

26. FRIDAY. Stressful. You may be feeling the accumulated stresses and strains of the workweek. Try to make as few demands on yourself as possible. If you have a chronic illness which has not acted up in a while, expect a mild recurrence today. Because there is a chance that the cause is psychological, it is a good idea to make more time for rest and relaxation. You need to make an important decision fairly soon. If you find this difficult, consult an expert, or at least someone who has specific experience in the matter. Be ready and willing to show off a talent you have been developing.

27. SATURDAY. Sensitive. Time spent on your own is sure to be productive. Take care of some private matters in peace and quiet. This is also the ideal day for cleaning out your closets and bureau. You are apt to be in the mood for those household chores which you usually leave until last. Friends may encourage you to go out this evening, which could be an exciting contrast in your day. However, if you do not really feel like socializing, decline the offer without making up an excuse. On no account should you go out just because others are urging you to do so.

28. SUNDAY. Buoyant. You should be in top form and raring to go. A health problem which has been bothering you is likely to clear up on its own. Getting into a different environment that is peaceful and relaxing is likely to be inspiring. Pursuits which only the brave will tackle may appeal to you. You could become intent on rock climbing or sky diving because of the allure of being away from it all. Or it could simply be the challenge which appeals to your Virgo sense of adventure. This is also a particularly favorable day for focusing on your personal ambitions and intentions for the long-term future. Do not discount the possibility of a career change.

29. MONDAY. Disconcerting. Squabbles may erupt over domestic or property matters. If you cannot pay your rent or mortgage on time, it is probably best to try to negotiate. Family members may not be as supportive of your plans as you hope, but try not to let this deter you. While loved ones may know best about certain matters, they do not know everything. Discussions with a friend who tends to have a lot of initiative should help you get fired up to try again. A buyer or seller with whom you are currently negotiating is likely to be pleasantly accommodating in terms of payment schedules or transfer date.

30. TUESDAY. Tricky. Focus hard on what you want to achieve. Competitors are likely to be quite challenging and could potentially throw you off course. Do not be persuaded by the argument of a so-called expert, no matter how clever it seems. Somebody in your midst may simply be arguing for the sake of seeing what you will say or do. You could be tempted to change your image. Consulting an expert is a good idea. Obtain a recommendation from a friend or you may end up with a consultant who only confuses you. It is you who must make key decisions on your own behalf; even an expert cannot make them for you.

31. WEDNESDAY. Lucky. Good fortune is coming your way in relation to money matters. If you are temporarily short of cash, be alert for an opportunity to earn a little extra on the side. If you have been out of work for a while, this is a favorable day for renewing job search efforts. Come up with people from your past who may be useful contacts. It could also be worthwhile knocking on doors and sending out resumes to major corporations. Prospective employers may be impressed by your determination and initiative. Trust your Virgo intuition; it should be a helpful guide. Relax with a good book this evening rather than going out.

APRIL

1. THURSDAY. Fortunate. Virgos can look forward to a pleasant financial surprise today. If you check through your bank statement, you could find that you have earned more interest than you expected. Or there could be a short-term, high-interest offer. Job prospecting can be very lucky for Virgo people in need of work. A colleague with whom you used to work could come up with an interesting proposition for you. It is also quite possible that you will benefit from your mate or partner's good fortune. There may be a genuine cause for celebration. Negotiations concerning a new enterprise should go surprisingly well; a deal can be sealed with a handshake.

2. FRIDAY. Confusing. On such a busy end to the working week you need to spend a lot of time on the telephone, sorting out difficulties and reinforcing recent agreements. Do not expect everyone to be as cooperative as you would like. Colleagues may feel pressured because it is Friday and there is still much to be done. It could be hard to pin people down. Be patient rather than knocking your head against a brick wall trying to get immediate results. Attempting to bully others into doing what you want is likely to backfire. Double-check any information passed on to you which seems hazy or very improbable.

3. SATURDAY. Stressful. You are likely to be busier and on the go more than you intend to be. Your routine could be knocked out of kilter as last-minute changes of plan become necessary. If you go shopping, be prepared for an argument with a salesperson or at the checkout. If you are returning an item, you may not get much satisfaction without a valid receipt. Resist a tendency to hurry around too much, which could leave you feeling exhausted. If you are planning to socialize this evening, do not expend all of your energy earlier in the day. Someone you used to work with may appear on the scene unexpectedly and should be treated with kid gloves.

4. SUNDAY. Variable. Local trips and errands could turn out to be more time consuming than you intend. It is possible that a detour or heavy traffic will cause delays. If you have the option to shop another time, do so. Socially, there is a good choice of many options. Friends who lives some distance away may invite you to a party. Much as you love them, you may not feel up to making the journey. It can be difficult sometimes not to offend sensitive people. Try to come up with an excuse that sounds valid if you feel that honesty is not really the best policy at this time. Get to bed earlier than usual.

5. MONDAY. Exciting. This promising start to the working week gives you sufficient time and information to allow you to finish up an important project. If you need repairs done to your home or vehicle, search around for the most favorable price. A specialist may actually be in a position to charge less than an all-around handyman. A flirtation between you and an admirer should be kept lighthearted. This is an especially favorable day for communicating something of importance to an older family member. Be more open about your feelings and you should receive a warm response and all the encouragement you need.

6. TUESDAY. Productive. Today is just as promising as yesterday for completing projects. If you are trying to purchase property, some favorable news is likely. If you intend to put your home on the market, be prepared to shop around for the best real estate salesperson. If a survey is being undertaken, the results should not reveal anything too negative. You may have to spend some time convincing your mate or partner to go along with your plans. Disagreements relating to domestic matters are likely, but these can be cut short if you manage to keep cool. Be diplomatic rather than critical; give in on minor matters.

7. WEDNESDAY. Easygoing. This is a more easygoing day than yesterday. If you use creative talents in your work, you should be especially inspired. Ideas are moving to the level of reality, and tangible results should come from your efforts. Leap at an opportunity for a change of scene, which should help you gain a better perspective on any worrisome situation. Children may need reassurance if they are going to be away from home. You may be given a choice of two equally attractive offers. Opt for the one where you may meet new people rather than confining yourself to your usual circle of friends and colleagues.

8. THURSDAY. Mixed. A child is likely to have a temper tantrum in your presence. Any behavior that seems unusual probably has a specific cause. If you need to restrict your children in any way, explain why. Laying down the law without reasonable justification can create new problems. You may be frustrated by not being able to do as you please, particularly if you have family members depending on you. While you may be concerned to protect them, this is a good time to let go of the reins a little. There should be less cause for worry if you are available to listen without offering any specific suggestions.

9. FRIDAY. Variable. You are likely to feel lazy. If you have time to spare, arrange to meet a friend for lunch. Stimulating conversation beyond what you share with your mate or partner may have been missing lately; catching up on a friend's news and views could compensate for this. Be careful with any contractual agreement, especially if you are shopping for major household items. While you may be feeling quite happy about your intended purchases, do not be lax about comparing prices and quality. You may need to return an item for exchange at a later date; a receipt will probably be required. Get your home filing system in good order.

10. SATURDAY. Demanding. It may be difficult to know where to start with household chores. Try not to schedule too much. You are apt to be more forgetful than usual. Sort out your priorities so that no vital matters are overlooked. If you feel sluggish, a change of scene could help restore your energy. Try to avoid the Virgo workaholic tendency to keep going despite feeling worn down. Be willing to delegate work that other people can do as well as you, or perhaps hire some help. Relentless mental work could be more taxing than you expect; your brain needs recharging just as much as your body does. Socializing as a twosome should be more enjoyable than going out in a group.

11. SUNDAY. Changeable. This is a good day for getting household chores out of the way. It is surprising how much difference an orderly environment can make to your state of mind. You will feel satisfied when everything is shipshape. If you have been suffering from a health problem lately, it should show signs of clearing up now. Expect last-minute changes of plan, especially with social arrangements. Be prepared for a visitor to arrive a little earlier than you expect. It is probably best if you aim to be ahead of schedule yourself. Share a secret hope with that special person in your life.

12. MONDAY. Confusing. This is a hectic start to the working week. You may have to fit new training into your schedule, or you may have to travel a long distance on short notice. Try to take all of this in stride. Although you probably cannot finish everything that you schedule, you should be able to complete the most urgent priorities. The afternoon is the best time for meeting with important people. There may be contact from somebody overseas. Make a point of discussing the future with those who are most likely to be affected. Paving the way now can make your path smoother later on.

13. TUESDAY. Disquieting. This is one of those days when you may feel that others are plotting against you. Being around people who tend to be clannish could be the reason you feel left out. Get involved more in other areas of your world and this should bother you less. If someone you know seems to be turning a cold shoulder toward you, you may have to acknowledge that they are not quite the friend you thought. Your mate or partner may seem emotionally closed down. It may be best to try to find out exactly what the problem is, although wait until tomorrow to do any deep probing.

14. WEDNESDAY. Buoyant. This is a much more positive day than yesterday. Family members and others you are close to are more inclined to discuss what is on their minds. It is a favorable time for making mutual plans with your mate or partner. You may hear from someone you have been thinking of getting in touch with yourself. Spread your social wings and issue some invitations. A favorable opportunity is likely in relation to joint finances or investments. Current conditions are excellent for getting a mortgage or other loan application approved. Superiors at work are willing to try any new approach you have in mind.

15. THURSDAY. Good. Potentially you could make a handsome profit on a wise investment today. An important business or property deal can now be finalized. In the workplace you may be surprised by how willing certain colleagues are to be helpful. The pressure which has made them less than accommodating lately is now lifting. The amount of effort you put into work is closely connected with the degree of satisfaction you receive in return. If you enjoy antiques or the arts, this is a starred day for buying but not for selling. Drop by a dealer based closed to home.

16. FRIDAY. Fair. You are moving into an important new chapter of your life. Concentrate on clearing out some of the deadwood; this applies to some of your relationships as well as to your material possessions. If there is someone in your life who seems to be more trouble than they are worth, now is the time to find a way to cut free. Sorting through your closets and clearing out unwanted possessions is a good idea. Bag up what you do not wish to keep and bring it to a thrift store or other charity. You may need to enter into an important legal agreement. A handshake is not enough when a significant amount of money is involved.

17. SATURDAY. Changeable. Do not expect business or social arrangements to be set in stone. This is one of those days when even the best laid plans are apt to go awry. So long as you remain flexible in your attitude, all should be well. If you are planning to travel quite a distance, make a preliminary, routine check of your vehicle; there is a possibility of breakdown if you neglect doing so. There may be delays on highways, so allow yourself more time than usual for your journey; an alternative route might be quicker. Your traveling companion can set the tone for the entire trip. Enjoy the ride as much as the destination.

18. SUNDAY. Pleasant. Although there are key responsibilities to handle today, you should gain pleasure in doing a job well. You may be the one who is called upon to organize a social outing for the family or the neighborhood. If you are planning to return an item to a store, you should get a better response if you speak to the manager rather than with an assistant. If you are going to an important social get-together, remain as relaxed as you can be. You will make a better impression if you do not appear to be trying to make an impression. Be sure to pay close attention to grooming and looking good.

19. MONDAY. Stressful. You have to juggle carefully in order to meet both work and domestic obligations. Be cautious about going too far in either direction. Your job is important, but your family needs you too. Collaborative efforts should be a big help, lifting some of the burden from your shoulders. If you can manage to share your load, you will save yourself a lot of time and a lot of mental stress. If you have a health problem which crops up intermittently, try to find help from a relative or friends for the times when it is confining. A professional consultation may bring to light a new procedure or treatment which could help solve the problem and give you much needed relief.

20. TUESDAY. Difficult. Somebody you thought was a friend may take action which makes you question their loyalty. If malicious gossip is being spread, either about you or someone who is important to you, now is the time to nip it in the bud. Focus on the side of your Virgo nature which is concerned with fairness, then confront the person who may be to blame. This should put a stop to it. This is not a favorable day for getting involved in a complicated financial deal, particularly with people who are friends. It may be difficult to say no to a request for help, but you can save yourself a lot of heartache in the long run by doing so.

21. WEDNESDAY. Variable. This is another day when you may be disappointed by a friend's attitude or behavior. Talking about what is irritating or hurting may lead to that person changing their behavior. However, it may be obvious that whatever you say or do, they are not yet ready to change. It is up to you to decide which course of action is appropriate. If it is clearly time to break away from one particular relationship, do not hesitate. In group efforts, you may feel that some of the others are not sufficiently committed. Nobody will really blame you for wanting to withdraw your cooperation, and it should give you a break if you do so.

22. THURSDAY. Frustrating. You need to spend some time alone. If you are going on a long-distance trip, opt to take the train rather than a quick flight. In this way you should be able to drift off into your own world for a while. If you have to drive, you must concentrate on traffic rather than daydreaming. Where work matters are concerned, you need to deal with people face-to-face rather than by telephone or letter. Once you glean the information you need, however, there should be a chance to bury yourself in facts and figures and future projections. Try not to take on more than you can comfortably manage.

23. FRIDAY. Exciting. You should be left to your own devices today, with an opportunity to hide away from prying people. You may be able to work from home or escape to the library. Concentrate on detailed work and fact checking. Being in a quiet environment should be a boon. If you recently argued with someone close to you, there should be an opportunity to smooth things over. An apologetic telephone call could do much to ease the situation. Socially, there are a number of enticing opportunities. Pick the one which seems most exciting and most likely to lead to meeting new people.

24. SATURDAY. Disquieting. An important matter needs further clarification. News you receive today may only serve to confuse you. Try not to worry too much about getting facts and figures; today is not the right day for this. Patience is the best approach to decision making. Be careful if you are driving. People who only drive on weekends may pose a road hazard. Try to avoid lengthy trips; you could find them quite tiring. Your peace and quiet may be interrupted this evening by noisy neighbors. To avoid a disagreement with them, get out of the house for a while.

25. SUNDAY. Fair. This is a good day to plan for the future. You should have time to pursue your personal interests. As a Virgo you sometimes lack confidence in your abilities and worry too much about failure. Today you should feel better able to take the initiative when it comes to matters which you previously avoided. Be careful how you approach family members with a new idea. Trying to storm your way through issues which have been difficult for a long while is probably not the best answer. It is better to take a more gentle and diplomatic approach to any sensitive situation, being willing to listen and to compromise.

26. MONDAY. Disconcerting. Difficulties in relationships with higher-ups are likely. You may be less inclined to follow the lead of others, causing the main problem. It can be frustrating having to toe the line when you feel that you have better ideas. Nevertheless, you need to be careful not to jeopardize your position by doing anything out of bounds. If you are supposed to obtain permission before you go ahead with a specific action, be certain to do so. Attempting to override established authority may backfire on you. Property negotiations are likely to proceed better than expected; hold out for what you want.

27. TUESDAY. Mixed. Somebody else's mistake may turn out in your favor where money matters are concerned. Any confusion that has arisen over your bank account or investments can be rectified now. Although you feel restless to get away from your usual scene or to begin a new project, leftover work may hold you back. You may also have obligations to other people which tie you down. Or you may lack the confidence to take that vital leap. Be patient. Trying to force the action is unlikely to achieve much. Work superiors are apt to be surprisingly helpful and understanding, but their hands may be tied too.

28. WEDNESDAY. Unsettling. Your patience in regard to a financial or property matter is likely to finally start to pay off. If you are having a survey done, do not worry too much about the outcome. Any expenditure required in order to obtain a loan should be minimal. Somebody in your family circle is determined to share a secret which would be better kept quiet. The burden of keeping this secret can be more than you realize. Point out that you would rather not know before you become encumbered with information you do not wish to hear. If you reveal a personal confidence, do not be shocked if it soon becomes public knowledge.

29. THURSDAY. Tricky. It is important to keep your cool. Although something said to you could be aggravating you are apt to regret any mean retort that you make. If you intend to go out with friends this evening, be flexible about the arrangements. Some people can become extremely flustered if they do not get their own way, but you can rise above the situation. At work you may be called upon to settle a dispute between colleagues. You probably need to take stronger initiative than usual in order to restore the peace. Teamwork can be tricky because of the mix of personalities.

30. FRIDAY. Changeable. As a Virgo you like to have everything in its place, including your social and business arrangements. Today, however, little is likely to go according to plan. Be prepared for colleagues and friends to be forgetful. Try not to rely too much on anyone else. If you have no choice in this respect, at least make a point of confirming arrangement details. This is no time to leave anything to chance. You may have difficulties keeping track of the key developments taking place in your life, but circumstances will remind you of your priorities. Put family members before friends if forced to make a choice.

MAY

1. SATURDAY. Unsettling. This rather unsettling start to the month may bring some surprising news your way concerning work or family matters. Because the information arrives out of the blue, it may come as a shock at first. Before panicking or deciding to take immediate action, consider all of your options. A letter which at first appears to be delivering negative news may not be as bad as you think. Before making any changes to joint financial arrangements, be cautious. Think long-term. A loved one may try to convince you to part with more money than you can afford; do not be persuaded against your best interests despite their persistence.

2. SUNDAY. Easygoing. Domestic and family matters should be a lot smoother today. Relax and enjoy life. This is a day for slowing your pace. If you have been working nonstop on a new project, take the time to look back over what you have done. This is an ideal day to correct any mistakes or make some minor adjustments. Someone you have not seen for years may reappear in your life, which should be a welcome surprise. There could be some encouraging news concerning property negotiations. The health of a member of your family, whom you have been quietly concerned about, is likely to show definite signs of improvement.

3. MONDAY. Lively. Looking for property to buy, be prepared to search quite long and hard for exactly what you want. If you have already found a place you are interested in, today is ideal for a second visit. Do not be embarrassed about taking your time looking or about going into a lot of detail regarding matters which really concern you, such as schools or taxes. Thoroughness in all respects is necessary at the moment. There should be a positive development in relation to joint finances or investments. You may receive an unexpected bonus or an inheritance. Aim to make family discussions deeper and more meaningful. A long-held secret may be revealed by an older loved one.

4. TUESDAY. Variable. There is a strong possibility of hearing from someone from your distant past. Any reunion which takes place now is likely to go well providing you do not focus too much on matters in which you always had a difference of opinion. Try to keep the conversation light. At work, you should be able to make good progress, finally reaching the end of a project which took a long time to complete. Relax and enjoy the slower pace this evening. If a family member brags about their recent success, enthusiastically acknowledge it without making any less than favorable comparisons.

5. WEDNESDAY. Useful. You have the opportunity to set your own schedule. With a lighthearted atmosphere at work, you can get quite a lot done. Structuring your day carefully should also help. Loved ones may be restless for a change of scene. Find the time to go out with them for a while; the break from routine will do you good. Romantic possibilities abound for single Virgo men and women. Someone from another country or culture may invite you to visit their home. This could lead to a love liaison as well as being a very pleasant glimpse into their life.

6. THURSDAY. Successful. This is another day with more potential for romance to enter your life. For single Virgos hoping to meet an eligible partner, there is good chance of doing so through socializing away from the usual haunts. For Virgos on vacation at the moment, there is a likelihood of linking up with a local person. Do not be too trusting of complete strangers, however. There are some individuals who will try to appeal to the romantic and compassionate side of your nature in order to extract money or gifts from you. Do not get involved in anything that might be risky to your health or overall well-being.

7. FRIDAY. Deceptive. If you are involved in a new personal relationship you may feel that it is moving at too fast a pace. Your new partner may try to convince you to make a commitment, and be quite pushy about it. Trust your good Virgo instinct. Make it clear what you want and what feels right to you. Work matters are not particularly straightforward. Details need to be double-checked. You may have to put up with frequent interruptions from various people. Resign yourself to the fact, that you may only make slow progress. Keep your goals for the day to a minimum so that you are not disappointed.

8. SATURDAY. Productive. You are likely to be in the mood to take care of household chores which you have been putting off. Once your environment is tidy, you should feel quite relaxed. If you are getting together with family members later today, your discussions may be intense. Try not to bring up any subject which you generally find hard to talk about with them. Otherwise you may end up feeling emotionally drained. It may be necessary to make a longer trip than you expect in order to find an item you want to purchase. Telephone ahead to ensure that it is in stock. For time-conscious Virgo people, there is nothing worse than a wasted journey.

9. SUNDAY. Sensitive. Shopping for supplies needed to entertain guests could turn out to be quite tiring. Try to get someone to help you out with the practical side. If you do not have that option, consider buying prepared food such as a party platter. This can help save your energy so that you enjoy being the social host. A family friend or even a neighbor may suggest an interesting business proposition. Your potential role could be quite special and financially rewarding, ending the weekend on a wonderful note. It is not often that you go to bed on a Sunday evening with great enthusiasm for upcoming meetings and negotiations.

10. MONDAY. Cautious. In an ongoing romantic relationship there is likely to be opportunity to put the partnership on a firmer footing. If you have been involved with someone for a short while, this should be a particularly reassuring development. In a longer term relationship, you and your partner may feel that it is appropriate now to formally tie the knot. Going through a ceremony and taking vows can cement your partnership in a way that makes you feel especially secure. The only person who may now need reassurance is a family member who is feeling rather negative but cannot give you any specific reasons.

11. TUESDAY. Demanding. A long-distance journey could turn out to be troublesome. Detours may take you away from the familiar route and throw you off course. If you have a map to consult you are likely to encounter fewer problems. At work, do not be too disappointed if colleagues are not as enthusiastic as you are about new developments and pending changes. For some people, the introduction of new equipment or procedures can be quite daunting. They may respond well if you offer to take up the role of teacher; try to explain details in a way that does not seem patronizing or know-it-all.

12. WEDNESDAY. Difficult. A friend or associate may be eager to get you involved in a project which involves working from home. It can be difficult to avoid being persuaded by the incentives being offered to you. However, there is little point getting involved in something which strikes you as being too much of a hassle. Be firm. Decline if this is not really what you want. A special offer you see advertised may seem appealing, but read the small print. It could turn out to be less of a bargain than it at first appears. If you are going shopping, it may be best to do so with a friend or with your partner so that you can get a second opinion.

13. THURSDAY. Rewarding. This promises to be a productive day for self-employed Virgo people. A cash-flow problem may now be resolved because payment reminders you recently sent out are beginning to produce checks in the mail. If you are taking new orders, secure as big a deposit as possible. Otherwise you may expend efforts or occur financial expenses and not be reimbursed due to cancellation of the order. Be a little wary about somebody who wants to mix business with pleasure; it is possible that they are after something quite different, which could put you in a ticklish situation.

14. FRIDAY. Deceptive. If you can avoid undertaking a long-distance trip it will be just as well. Lengthy travel could turn out to be more tiring than you expect. If you have to make such a journey, it should be more enjoyable if you are traveling with a friend or compatible colleague. Try to arrange to share the driving if going by car. Having company will make the time go faster. A delay in communications at work could lead to temporarily holding up a pet project. Although you want to get everything tied up before the weekend, try to take the forced delay in stride. There is little point in fraying your nerves by worrying about a situation out of your hands.

15. SATURDAY. Sensitive. You may be surprised by a communication from a friend who asks to come stay with you on short notice. The main problem is that this person is not giving you much time to prepare. Much as you may feel an obligation, do not commit yourself to a visit that is going to be stressful or uncomfortable for you and for other family members. As a Virgo you need to learn to be discriminating. Part of this process involves knowing when to put your own needs above someone else's. Attending a concert or sporting event can be a good way to relax this evening.

16. SUNDAY. Useful. Do not put off taking care of a number of tedious tasks around the home. Once you make a start on housework and other chores, you are likely to make good progress. In addition, getting your environment in good order could be quite therapeutic. There may be a surprise visitor before the day is through, making you even more pleased that you have made the effort to tidy up. A shopping expedition is likely to be more enjoyable if you include plans to meet a friend for lunch or dinner. If you are planning to buy a special outfit, it could be useful to have a second opinion. Affection highlights this evening's activities.

17. MONDAY. Challenging. Attempt to take charge in the work environment. It is not a good idea to allow responsibilities to mount up. Come to grips with projects and tasks which you have been putting aside. Be prepared to take more initiative; is likely that you will be rewarded for doing so. A beneficial friendship which you recently formed should be gaining momentum. Together you can find the courage to do something together which previously you have each feared. A communication from someone out of state or abroad is likely to give you a challenging new option.

18. TUESDAY. Manageable. Today gets off to a busy start. You should be able to take everything that comes along in stride, but your mind is apt to be preoccupied. You cannot do much wrong at the moment if you get involved in team effort. Tedious or difficult tasks should be much easier to carry out if you have some moral support. It is possible that you will at last be able to make a key connection with a distant contact. Any relationship which begins now, whether of a personal or business nature, is likely to become increasingly important to you in the future. Be generous in donating your time or money to a worthy cause.

19. WEDNESDAY. Disquieting. Group involvement should be just as useful this morning as yesterday. Hearing a range of alternative points of view can be very helpful. You can probably find the solution to a problem through a general discussion. A friend who has asked you before to get involved in a shady business deal may approach you again. This new venture is probably going to be more effort than it is worth, but it may take a while to convince your friend. You can be more persuasive if you do not stick entirely to facts but also show the annoyance or anger that you feel.

20. THURSDAY. Demanding. A recurring health problem could start to trouble you again. This may be linked to your emotional well-being. Think back to a recent difficult event which you tried to ignore. If you can identify what has troubled you and counter the situation, your health problem may miraculously clear up. You are likely to take on more than you can manage at the moment. Be aware of the limitations imposed by your backlog of work. If you do not recognize when to stop, nature has a strange way of letting you know. Virgo people who work from home might consider taking an extra long lunch break or an afternoon nap.

21. FRIDAY. Changeable. Work is likely to pile up. The absence of certain colleagues may be the main problem. Although you may think that you have no choice but to buckle down and do it all yourself, there could be alternatives. Consider asking your boss about hiring a temporary worker or extending a deadline. For Virgos currently looking for a job, a temporary assignment could be the way to get a foot in the door. Communications with distant contacts may be difficult due to bad telephone lines or a computer glitch. This is a good time to begin learning a second language.

22. SATURDAY. Mixed. This is a weekend to do your own thing, although there may be responsibilities you must deal with first. Try to get your priorities in good order. If you have a job interview coming up, it may be necessary to purchase a new outfit. Look for a suit or shoes that you want for personal use as well. Whatever you wear for an interview should also be appropriate for your future job. Find time to get away to a different environment. If you have been feeling sluggish lately, a new locale should be a good way of recharging your batteries. If socializing this evening, be wary of eating or drinking too much.

23. SUNDAY. Pleasant. This promises to be a very pleasant day for social events. It is likely that you will make a new friend or become closer to someone you already know from the neighborhood. Family gatherings should also go very well. Take good advantage of the opportunity to relax and bask in the simple pleasures of life. Enjoy a walk or working in the garden if the weather is good. As a Virgo you sometimes find it hard to relax. Today you may be inspired to begin a home decorating project. You will also appreciate having some time to yourself to catch up on correspondence or just to get your thoughts together. Begin now to make plans for a future move.

24. MONDAY. Good. There should be a heightened sense of positive movement for the week ahead. Where business matters are concerned, there is some easy money to be made. An influential figure may suggest an interesting proposition. If you have had a problem getting paid on time, or have suffered through other disputes over pay, this is a good day to tackle the issue. The clarification of any matter which has been confusing should be quite straightforward. Strive to tie up a number of loose ends. A discussion with an expert could help to unravel financial complexities. Conditions favor buying stocks or property if you have cash to spare.

25. TUESDAY. Fortunate. It is time to start thinking differently about your financial situation. There could be an opportunity to wipe the slate clean and begin all over again on a more positive note. A family discussion is likely to be helpful. If you are looking for property to purchase, take a family member along for a second opinion. For Virgo people who have been out of work, this is a very positive day for job hunting. It is likely to be worthwhile to contact companies that you have avoided before. A longshot could turn out to be quite a fortunate bet. A family heirloom may be worth a lot more than you think.

26. WEDNESDAY. Unsettling. As a Virgo you try to be prudent with your money. There are times, however, when the spending bug can get the better of you. This is a day when you would be wise to stay away from tempting stores. You may see a beautiful item on sale which is hard to resist but which you cannot really afford. If you must go shopping, carry cash and leave your credit cards at home. Bills which arrive now could be larger than expected. This may force you to reassess your budget or create a new one. You may need to cut out some nonessential items and postpone a major purchase for yourself or your home.

27. THURSDAY. Frustrating. It is likely that you have a lot to get through and less help than usual. Getting to the point in telephone conversations can be difficult, leading to more wasted time. It may be necessary to avoid spending much time on general niceties. Knowing exactly what information you need should make things easier. A long-distance trip may turn out to be more tiring than you expect. Try not to put yourself under too much pressure. Avoid arranging appointments one after the other; schedule a few definite breaks in your day.

28. FRIDAY. Demanding. Be prepared for unexpected visitors. People you know are coming to visit are likely to turn up surprisingly early or irritatingly late. Once the socializing gets under way, however, all should be well. The work scene is likely to be very busy. There could be extra duties to handle which you have not scheduled. Colleagues with time on their hands may be in a position to help; do not be too proud to ask. Discussions with superiors can be stressful. This is not a time to issue ultimatums. Being a little more subtle in your dealings should help you get better results.

29. SATURDAY. Enjoyable. This promises to be a happy start to the weekend. Home and domestic affairs are likely to run smoothly. Spend some quality time with family members. Youngsters may need new clothes for summer and will probably enjoy a trip to purchase them. You may be reminded of the past in more ways than one. A friend you used to get along with well could be back in touch. If you have already planned a reunion, it is likely to be enjoyable to reminisce and catch up on old times. If you are thinking of planting some flowers in the garden, let your imagination run wild when choosing the colors and varieties; also plant some vegetables.

30. SUNDAY. Tricky. There may be tensions on the domestic front. Repairs that need to be done around the house may keep you busy for longer than you expect. It is a good idea to set yourself a time limit, especially if you have a social event planned for later in the evening. You may feel irritated because others are not pulling their weight around the house. However, this may not be the best time to talk about it; you are apt to blow your top just now. If you go about things in the wrong way, you may not get the results you want and deserve. If you know that you are too angry to have a rational conversation, wait until you feel calmer and back in control.

31. MONDAY. Easygoing. Family and domestic concerns should be easygoing. If you recognize that you have created some of the recent tensions yourself, take the initiative to smooth things over. If your home or car is up for sale, there is a good chance that a buyer will come along now; you may even be offered a better price than you expect. The work environment is likely to be hectic. Higher-ups appreciate the problem you are facing of needing to cope with personal concerns during work hours. It should help to demonstrate that you are in no way letting down on the job, although it is still important to limit your phone calls to home.

JUNE

1. TUESDAY. Calm. There should be a serene feel in your world. No matter how flustered other people may be, you can remain calm and composed. For Virgos who utilize creative talents at work, this is likely to be an especially productive time. Your imagination is firing on all cylinders. New ideas should take shape quite easily. There could be enough spare time to do something a little special, such as having lunch with a friend. Children are likely to be in a happy frame of mind, especially if they receive praise from school and from you for work well done. You deserve to compliment yourself, too, for the encouragement you have provided.

2. WEDNESDAY. Buoyant. You should be able to take life in stride once again today. With any task that you usually find tedious, you can now sail through it with ease. It is not so much that you are working faster but that you are prepared to simply plod through; you will achieve your goals in the end. Not much is likely to throw your world into chaos. There could be an exciting offer but even this is not likely to unsettle you. Because your feet are very much on the ground, this is an important time for key planning and decision making. Keep future goals firmly in mind.

3. THURSDAY. Disconcerting. Family members are likely to be more sensitive than usual. You could be rushing around a lot trying to fulfill all of their needs. This is one of those days when if there is anything to cause a temper tantrum, it will probably occur in your presence. One problem could be that you cannot afford an item you wish to purchase, or perhaps you simply are not prepared to pay full price on principle. The choice is entirely yours as to whether you give way and feel ripped off, or stand your ground and have to put up with bad behavior. Offloading your burdens to a friend can be a great release; their perspective can restore your good humor.

4. FRIDAY. Variable. On this positive end to the working week a project which has been difficult may suddenly come together. At the eleventh hour you may realize the simple solution. It could be one of those situations where you have to get frustrated before a solution comes to mind. Talking it over with a colleague can help you see the light. A long-distance trip could be stressful. There are likely to be delays, perhaps due to road repairs. The less crammed you make your schedule, the better. Work superiors are open to new ideas. Be prepared to strike while the iron is hot; you have more power and influence than you might imagine.

5. SATURDAY. Satisfactory. You ought to be able to speed through any household chores which need to be done. This is one of those days when you have more energy and can therefore fit in more activities. If you are entertaining guests this evening, everyone should have a good time, including you. There should be a lively atmosphere, making all your advance preparations well worth the effort. You may be introduced to somebody quite important. If you are looking for work, this person could be instrumental in helping you move into a new job in the future. And Virgo singles looking for love can be helped by a practicing matchmaker.

6. SUNDAY. Unsettling. There may be a tense atmosphere, with partnership matters under particular strain. If there are disagreements between you and your mate which have been bottled up, these may come to a head now. It is best to clear the air, but be careful about what you say and how you phrase it. Try to be broad-minded. As a Virgo you sometimes get fixated on details and cannot see beyond them. Now it will benefit you to try to see a stressful situation from the other person's perspective. A change of scene is likely to make it easier to talk. Keep spending within reasonable limits. Do not buy anything over the phone.

7. MONDAY. Unpredictable. Partnership difficulties may continue to cloud your horizons. You may feel that you are right, and that until the other person gives way nothing can be done. Decide which is worse: giving in to a compromise or feeling constant background stress. You may absolutely be right, but that may not be the most important factor to consider at this time. An exciting development is likely in relation to career matters, which should lift your spirits and help you ignore minor concerns. An ex-colleague may unexpectedly reenter your life, bringing positive news or helpful information as you consider your next career move.

8. TUESDAY. Rewarding. This is a helpful day for dealing with finances. If you have been thinking of making new investments, look at all the options currently available. There are apt to be especially beneficial offers now. Meetings behind closed doors are likely to produce favorable results. Discussions in which a lot of people are involved could be quite hard to manage, however. You may find it difficult to get your voice heard and your point across in a large group. Subtle tactics may be the best solution; whispering instead of shouting can be a good way to get attention.

9. WEDNESDAY. Mixed. You may receive an unexpected financial bonus. This may be due to a favorable interest rate increase on a fund in which you have invested or a lower mortgage rate. Be careful with your money, however. Any additional cash that comes your way may seem like an incentive to spend more. First, consider your overall financial situation. If you have outstanding debts, reducing these should be a priority. If you now receive items you ordered by mail, check right away for any unwanted returns. It is possible that the deadline for returning merchandise is shorter than you expect.

10. THURSDAY. Cautious. Be more careful in handling joint financial matters. If you are consulting with an adviser about pension or insurance plans, you may be talked into parting with more money than you intended. It is not so much that you are gullible as that the person you are dealing with has very outstanding powers of persuasion. If you intend to travel a long distance by public transportation, be sure to check the arrival and departure times well ahead of your journey. Any timetable you have may be out of date. Allow more time for any journey where difficult connections are involved. Try to relax in mind as well as body.

11. FRIDAY. Stressful. Any long distance journey you have to undertake is likely to be stressful. If you are traveling by car, there may be a lengthy delay due to road repairs or an accident. If you are using public transportation technical hitches may affect the smooth running of the service. Your best bet is to allow more time than usual to reach your destination. This may not be a very satisfying end to the week for business affairs. If you have been waiting for news from overseas, the response you receive may not be what you were hoping for. Keep your expectations on the low side and there is less chance of disappointment. Do not make any promises or new commitments.

12. SATURDAY. Fair. There may be an opportunity to mix socially with colleagues from work. Look your best, especially if there is a possibility that you will be hobnobbing with a superior. It is important to make the best impression. Because Virgo people are often storehouses of information, others are apt to turn to you for advice; someone you do not know well may do so today. Or a close family member may have a private problem or dilemma which they need to discuss. Your discretion in the matter is highly important. You are apt to be more tired tonight than you realize. A late call raises your hopes about an upcoming event.

13. SUNDAY. Happy. On this pleasing end to the weekend it is likely that there will be an opportunity to go somewhere exciting or do something unusual. As a Virgo you never like to be bored; today's change from routine should suit you perfectly. It is possible that you will soon be able to start out on a new career path. Work on developing ideas that form the seeds for a more rewarding future. Contact with influential people also contributes to the overall possibility of change. If there is a problem which you need to discuss, choose a loyal and trustworthy friend you have known for a long time rather than a family member.

14. MONDAY. Rewarding. Get an early start to this positive beginning of the workweek. It is likely that you will be praised for your recent success and possibly also receive material acknowledgment, especially for effort you have put in beyond the call of duty. If you have recently moved into a new job, you may now be eligible for profit sharing or stock options. Take full advantage of this. If you are self-employed, it may dawn on you that business profits have increased substantially. Now is the ideal time to think about a tax-deferred savings plan or retirement scheme, or busines contributions for health insurance.

15. TUESDAY. Enjoyable. Today is ideal for getting together with friends or colleagues you have not seen in a while. There is bound to be a lot of news to catch up on and lively gossip to exchange. The opportunity to go on a trip is likely to come up spontaneously. Even if you feel a bit apprehensive about what is involved, go anyway. Sometimes actually doing something is less daunting than the initial apprehension about it. Virgo people who are bored with the usual activities should consider joining a group, club, or society which focuses on a subject you find especially interesting.

16. WEDNESDAY. Frustrating. Teamwork is often useful because it saves time and overall effort and can also make tedious tasks more palatable. Today, however, you are likely to find it difficult to get along with others in any assigned group. You may not agree with overall policies and may feel that your voice is not being heard. Taking a more aggressive stance is not the answer. You can gain more by having a private conversation with the person who is in charge or is the natural leader. When a straightforward approach is achieving little, slightly devious methods can sometimes be both justified and successful.

17. THURSDAY. Changeable. This starts out as a rather quiet day, making you imagine that not much is going to happen. However, do not be mislead by this lull. Some last-minute deadline work is apt to come your way. Tasks which are assigned to you at the eleventh hour could turn out to be much more urgent than anything else you have to handle. Try to conserve your energy earlier in the day for what is in store. Rumors spreading around the workplace may have no real basis in truth, or the facts may be twisted. Do not pay too much attention to them. If you are waiting for an answer on a legal matter, be prepared for delays or false reports.

18. FRIDAY. Buoyant. You may be surprised at how much energy you have at this late stage in the week. This is a starred day for catching up with tasks which have gone by the wayside as other priorities took precedence. You may be able to make a little extra cash on the side. Joint business enterprises are likely to be surprisingly profitable. Money which you have earned quite quickly through investing can now return handsome interest. Some time spent alone is likely to be useful. You tend to get more done when you are not distracted by someone looking over your shoulder or offering advice.

19. SATURDAY. Demanding. Although you probably want to do your own thing this weekend, family obligations may have to take priority. With many demands being made on you, it is better to try to negotiate rather than bottle up your feelings. The alternative is that your negative emotions could emerge in ways and in circumstances which are inappropriate and may embarrass you. Feelings connected to events from the past which you have tried to suppress may likewise influence your reactions today. Before losing your temper, for no truly justifiable reason, get control of yourself. An apology may be in order, or at least an explanation. Stay away from crowds tonight.

20. SUNDAY. Easygoing. Today should be calmer and more peaceful than yesterday, probably because you have identified exactly what has been bothering you lately. Time spent in the company of good friends should be especially enjoyable. Take advantage of an opportunity to discuss personal matters with someone who really understands you and takes a genuine interest in your affairs. Although you may be inclined to get more involved in a club or other group, be sure to check out admission or membership details before turning up for a meeting. Otherwise you could be upset at being refused entry or at having to ask for a special exemption.

21. MONDAY. Profitable. Your ability to improve your financial status is increasing. You may be offered a high-paying work opportunity. Somebody you know could need help part-time and be willing to take you on with hours fitted around your regular job. If you have been out of work, this is a favorable day for investigating new job possibilities. Be prepared to try all sorts of approaches, including the unorthodox. It may be worth your while contacting higher-ups from previous places of employment. They may be able to give you insider information which puts you ahead of the crowd. Also consider signing up with a temp agency.

22. TUESDAY. Useful. You can expect some good fortune in relation to financial matters. If you go out shopping for household articles, gifts, or clothes, you are apt to stumble upon an unusually good deal. This is another favorable day for Virgo people who have been out of work to seek out a new job. Pay attention to casual conversation; it is surprising what people can let slip. You are likely to pick up a useful hint or tip if you heed what is said by a company bigwig in your presence. You may decide that the cost of relocating is too high, but do not rule out the possibility entirely.

23. WEDNESDAY. Unpredictable. Be careful not to allow recent financial good fortune to go to your head. You are likely to be tempted to go on a buying spree rather impetuously. You do deserve some kind of a treat, but try to keep the cost in perspective. After all, there are bills to be paid and debts to clear up as well. If you are basically struggling to make ends meet, focus on ways to improve your situation. It is possible that you can add to your current income by taking an extra part-time or a temporary position. Also look for ways to trim your budget, perhaps by bartering services with a friend.

24. THURSDAY. Unsettling. A dispute may arise with either neighbors or relatives. The main difficulty may be that everyone thinks they are totally right. It is not in your best interests to pursue an explanation or defense which is not being heard. No matter how hard you try, you may end up feeling that you are banging your head against a brick wall. The key to success involves either changing your tactics or being willing to ignore the matter and compromise in order to keep the other side happy. No matter how strong your principles, sometimes it is not worth fighting for them at a particular moment; bide your time.

25. FRIDAY. Excellent. This is quite a sociable day both within the workplace and outside of it. There is an opportunity to get to know a colleague better through joint social activities. Conversations and discussions, whether they take place in a restaurant or in a board room, are likely to yield invaluable information. If you work directly with the public, your contacts may suggest a favorable new job opportunity or work contract. Friends of friends can also be a helpful source of information, tips, and new work prospects. Enjoy evening socializing where you have a chance to meet new people.

26. SATURDAY. Slow. This is a home and family-oriented weekend. Focus on getting chores and do-it-yourself tasks completed around the house. You should be able to make a good start and then, by working intensively, get a lot completed in a short space of time. Try to alternate or combine tasks which are monotonous or repetitive with more pleasurable activities. For example, get through a pile of ironing while listening to the radio or catching glimpses of a television show. Getting together with a friend should be pleasurable this evening, but if you stay out too late you could be too tired to enjoy what tomorrow has in store.

27. SUNDAY. Pleasant. This is a very favorable day for surprising your family with an unplanned visit. Older relatives who do not get out much may especially appreciate hearing your latest news and perhaps going out to eat. If you have small children, a family trip to an amusement park or to the zoo should bring everyone a lot of pleasure. If you do not have much time during the week to spend with your children, make the most of the opportunity now. Nothing major should go wrong today. If there are any minor hiccups, you should have no problem handling them quickly and effectively.

28. MONDAY. Variable. You can make a good start to the working week by focusing on tying up any loose ends left over from last week. If you have been out of work, this is a favorable day for taking initiatives to get a new job. It might be worthwhile contacting companies who are not actually advertising vacancies at the moment. Especially in the corporate world, a new boss may be willing to make changes and employ more additional people than the previous person. Socially, it is in your best interests to keep your friends and your lover apart for now. Family members, too, should be kept in a separate compartment of your life.

29. TUESDAY. Happy. You should feel pleasantly in control of your universe. With any task which seems the least bit daunting, work out a detailed schedule. Once you can see the entirety of the task ahead of you, the strategy to succeed will become obvious. So long as you take your time and sustain your concentration, you will make good progress and succeed in the end. Hanging around the house can be a bit too dull for your children. They are likely to be happier if you take them somewhere for a change of scene or give them the money to go alone if they are mature enough.

30. WEDNESDAY. Easygoing. You may be criticized at work for being too relaxed in your attitude. It is not normal for Virgo people to take life easy. Other people are probably so used to seeing you hard at work that, if you appear to be taking a few too many breaks, they may get the impression that you are shirking your responsibilities. Higher-ups, in particular, are likely to equate time with money. Your key to success lies in spreading out your activities and taking each task in stride. In this way you do not have to feel stressed and everyone else will think you are consistently busy.

JULY

1. THURSDAY. Disquieting. This is one of those confusing days. It is possible that you are as much to blame as anyone else because you are seeing the world through rose-colored glasses. Although it is nice to approach life optimistically, be watchful that you are not making foolish judgments about other people or about the situations developing around you. Someone who appears to care for your interests may be primarily self-centered. A discussion with a family member may be difficult as you fail to see eye-to-eye with one another. Be ready to face facts rather than relying on hopes and wishes.

2. FRIDAY. Sensitive. On this up-and-down day your schedule is apt to be thrown off by unplanned developments. As a Virgo you are a flexible person by nature, so it should not be too difficult to cope. A lot depends on who are you dealing with, however. An individual with a tendency to use shock tactics may get in touch with you, probably by phone. Be prepared for a call which you do not entirely understand at the time. Someone could even hang up on you. Although you may initially feel that it is up to you to smooth things over, the other person will be doing the apologizing by the end of the day. In the meantime, prepare to meet them halfway.

3. SATURDAY. Fair. You should be able to make good progress with whatever you undertake. For Virgo people who are self-employed, there may be loose ends of a contract to clear up. Tackle this first, when you can concentrate best. Strive to get all outstanding and urgent matters out of the way, leaving the rest of the weekend clear for personal interests. Partnership affairs are optimistic. You will enjoy getting away with your mate or partner for a break and a change of scene. However, avoid using a family visit as an excuse to ignore a problem that needs to be resolved.

4. SUNDAY. Pleasant. A personal relationship is moving from strength to strength. If you recently became romantically involved, there is an opportunity now to make the relationship more settled and constant. If you have been closely involved or married for some time and there has been some rockiness in the relationship lately, this can be smoothed out on this holiday. The intervention of a mutual friend can be most helpful. Find some time to talk about your mutual aims for the future. It is likely that you are now seeing eye-to-eye about your plans, hopes, and dreams. Discuss ways to turn them into realities.

5. MONDAY. Cautious. This is an unusual start to the new work-week. You need to clear up old debts and start fresh. It is a good idea to work out how you are going to repay any outstanding accounts. Working from a clean slate is a necessity at the moment. You are close to being in a position to invest in a new company or even to launch your own business. Concentrate on the benefits and weaknesses of a prospective new business deal. You do not have much time to make up your mind about whether it is worth-while and then to announce a final decision. If unsure about what to do, err on the side of extra caution.

6. TUESDAY. Changeable. Aim to conserve funds rather than indulging in extravagant spending. Keep at least a little in reserve in the bank. Negotiations concerning a joint business enterprise are likely to go well. Some matters simply cannot be discussed in the open, however. You can get to the bottom of a confusing matter once you are behind closed doors with the person or people involved. It is not advisable to try to mix business with pleasure just now. A friend promoting a joint venture may turn out to be more of a hindrance than a help.

7. WEDNESDAY. Challenging. The day starts out well. You are apt to receive an encouraging morning telephone call from someone you are contemplating joining in a business or property venture. Details may have to be kept hush-hush for the time being. Later today you need to move your thinking and planning to a much broader level. You may have to travel a long distance on short notice. It is not in your best interests to rush around too much and try to do a lot in a limited amount of time. Spread out your activities so that you have time to think as well as time to travel in a relaxed fashion. Do not trust your intuition later in the day.

8. THURSDAY. Disconcerting. You have a lot going for you, but do not get carried away with the idea that the whole world is at your feet. Other people are equally as ambitious as you and as determined. Someone with secret plans may be working against your interests. Guard against jumping to conclusions. This is one of those times when other people may be lax about filling you in on key information. In order to set a new plan or project in motion, it is necessary to show that you believe in yourself even if secretly you are harboring a few self-doubts. Your positive statements can help convince even you.

9. FRIDAY. Mixed. There is little that you cannot conquer at the moment if you put your mind to it. You may feel, however, that you are lacking certain abilities, or that there are certain individuals you cannot entirely trust. You are right to be a little suspicious of other people's motives. However, you have nothing to lose and more to gain by having faith in your own capabilities. You are now very close to making a dream come true, but a little backtracking may be required before you take the final step. An influential figure may be able to help you in an indirect, unspecified way, or new government regulations could be advantageous.

10. SATURDAY. Variable. People who have a positive influence on you can now be instrumental in helping you take care of a neglected area of your life. It is not wise to be overly influenced, however. Steer clear of those who may have ulterior motives. Be careful about putting your trust in someone you do not know very well or for very long. Find out more background information before making any kind of a commitment. Family and domestic problems may hold back your progress. You need to balance your private and professional interests with your regular home obligations. A sporting event can be special fun this evening, but do not bet on the outcome.

11. SUNDAY. Rewarding. You can fulfill a key ambition today so long as you find some time for yourself. If you have troubling matters on your mind, a conversation with someone older and wiser will help. Friendships are likely to be extra rewarding. Sometimes you feel you are doing all the giving, but today it is likely that a few favors will be returned to you. Socially you can look forward to quite a busy time. Several different activities should be both exciting and enjoyable. All kinds of group involvements are likely to be rewarding personally and perhaps providing a business advantage.

12. MONDAY. Successful. This is a positive start to the working week. An event that happens today in connection with a cherished aim is likely to make you feel very optimistic. An appealing possibility which was suggested recently may now become a concrete offer. A friendship which recently began is likely to start to blossom as you get to know one another better. Sharing activities in which you are both interested is the best way to break the ice and get past certain barriers. Take advantage of an opportunity for a change of scene this evening, perhaps at a new restaurant or health club.

13. TUESDAY. Sensitive. You are likely to become involved in a new relationship, with romance or business the basis. This new person could turn out to be an important friend in the future. Turn your attention to personal matters. Get in touch with your dreams. Some of your aims and ambitions have altered over the last few months based on all of the changes going on around you. It is best to shift your thinking now and adjust your perspective to take into account the new situations which are developing. Find time to be alone later, when you are apt to be very sensitive to any criticism or even to helpful suggestions.

14. WEDNESDAY. Satisfactory. Behind-the-scenes discussions are important and should be quite revealing. Problems which others have not been able or willing to discuss in casual conversation could now be aired fully. You need to thrash out important issues in some depth. Postpone activities which may disrupt the momentum which is building. If you are involved in key business discussions, this is not the time to take a break or to stall. Once you lose momentum, ideas could end up on the back burner. You have every reason to feel confident that a certain dream will be realized if you keep urging them onward.

15. THURSDAY. Easygoing. This is a good day for tying up loose ends, then taking time out to do something a little special for yourself. If you are not feeling too active, you may want to spend time simply relaxing and daydreaming. It is a good idea to give your mind and body a rest for a while. A trip to a peaceful destination would be ideal. Lounging around at home, if you have the opportunity, should also be very relaxing. Keep any social arrangements for this evening intimate and low key. You are not likely to be in the mood for a large, raucous get-together or for spending time with an argumentative person.

16. FRIDAY. Fair. You should be able to make good progress with personal projects. Your various contacts and associates are ready and willing to help you. Your Virgo charm can also be instrumental in helping you get what you want. If you work from home, there may be too much disruption and noise to concentrate effectively. Rather than tearing your hair out and becoming stressed, take a break. A drive may turn up some exciting possibilities for the future while clearing your mind and calming your emotions. If you do not want to travel, visit a neighbor or a friend who lives nearby.

17. SATURDAY. Excellent. You can make significant progress with whatever you set out to do, but be aware of your limitations. To make the best headway, do not set too rigid a schedule for yourself. You may have to make an important trip, but this should go well. Although you may anticipate delays, it is likely that your journey will not be held up after all. A break from weekend routine is likely to do you a world of good, even if it is only a trip to run a few errands. Arrange to spend this evening with friends who always lift your spirits.

18. SUNDAY. Manageable. Trust your own judgment; it is the best measure you have at the moment. Your insight is keyed in to all that is going on around you. Pay close attention to what you sense at an intuitive level. Your current sensitivity enables you to act on a hunch or even a vague notion. You may be introduced to an important contact, probably at a social event. This person could become significant in your life in the not too distant future. Be prepared for a change of arrangements halfway through the day. It is unlikely that everything will go entirely according to plan, which can actually be advantageous for you.

19. MONDAY. Buoyant. Life may not be totally peaceful but it should be trouble-free. There is apt to be a pleasant surprise where finances are concerned. Someone or some company may have made a mistake which, when rectified, turns out to be in your favor. Attend to any money-related matters which have been neglected. If you are behind with personal or business accounting, make an effort to catch up. A behind-the-scenes meeting is likely to reveal some very interesting information. This is a day when new and exciting developments in relation to work matters can be a boon to your career.

20. TUESDAY. Disquieting. You may not have as much clout in a group as you once thought. Be careful about the number of demands you make at the moment. If you are willing to take a back seat temporarily, you will get a much clearer perspective on the overall situation. Those who cannot directly help you right now may be able to do so in the future. Both at work and socially, do not expect a tranquil day. There are likely to be tough decisions to make and mistakes to rectify. You could be doing a lot of chasing down other people. Keep your energy high by eating a good breakfast and lunch. If you must skip a meal, make it dinner.

21. WEDNESDAY. Disturbing. It can be difficult to keep your focus on mental tasks and paperwork. You have to work in a hurry and may not have time to check thoroughly. Try not to make mistakes in the first place by using a calculator or spell checker. Somebody at work may be spreading a lot of rumors; do not pay a great deal of attention to gossip. This person may have malicious motives. It is best to keep out of the situation as much as possible. Although you may feel like standing up for someone whose reputation is being smeared, you could be getting into hot water. Be sure to keep negative opinions to yourself.

22. THURSDAY. Quiet. You have time to work out strategies and mull over decisions today. So take no rash action. If you are thinking about making a key financial or business investment, think the matter through in greater depth. Compare the various plans and deals being offered. Negotiations may delay you but can lead to a better deal. If you work for yourself, someone may show an interest in becoming your agent. This could genuinely help you ensure increased profits and perhaps more financial security. Weigh this against the percentage that this person wants, then decide what is most advantageous for you right now.

23. FRIDAY. Variable. This is a particularly favorable day for getting out to see people. Do not neglect close relatives or neighbors whom you have not had time for lately. Virgo singles, or those who are new to the neighborhood, should accept an invitation to a local celebration. It could provide an excellent opportunity to meet new people and also get to know acquaintances a bit better. For single Virgos looking for love, events taking place close to home may lead to meeting a new partner. Just finding a wider circle of friends whose company you can enjoy socially should be a boon.

24. SATURDAY. Enjoyable. A trip with family members can be very enjoyable. You may also be in the mood for entertaining at home. If there is a specific project which you want to get finished around the house, get an early start. Make do with supplies already on hand. Self-employed Virgos should be able to make good headway with chores that have not been tackled for some time. This is also a day when an important business deal can be finalized with a handshake. A loved one has a lot of ingenuity, which may be helpful in ensuring that your interests move forward. Be willing to seek advice and to then act on it.

25. SUNDAY. Useful. This is another favorable day for getting home-based work and projects finished and out of the way. A contract can now be signed and sealed. You should again be able to make good headway with completing chores at home. If you have recently begun a decorating project, do not quit until you apply those finishing touches. If you are planning a new decorating project, opt for something simple which will not involve a lot of detailed work. You may not have the patience for creating special effects. Choose painting rather than wallpapering, perennial plants rather than annuals.

26. MONDAY. Tricky. Children are likely to be a source of great pleasure. If there is something special that you want to do for yourself, perhaps go to a home or crafts exhibit, invite family members to come along. Those who have never been to such a show before may be intrigued by all that is going on. Virgo parents may be asked for advice by an older child. Together you may want to go out and choose some new items that you both like. If you yearn to turn a hobby into a money-making business venture, look into the sale of products which attract you.

27. TUESDAY. Deceptive. A discussion which takes place behind the scenes may be disconcerting. Someone close to you is struggling with a difficult problem. If you feel that you are not the right person to give advice, do not attempt to do so. Although you may not enjoy discussing sensitive subjects, if a family member is involved you can help clear up the problem by talking it through. Ignoring the matter may only make it worse. You are apt to feel quite restless; a change of scene could be helpful. Your mind should clear and you should start to feel more relaxed in wide-open spaces where you can commune with nature.

28. WEDNESDAY. Disquieting. Although you are restless to make headway with work endeavors, you are apt to feel tired and have reduced powers of concentration. Try to find time to eat properly, which should help keep your energy level raised. Problems you are mulling over in your mind can have a debilitating effect on how you feel physically. It may be helpful to write down your thoughts and worries. Seeing them on paper should give you a more objective view of them. You may even be able to ignore some of the problems that you decide do not really matter. Concentrate on doing the best you can under current circumstances without thinking too far ahead.

29. THURSDAY. Unsettling. There may be one or two tricky problems to handle at work. Higher-ups or customers who expect everything to be done at the last minute, when there is not enough time, can stress you out. However, you may not feel that you can let them down at the moment. The less you plan the day, and the more open you are to change, the better. Crossed wires with a colleague could lead to an argument. It is best to approach any confusing matter delicately. If you start by criticizing, you may only get a lot of defensive excuses in return. Taking the role of a dictator is likely to create more problems than it solves.

30. FRIDAY. Sensitive. You could be at loggerheads with your mate or partner. It is probably a question of not seeing eye-to-eye on one particular matter. Do not press the issue. You are likely to get better results by concentrating on your own activities. A change of scene is bound to be healthy, whether you go alone or with company. If you are trying to get to know somebody better, you can be most at ease when you are both away from your home territory. Other people are likely to be generous today, but do not take too much for granted. Although someone may go out on a limb for you, assuming this is going to be repeated would only be fooling yourself.

31. SATURDAY. Stressful. Avoid discussing important matters with your mate or partner. If you have decorating ideas, keep them to yourself for now. You and your loved one still have a problem seeing eye-to-eye on anything. If a family member is especially moody at the moment, it may be due to a physical problem. If stress and pressure are the cause, try not to add to this. Take on tasks at home that are most often done by someone else, such as cooking or gardening. However, do not force anything that is not readily accepted. Keep evening plans simple and on the quiet side.

AUGUST

1. SUNDAY. Buoyant. This positive start to the new month promises smoother relationships in all of your partnership affairs. You can now discuss your most cherished dreams without fear of them being disapproved or dismissed without any thought. Be open to experience some emotional moments; there is likely to be more openly expressed love and affection between you and your loved ones. For single Virgo men and women, this is a starred day for getting closer to someone you admire and also for meeting new people. Business matters also are promising. A golden opportunity could come your way; do not let it slip through your fingers.

2. MONDAY. Favorable. Get up early to take full advantage of this optimistic start to the working week. Helpful developments are likely in connection with all of your business matters. It is important to establish the right atmosphere, however. Entertaining at lunch or dinner is a good way to get a new working relationship off on the right foot. People warm to your more personal touch even in a business context. The signing of a contract is likely. As always, it is advisable to study the small print carefully, but do not belabor the matter; others may be offended if you do not appear to trust them.

3. TUESDAY. Confusing. This is a day of ups and downs where money matters are concerned. What you gain through shopping for one item you may lose by not having time to do other work. Haggling can be helpful, but try not to waste your time with trivial matters. There may be problems with a partner's spending, especially if you suddenly discover that there is not much money left in the kitty. It is a good idea to review your joint budget before splurging on anything new. Avoid any business deal involving friends; it could turn out to be quite complex and put stress on your relationship.

4. WEDNESDAY. Disquieting. A trip which you have had your heart set on may not turn out quite as you expect. Rather than excitement, you could be bored. It may just be that your expectations were raised too high. Keep in mind that the grass is often greenest close to home. Make the most of what is available. At a later date you may want to reassess why you were misled. Your resourcefulness is likely to do wonders to get you out of an unpleasant situation. As a Virgo, your knack of finding the best in people can save the day. Do not count on a promise being fulfilled or even recalled.

5. THURSDAY. Enjoyable. This is a much more favorable day for out-of-town pursuits. A visit to a locale you used to know well could be very enjoyable, especially if you get a chance to catch up with old friends. A plan you have been working on is finally beginning to come together. Seeds you have sown in the past should be bearing fruit, particularly in relation to career or educational matters. If you recently took an examination and expect to hear the result soon, you have every reason to feel confident. Whatever has been a long, hard grind is apt to produce the kind of rewards that convince you it was well worth the effort.

6. FRIDAY. Variable. Morning hours should be quite straightforward in relation to business matters. A meeting with an influential person is likely to be surprisingly fruitful and helpful. Somebody could end up doing you a big favor. Do not expect to make as much progress in the afternoon, however. You may not be able to close a business or financial deal because you need more time to thrash out the terms. Hold out for an agreement you feel comfortable with in all respects. Do not hesitate to draw up a new contract if one currently in effect is not meeting your present needs.

7. SATURDAY. Disconcerting. A mix-up in arrangements could leave you wondering why you ever got involved in the first place. You could end up financially out of pocket or stranded out on a limb socially. Be prepared for a change of plan. Either decide that you can adapt to the new arrangements or that they do not suit you and you should opt out. It may be difficult to relax because there is so much on your mind. Sudden news can leave you feeling upset. Try not to dwell on information which has not been confirmed. In all probability the situation will change yet again. There is no point worrying about something that is likely to be resolved naturally without any intervention on your part.

8. SUNDAY. Pleasant. Friends and acquaintances are the best company today. Someone in your social circle could be a source of inspiration for you. If you have the chance to go on a group outing, do so; you are likely to enjoy yourself more than you imagine. If you are fairly new to your neighborhood, this is a key time for making new contacts. One person to whom you are introduced may become a key figure in your life in the future. If you hit it off right away with this person, work to develop this friendship or romance by issuing a casual or open invitation to go to lunch sometime or to drop by your house for coffee.

9. MONDAY. Frustrating. The first half of the day should go quite well. Make an effort to cultivate relationships which you sense could be highly useful in the future. You have the potential to achieve an important goal which you have only dreamed about. It is important, however, to work at getting a definite plan in place. Without a firm foundation your ideas could evaporate into thin air. Achievements may get harder as the day progresses. Colleagues and others may be hard to pin down, and your own ideas may become just as elusive. Frustrating as this seems, it is not a signal to give up. Hold tight to your dreams despite stumbling blocks.

10. TUESDAY. Mixed. Important conversations which have a bearing on your future are likely to take place. Listen more than you talk. Someone in your circle of friends and acquaintances has the potential to unlock a door for you. If you are starting out on a new career path, it might be helpful to seek some expert advice. A local social event may turn out to be quite interesting. For single Virgo men and women, a meeting tonight may be the place where you meet a potential mate. Be prepared to struggle as you did yesterday when it comes to trying to get new ideas accepted and off the ground.

11. WEDNESDAY. Difficult. You may be starting to wonder if a new project is such a good idea after all. Give it a chance. If you are not feeling in top form physically, your emotional and mental strain is likely to be casting a negative cloud on your plans. It may be a vicious circle, where the harder you try, the more stress you put upon yourself. If you have an opportunity to get away from it all for a while, do so. A change of environment could change your perspective as well. It is important to make it a complete break so that you can switch off for a while. Avoid mixing friends and money matters; neither loan nor borrow.

12. THURSDAY. Fair. Compliments are likely to fly your way. If you make an extra effort with your appearance, others are bound to notice. And you may discover a secret admirer in your midst. One way or another, your self-esteem should receive a boost. This is another propitious day for getting away from it all if you can find the time. Even if you think that you cannot do so, once away from your usual environment your perspective will change, making you realize that a problem is not that important after all. Avoid getting embroiled in family disputes. It is best to keep some of your ideas and notions to yourself for now.

13. FRIDAY. Favorable. You are in a strong position to consolidate your past experiences and make definite plans for the future. Your thinking at the moment is far-reaching but sound. There is little point having brilliant ideas if you cannot start to back them with solid progress. Social and business contacts are apt to contribute to your success. Spend more time discussing plans with those you are closest to professionally or emotionally. Much that has been hanging in the air in your personal and business life is starting to come together now. Plans can be moved along by working out a mutual agreement with those whose help you need.

14. SATURDAY. Manageable. A discussion with your nearest and dearest may be helpful in solving a financial difficulty. This should be a productive day if you concentrate on getting practical tasks completed and out of the way. However, be careful that you do not take on more than you can comfortably handle. Do not overestimate your stamina. An idea may seem simple at first, but once you get into it you could discover that there is a lot more involved. Research the project beforehand rather than jumping right in. Make the time to do someone a favor without expecting anything in return.

15. SUNDAY. Good. If there are sales going on, this is a propitious day for going out shopping. You could pick up some real bargains in home furnishings or clothing. Warehouse clearance stores may be a good bet, particularly if you want designer fashions. And sometimes you can end up with a great deal if you shop at thrift stores or consignment shops. For Virgo people involved in property negotiations, there should be some encouraging news today. Water-related activity can be fun for the whole family, especially boating. Pay close attention to safety rules and regulations, however.

16. MONDAY. Disconcerting. This may not be the most easy-going start to the workweek. It is important to keep most matters to yourself; talking to the wrong people could cause a lot of problems in the future. People may pry into your affairs, but you do not have to respond. If you are asked to use discretion, do not ignore the plea. Be wary of spending too much time trying to tie up loose ends. It is important to devote your energy to more important, future-based projects. As a Virgo you sometimes get lost in petty detail. This is not a time to allow yourself to get wrapped up in matters which are not of high priority.

17. TUESDAY. Unsettling. It is a good idea to double-check meeting times and places. Do not leave this to the last minute; verify arrangement details a good while before you are due to start out. If you are using public transportation but infrequently do so, do not rely on an old timetable you happen to have around; it is apt to be out of date. A few telephone calls can save you a lot of bother. A problem you have been sweeping under the carpet needs in-depth analysis. Be prepared to slow down and consider matters carefully. Rushed ideas or decisions are unlikely to work out well in the end.

18. WEDNESDAY. Stressful. Plans and arrangements are prone to change. You may not have much control over this, but you can improve the situation by remaining flexible. Single Virgo men and women should avoid being taken in by a fast-talking individual who may be after something more than you realize. Opportunists usually have ulterior motives, so be warned and be cautious. A long-distance trip could be quite tiring. There may be more traffic delays than usual and more crowds. If listening to music or a recorded book helps you cope with traffic jams, plan to take extra tapes to play in your car. Get to bed early tonight.

19. THURSDAY. Changeable. The day starts out on hold. You probably cannot easily get in touch with the people or obtain the information you want. Try to be patient. There is little point knocking your head against a brick wall. Evening hours are especially favorable for entertainment and leisure activities. It is likely to be worthwhile attending a neighbor or relative's gathering. If you are hoping to get to know others better, this could be the event which allows you to discuss personal interests. You could also be in the mood for entertaining at home. If you host an impromptu gathering of friends, consider inviting a few neighbors as well.

20. FRIDAY. Pleasant. The working day should go well, with a lot of progress in tying up outstanding matters. If you spend time at home you are likely to be inclined to get chores done so that you will be free for the weekend. Be careful about being overly thorough in any of your activities. A tendency to be rather ruthless at the moment means that you could end up throwing out something which you later regret getting rid of. Try to be moderate in all of your activities. If you are entertaining at home this evening, asking others to help with the advance preparations could make the get-together easier and more enjoyable for you.

21. SATURDAY. Useful. Hard work you are exerting to bring a project to an end will be worthwhile. You cannot reach the expert stage on the first try or even the second, so be patient with yourself. Pursue and develop interests which will broaden your horizons. Socially, this is another excellent day for entertaining at home. If you want to get to know a certain person better, inviting them to a social occasion might be the best way. Somebody close to you is apt to turn up with a lovely gift. Although this may not be anything of long-term significance, it should be a delightful expression of their feeling for you.

22. SUNDAY. Happy. Your social life should be very pleasant. There is opportunity to travel farther afield than usual. Any broadening of your horizons is likely to be enjoyable as well as a real eye-opener. You probably feel that you can take on the world at the moment. Concentrate on making the best possible use of your spare time. For Virgo parents, this is the perfect day for organizing a family trip. Children who are on school vacation may be tired of staying around home. An adventure park meant to appeal to children may have a clever way of appealing to adults, too. Do not neglect a pet; grooming can ease the heat of summer.

23. MONDAY. Changeable. If you have the chance to do something special with your mate or partner, make the most of it. Perhaps you can meet for lunch for a change. Today starts out well thanks to your optimistic outlook on life in general. Contact from someone special should put you in a happy frame of mind. However, do not expect the entire day to go smoothly. You may have to cope with excessive noise and disruptions, which make it hard to concentrate. If you need to sort out detailed work, find a quiet place such as the library or a vacant office at work. Do not base future plans on vague promises. Make some timely resolutions now as your Virgo birthday period starts.

24. TUESDAY. Stressful. Virgo people have a tendency to be workaholics at times. You may find it difficult to separate your private life from your work. Ignoring your mate or other loved ones can lead to unrest at home. Children, in particular, may need and demand extra attention. You may get quite stressed as the day wears on. It is probably best to force yourself to take a break. Keep in mind the old saying about a change being as good as a rest. Just switching tasks can perk up your energy. News from someone at a distance could put you in a serious frame of mind but try not to worry; conditions are apt to change for the better before you know it.

25. WEDNESDAY. Rewarding. There should be fewer problems to contend with at work, allowing you to finish up an important project you have been working on intermittently. If you are involved in anything new, do some in-depth research right at the start. The day gets more complicated later due to unplanned events. You may be loaded down with more work than you anticipated due to the absence of a vacationing colleague or relative. If you start to feel hassled, you may make mistakes or react too abruptly, so be careful. If a loved one leaves you an abrupt message, do not jump to conclusions. The tone of a comment can seem quite different on paper than in regular conversation.

26. THURSDAY. Demanding. Although you may feel concerned about having a lot to do and not much time to do it, those you can usually rely on for support are likely to be unavailable. Try not to panic. Take the attitude that what gets done will be whatever you can manage. The irony is that once you relax, you are likely to be able to work faster. Be careful not to skim over details. In your hurry to complete a project you may cut one too many corners. This might work out, but keep in mind that you are taking a risk. If a new partner figures in your plans, know exactly how much authority you are willing to give away.

27. FRIDAY. Fair. It is best to avoid picking fights with people you disagree with. While you need to eventually get to the bottom of a problem, it is not worth stirring up trouble at this late point in the working week. If you have been out of work, an interesting opportunity could come your way. However, it is not likely that you can look into it before next week. At least the weekend should give you time to think out how you want to proceed. You and your mate or partner may find it difficult to agree on home-related matters. Be willing to give unless you truly care a lot.

28. SATURDAY. Lucky. This is an especially favorable day for travel with your loved one. If you cannot actually get away, consider where you would like to go in the future. Strive to bridge the gap with someone you recently argued with. A heart-to-heart talk about matters which are quite personal to both of you is likely to bring you closer together. Socially, involvement in sports activities is bound to be fun. If you are thinking about losing weight or getting more fit, this weekend is a good time to try out a new physical activity, especially one that involves a team.

29. SUNDAY. Challenging. For self-employed Virgo people, today is ideal for settling down to sorting out accounts. With less commotion than you usually experience during the week, you should be able to concentrate on detailed figures. If clients are behind in payments due you, send out reminders. Also pay your own bills before the deadline to avoid high interest charges. This is a favorable time for working out a new budget. It may not be simple to figure out how you can get the money to pay off a debt, but finding a way should be a relief. A part-time job or selling an item of personal jewelry could give you the influx of cash that you need.

30. MONDAY. Productive. Start the working week by tying up a mountain of loose ends. Other people's neglect or mistakes could cause you problems. It is frustrating to realize that you cannot always trust others to do as you ask. However, there may be a good reason why one particular person has been lax. Before launching a critical attack, find out more information. Although you may have to make an important decision, take the time to weigh all aspects of the situation. This may be time-consuming but is necessary if you want a decision you can live with for a long time.

31. TUESDAY. Satisfactory. Key discussions are likely today in relation to a new business or financial interest. It should be possible for everyone to agree so long as the most sensitive issues are handled with care. If you are going to be traveling on an unfamiliar route, take along a detailed map. If the map you now have is no longer up to date, buy a current one. Otherwise you could end up on a road you did not even know existed. This is a testing day where your personal resources are concerned. It will pay to keep your spending to necessities only. Avoid adding any new purchase to your credit card.

SEPTEMBER

1. WEDNESDAY. Tricky. Any travel plans might be upset through no fault of your own. It is also possible that if you have not been taking good care of your car problems could arise now or your gas mileage could be very poor. A breakdown in basic mechanics could set you back in both time and money. Do some routine maintenance checks before you set off. If you do not have plans to travel, you may be called upon to do so at the last moment. It can be helpful to keep an overnight bag packed and ready for instant departure. Be prepared for a last-minute debate with a workmate or a family member just before you leave.

2. THURSDAY. Disquieting. Do not expect any journey to go entirely smoothly. Although it is probably good for you to have a change of scene, you may be rather rushed. If you are working away from your usual base of operations, there could be constant interruptions due to phone calls from those people you left behind. While you thrive on new stimulus at the moment, too much stimulation can make you frazzled. Inwardly you probably feel a need for complete freedom. However, if you do not keep in touch with others it will cause problems. Try to strike a happy balance between independence and responsibility.

3. FRIDAY. Exciting. Sensitive negotiations should produce favorable results. If you can manage to stay on good terms with both your backers and your foes, you can keep everyone happy. Tempting as it may be to voice your thoughts, if they could appear overly critical it is best to avoid doing so. An exciting development is likely in connection with your career matters. This should help make the last day of the working week end on a high note. A break you have been waiting for since early in the year is finally about to materialize. Gear up to take full advantage of it later this month in your Virgo birthday period. For now treat yourself to a change of scene on this long holiday weekend.

4. SATURDAY. Variable. Some of your most important hopes
and wishes show signs of being fulfilled. You have every reason
to feel optimistic. As a Virgo you sometimes cannot get a good
grasp on the overall picture as you worry about details, but this
is not the case at the moment. Your ability to maintain a broad
view and keep an open mind is bound to be helpful. Although
many things seem to be going your way, little in life is straightforward. Before today is over you are likely to take a wrong turn.
Fortunately, you can get around this temporary obstacle with a
little thought and some swift maneuvering. Keep all of your options open.

5. SUNDAY. Satisfactory. The opinion of a good friend can be
reassuring if you have a few doubts; do not hesitate to discuss
them. You may be reminded of the past. Review a plan you put
in place long ago and you may see that the seeds you planted then
are now starting to germinate. Seeing them come to fruition can
be quite encouraging. Home and family life should be easygoing,
with a more intimate feel. You can get a lot of creative work done
at home if you put your mind to it. Mixing your firm practicality
with your sensitive Virgo imagination should be a winning combination for redecorating. Consider ways of earning some money
with a favorite hobby.

6. MONDAY. Mixed. There could be a confusing start to the day.
Garbled messages may be the problem. It is best to double-check
information which seems dubious. A relative or neighbor who has
a tendency to be too talkative for their own good may reveal a
secret. Although it may not be easy for you to turn a deaf ear, try
not to dwell too much on what is said. Because other people's
opinions are not necessarily an accurate version of the facts, pay
little heed to rumors. Someone who knows you well may assume
that you have already heard a secret relating to a mutual acquaintance. If you have not heard it, pretend to know.

7. TUESDAY. Slow. Take advantage of any opportunity to put
your feet up and enjoy life. Lately you have had to work very
hard to achieve your goals; any rest you get now has been well
earned. There is likely to be some reassuring news from someone
at a distance which puts your mind at rest in regard to a matter
you have worried about for some time. As a Virgo you have a
tendency to worry needlessly at times. Now you could realize that

you have been wasting time in this way. Do not be hard on yourself; just vow to try not to get so single-minded next time. Efforts to tie up business plans or social arrangements should be productive if you remain as flexible as possible.

8. WEDNESDAY. Frustrating. Life at home could be a little difficult. Someone close to you is apt to be in an irritable frame of mind, forcing you to be extra careful about what you say and do. Because family members may argue about your personal plans, it may be useful to keep them to yourself at the moment. Wait until the commotion has died down and the dust has settled before saying anything that could upset them further. If you go out shopping, aim to keep your spending to necessities only. It could be tempting to splurge without planning to do so, but try to resist even a sale. A good book is your best evening companion.

9. THURSDAY. Useful. This useful day allows you to further some of your more important plans. Look to the future. If you have felt as though you were hitting your head against a brick wall, there should now be signs of a breakthrough as other people begin to give in a little. Someone new is likely to be quite an inspiration to you. However, do not be entirely trusting of new information or new people. Do your homework before making any kind of an agreement. Avoid revealing too much about yourself, your thoughts, and your own plans right now; bide your time and see what other people are planning.

10. FRIDAY. Rewarding. Although it is the end of the working week, you can make some sort of a fresh start. Discussing your most important personal plans with someone who understands, and perhaps can help you out, should be worthwhile. If you are undecided about a decision you have to make early in the day, do not worry too much; news or developments later in the day should prove reassuring. Even if you are forced to make a decision this morning which you wonder if you will regret, you should have reason to believe later today that you made the right choice. Figure out how much you are willing to give up for what you want, then hold your ground.

11. SATURDAY. Challenging. This is a helpful day for sorting out financial matters. Put some time aside to settle your accounts. If you are thinking of buying or selling property, now is the time to look at the various options open to you. If you cannot find what you want in one particular area, or it is not affordable, consider an alternative. There is an opportunity to put your financial situation on a firmer footing by realigning your investments. Or a part-time job might give you the cash cushion you need. A special gift could come your way, perhaps through an inheritance. Stick to your budget despite temptations.

12. SUNDAY. Satisfactory. If you are having second thoughts about an item you looked at but did not buy recently, today you will probably give in to your desire to possess it. Any emotional involvement which is developing at the moment is apt to be well worth the extra effort you are putting in to make it work. There is a good reason why you have not so far revealed your feelings. Now, however, you can express them without worrying about the reaction you will get. There is a good chance of receiving a positive response, so look for the signals. It is also possible to make a pleasant new social connection through a friend of a friend. Strive to expand your social circle.

13. MONDAY. Confusing. None of the information which comes your way today is likely to be straightforward. Whether you are at work or at home, be prepared for mixed messages. Anything important should be put in writing, not trusted to oral communication. Your thinking may not be as incisive and precise as usual. If possible, wait a few days to write a letter of complaint or apology. In the meantime, greater clarity may evolve in your thinking as you mull over ideas for a while. If family members are restless, go out together this evening for dinner or a movie if you have the time to do so. If time is at a premium, maybe an offer to pay their way will be an acceptable substitute.

14. TUESDAY. Demanding. Be prepared for a busy day. You are likely to be kept on your toes. The problem is that your schedule is likely to change on very short notice. It could be hard managing to keep up. Try not to put too many extra pressures on yourself. The less you have to do, the better. And the less you expect specific results, the easier things will tend to be. Telephone calls from friends or relatives are likely to be pleasant interludes, providing some light relief to simply gossip for a while. If you lack certain tools or other equipment for a new home or gardening project, consider borrowing what you need from a neighbor or renting it instead of buying.

15. WEDNESDAY. Enjoyable. Today should be pleasant for all kinds of socializing. You may particularly appreciate getting together with people you have not seen in a while. This is a generally favorable day for traveling. Any change of scene will probably do you good, even if it is only to run errands. Consider doing routine shopping in a different store for a change. You should be able to make good progress with home-based projects. If you have been thinking about redecorating, this is the perfect time to get an exact plan down on paper. Before buying new furniture, try rearranging what you have.

16. THURSDAY. Changeable. If you are rearranging furniture and decorating around the home you should make some favorable progress. You now have the patience to tackle any special effects which require a lot of concentration with paint or paper. If you are considering new window treatments, check decorating magazines for updated ideas. Consider starting from scratch with a whole new concept. Remaking curtains or drapes may seem more economical, but it could be a lot of work for a not very satisfactory result. If there are any safety hazards, such as loose carpet or tiles, you would probably be better off replacing them.

17. FRIDAY. Lucky. If you are looking for property to purchase, you are apt to be in luck today. You may find just the right place at just the right price. There is no need to rush a decision, however. Be sure to look at all your options so that you are certain about your choice. This should be a useful day for catching up on neglected jobs around the house. Later you could be in the mood to entertain. The tidier the place is, the more organized you will feel. Make an effort to stay in touch with old friends. If there is someone you have been meaning to call for ages, tonight is prime time for a long talk.

18. SATURDAY. Mixed. This is an unsettling day for romantic matters. You may have to rethink your ideas about someone you wanted to get to know better but who remains distant. You may decide that the person is not worth the effort and that you are wasting your time. Married Virgos may be irritated by lack of care and consideration, especially in regard to joint finances. Avoid a tendency to criticize and nitpick. Try to find a more subtle, gentle way of discussing the issue. This afternoon is ideal for getting out of town for a change of scene, perhaps to a restaurant noted for foreign cuisine or to a dinner theater.

19. SUNDAY. Happy. The children in your life are likely to be a joy to be around. You can all enjoy a trip to a new and exciting place. If you have never visited a theme park, this is the ideal time to go. For Virgo men and women who are romantically unattached, today could bring an opportunity to meet and get to know someone with partner potential. It is more likely that you will meet someone compatible away from your home ground and usual haunts. Introductions can sometimes happen in the most unusual places. You could be jogging in the park or walking the dog and end up with pleasant company. Creative interests and hobbies can be especially rewarding if you break with tradition.

20. MONDAY. Uncertain. The working week starts on an upbeat note. The earlier part of the day is most suitable for creative endeavors. You may be inspired to begin a new project or to tackle an old one from a new angle. Life gets more hectic as the day progresses. Get your schedule organized and specific details tied down this afternoon. It may be difficult to obtain definite commitments from other people, however. Try to be understanding with those who have good reasons for not being able to give you a firm yes or no. If a telephone message seems confusing, double-check the details before taking action.

21. TUESDAY. Good. Do not expect work matters to be entirely easygoing. This is one of those days when your progress could be slower than you would like. It may be that colleagues are less cooperative or simply too rushed to be able to spare the time you need. In the meanwhile, focus on smaller jobs if you are having problems getting larger tasks completed. A break from one project can refresh you as well as relieve any sense of frustration due to other people not being very helpful. The afternoon should bring some good news relating to your finances. There may also be an acknowledgment of your efforts from a work superior, perhaps with an accompanying bonus.

22. WEDNESDAY. Disquieting. You may feel hemmed in by the number of responsibilities that have been heaped on you. You are likely to be working against the clock, under more pressure than usual. Much as you may desire a change of scene, it is necessary to simply keep going. If you do not manage to get any break during work hours, compensate for it this evening by putting your feet up in front of the television. Or you may decide to go to bed early and read a good book. Signs of stress may manifest themselves as a minor health problem or a steady headache. This is a signal to get some extra rest.

23. THURSDAY. Rewarding. All of your partnerships are likely to be rewarding. Relations with colleagues should be smoother than they have been. If you put your heads together on a new project, you should come up with some dramatic results. In your more intimate relationships there is likely to be wonderful rapport. If you are unattached, you can now get closer to someone special. For married Virgo men and women, there can be some very rewarding moments providing you do not bring up issues which have been a problem in the past, particularly spending above and beyond an agreed budget. Still, as your birthday period ends, you are counting more assets than liabilities.

24. FRIDAY. Exciting. This is one of those days when you may find it harder than usual to get along with your mate or partner. One or both of you may be sensitive because you are overly tired or are being pressed by events taking place around you. It may be beneficial to have a little more time to yourself. If there are specific issues which need to be addressed, talk about them rather than trying to ignore them. By taking a practical approach, you should be able to iron out emotional difficulties or differences of opinion. This may come as a surprise, but there is likely to be some favorable news in relation to money matters; a bonus or cash prize is possible.

25. SATURDAY. Disconcerting. You have to move quickly and think on your feet in order to sort out a financial difficulty. A friend who lent you money a while ago may now demand it back in a hurry even though the original agreement was that you could repay it when you could. Do not panic. If you put your mind to resolving the problem, you should not have too much trouble finding an amicable solution. If you have been waiting for news in relation to buying or selling a property, what transpires today should put your mind at ease. Enjoy the company of one or two good friends this evening.

26. SUNDAY. Fair. Spend time clearing out some of the deadwood that has been building up in your life. After a fall cleaning and sorting out you will be able to more easily locate items which you usually have a problem finding when you need them. As a

Virgo you tend to function a lot better when you are well organized. You may be able to say goodbye to a financial burden which has been hard to cope with for a long time, such as a car payment or college loan. For self-employed Virgo men and women, new work coming your way now is the key to getting rid of a debt that has haunted you for ages even if there has been no demand for payment.

27. MONDAY. Mixed. You are likely to be in the mood for adventure and excitement as this workweek begins. You may have the opportunity to get involved in a new work project which will stimulate your mind. The only problem is that while the opportunity is there, you may have to cut through a lot of red tape before you can begin the actual work. Try to be very well organized from the beginning. Your efforts are likely to pay dividends down the road. Travel to a foreign or distant place can put you in touch with people who will be useful contacts in the future. However, do not rely too much on promises made by people you barely know.

28. TUESDAY. Cautious. This is another day when you are in the mood for change and excitement. Events are apt to bring both into your life, but probably not in the way you expect. Be prepared for a minor shock. Someone whose help you need may get the wrong impression from a letter you sent. They could vent their anger at you and even end up slamming down the telephone. As a Virgo you have a tendency to worry, but do not waste your time fretting over someone who behaves like this. Conditions are very changeable. Whatever bad behavior you have to put up with one moment is likely to be smoothed over the next with a sincere apology.

29. WEDNESDAY. Reassuring. You may have mixed thoughts at the moment. Although life has a wonderful expansiveness about it, your long-term ambitions are likely to be stymied by self-doubts. Try not to allow concerns about the past to interfere too much with the present. It is one thing to learn a lesson from the past, another to brood about what has gone wrong. Virgos usually function a lot better when someone takes the time to offer positive feedback to you. A pat on the back from an authority figure later in the day should convince you that you are doing something right and are appreciated.

30. THURSDAY. Changeable. Be prepared for a blowup at work or at home. Negative feelings which have been bubbling below the surface may now be revealed. Try not to react too abruptly to what seems to be negative criticism. If you think for a moment about what is being said, and by whom, you may see that this is intended to help. Changes to your regular routine are unavoidable. You need to shuffle appointments and meetings in order to fit everything in. It is seldom a good idea to neglect a request for help. Make time to sort out a problem affecting a colleague or relative before it builds up into something worse.

OCTOBER

1. FRIDAY. Successful. This promising start to the new month should produce at least one positive development in relation to your important career interests. Behind-the-scenes work and negotiations promise excellent results. There may be discussion of a salary increase or a stock bonus. Play your cards close to your chest when negotiating any new deal. It is best to bide your time, being careful not to say too much too soon. This is also a key time for focusing on important decisions you need to make in relation to your personal life. You have every reason to feel positive and not to delay taking action.

2. SATURDAY. Useful. It is best to keep business and pleasure interests separate. For self-employed Virgos, this might be the only day of the week that you are free to sit down and talk business. Make sure that you do not pick a setting which makes others think the discussion is merely a pleasant diversion. Although a friend may urgently need money, you may not be the right person to offer a loan. Financial arrangements which cross over the boundaries of friendship can sometimes turn more complicated than you ever intended. It is probably best to steer clear, with a diplomatic excuse, or else to make a monetary gift if you can afford it.

3. SUNDAY. Variable. Relationships with friends and acquaintances are under some extra strain. Someone who has become involved in a business arrangement may want to get you involved as well. It is not always easy to say no to those who are charged up with enthusiasm. However, if your instincts tell you to back off, trust them. Somebody trying to obtain money or other resources in a hurry may call upon you. If you do not feel comfortable about helping out, do not be pressured into doing so. After all, you may not be in the best position to help. Try to find some time to yourself later today, even if you have quite a lot to do around the house; let it wait while you pamper yourself.

4. MONDAY. Tricky. This fairly quiet start to the working week offers opportunity to catch up on neglected tasks. You should get encouraging results from working behind the scenes. You could be offered a new project which is beyond the normal scope of your duties. Anything which takes you away from routine should be particularly stimulating. Try not to worry about a lack of experience or expertise. You are sure to gain useful knowledge for the future from new endeavors which you undertake now. The earlier part of the day is the best time for concentrating on long-term planning in relation to business and financial matters.

5. TUESDAY. Manageable. You are ready to leave one set of tasks or work behind and begin a new chapter. This is a helpful day for establishing new aims and goals in most areas of your life. If you feel at all sluggish this morning, the excitement of a new beginning can be a good way of motivating yourself. News concerning a family or property matter which has been troubling you is likely to come now and be reassuring. Strive to make some inroads in tying up a business or property deal which has been in pieces for some time. This evening favors a lighthearted get-together with friends, but do not stay up too late.

6. WEDNESDAY. Mixed. You can benefit by concentrating on doing your own thing. If you feel ready to turn over a new leaf in your personal life, one way might be to revamp your image. Search through your closet and try on clothes you bought but never wore. If you are serious about a change of style, it might be worth consulting a professional who specializes in color choices. Magazine offers for a makeover may also be worthwhile, particularly if you are a little short of money. Your energy should be higher overall, but be prepared for a family upset this evening to drain your emotional reserves.

7. THURSDAY. Cautious. If you are in the mood for some excitement, long-distance travel is likely to perk you up providing you do not have to drive. Getting into a different environment can refresh your perspective on life in general. Find time to concentrate on your longer range plans. In career and business matters you need to be cautious and conservative. If there is new work in the pipeline, be wary of simply dropping an old contract which has become a bore. In good time you should be able to even out the balance and enjoy the challenge of both the old and the new.

8. FRIDAY. Lucky. Financial speculation could be quite fortunate for you. Your clever Virgo judgment is apt to have as much to do with favorable results as a spot of luck. It is never a good idea to take big risks with money; no gamble can ever be considered a certainty. You should be able to make good progress with routine work matters. Strive to tie up loose ends and get a particular task finished once and for all. For self-employed Virgos, this is a day for finalizing a favorable business deal. A family get-together is likely to be rewarding this evening, or you may want to make plans for a reunion.

9. SATURDAY. Buoyant. If you go out shopping you should be able to pick up a few exceptional bargains. Stores in which you do not usually shop might be the best bet. Guard against getting totally carried away with spending. Now is the best time for putting a new budget in place. If you are tempted to spend more than you can afford, it may be possible with a store's offer of interest-free credit. Keep in mind, though, that you will have to pay it off. Protect your valuables if you are out in public. Pickpockets often operate in unexpected places. So long as you stay alert, all should be well. Enjoy a quiet evening at home rather than going out.

10. SUNDAY. Profitable. Any new work which you are offered could be quite profitable. However, it is up to you decide if you want to take it on or if you would prefer a relaxing day. If you are short of money, it might be worth putting in the time to bring in a useful cash bonus. Neighbors may get on your nerves in subtle ways, perhaps by playing loud music or letting their dog run loose. It is best to take a charming and gentle approach if you decide to confront them. Avoid making a scene when you are still angry. Offer to compromise if you could be happy with that solution. At all costs, do not threaten a lawsuit.

11. MONDAY. Misleading. There is good opportunity to network and meet new contacts both in business and in your personal life. However, be a little dubious of people you do not really know. Sometimes individuals give themselves a good press but have nothing behind them to back it up. A long-distance journey you are getting ready to undertake may turn out to be a lot more complicated than you expect. If driving, it is possible that there will be a long detour; be sure to bring along a map, especially if you are traveling far from home. Be prepared to have to alter your basic schedule to accommodate another person.

12. TUESDAY. Quiet. On the whole this should be a quiet, easy-going day. However, because you have extra time on your hands there may be a tendency to try to catch up with neglected matters or take on new tasks all at once. Be careful not to spread yourself too thin or you could end up feeling stressed out. Neglected family issues deserve some attention. Focus your mind on the future and try to prepare for potentially busy periods ahead. Casual conversations with colleagues at work are likely to be surprisingly informative. You could pick up some helpful clues to future realignments. Take a moment to get in touch with an old friend you have not talked with in a long while.

13. WEDNESDAY. Stressful. If you commute to work, you may start the day with unexpected upsets. Road repairs or public transportation cancellations could cause delays which make you late for work. Try to take a little while to calm down and regain your perspective for the day ahead. If you have the option to work from home on occasion, this could be a favorable time for doing so. Property-related matters need careful handling. If you are going to be moving, be sure that you are informed of all relevant terms and conditions before signing a lease or a mortgage contract.

14. THURSDAY. Changeable. If you are looking for property to purchase, you may find somewhere quite unusual. Think twice, however, about taking a place which needs a lot of work in order to meet your needs. This place may look like a bargain, but you could end up forking out a great deal more money than you expect on improvements. If someone in your family has special talents such as carpentry, plumbing, or landscaping, take advantage of their expertise. They may be able to give you a more realistic price than someone you do not know. Unexpected news is likely to come in the mail; read a letter through twice to be sure you catch the undertones.

15. FRIDAY. Sensitive. Although you may be eager to move, be careful not to act too impulsively. You still need time to get to know a locale better. If you are planning to share the home, bear in mind that living with someone can be quite different from seeing them purely socially. For Virgo people who are unattached, there are opportunities to meet someone attractive this evening. Traveling to a distant place may bring you into contact with such a person. Any romance which begins now is likely to be fast-paced and exciting. Watch out for a marriage trap if you are not ready to settle down.

16. SATURDAY. Enjoyable. If you spend some time with youngsters, this should be a particularly happy day. You may have the most fun if you are not stuck inside. Consider taking a drive in the countryside or to the mountains. If the weather is bad, going to a child-oriented restaurant or to the movies is a good option. There may be special-offer prices on in your local newspaper, which should be worth the look. Be willing to show your true feelings in a love relationship, even if it is a recent relationship. Chances are you feel the same way about one another. Working on a creative hobby can be very rewarding, especially an item intended as a gift.

17. SUNDAY. Sensitive. It may be difficult to keep your thoughts off financial and business concerns, especially if people call you on this nonbusiness day to talk about them. Also try to get some extra rest and pure relaxation today. If you can manage to put worries out of your head temporarily, you should end up with a clearer perspective when you return to them after the weekend. You need to switch off from pressure and take life at a slower pace. Aim to devote the day to pleasure and rest. If a love interest is costing you too much emotionally and financially, perhaps it is time to back off for a while and reassess your direction.

18. MONDAY. Frustrating. Although you may be hoping for a relatively easy start to the working week, do not be too optimistic. It is likely that your workload will increase before the afternoon. Sort through the pile of work and decide what should take priority. Consider delegating some of the tasks to colleagues who have time on their hands or at least less pressing deadlines. Routine tasks may have to be temporarily put aside while you cope with more important and urgent matters. If you have been hoping to get some freelance work, you may be lucky today, but expect to have to work hard and fast.

19. TUESDAY. Disquieting. Routine matters may have to be put aside again today in favor of urgent work. You may also have to juggle your schedule in order to attend one or two key meetings. If you are trying to develop independent opportunities, you will have to give up some of your spare time, in order to go in search of work. It would be a shame to miss out on a good contract simply because your regular schedule is too tight to accommodate additional work. If you are asked to commit to a detailed contract, delay could be your best tactic. You need a little more time to get the future in proper perspective.

20. WEDNESDAY. Successful. You should be able to make excellent progress with work matters. If you have been temporarily out of work, a golden opportunity could arise today. There may be unexpected help from someone in an influential position. With this assistance, frustrated plans which you have been struggling to pull together could become much simpler. Partnerships are likely to be smooth. Work together with your mate or other loved one to get ahead with routine chores. This will free up more time for you to entertain and be entertained on the weekend. This is a day when acting on impulse should work in your favor.

21. THURSDAY. Variable. For single Virgos there may be difficulties in a romantic relationship. Someone you recently became acquainted with may not have made their intentions or their current situation completely clear. Perhaps they want something more or something less than you can offer. If you only want a casual relationship, they may be looking for permanent commitment. Or it may be that the other person only wants a friendship. This is a time for being blunt and finding out what is really going on. It is better to face the music and then make a clear-cut decision rather than hang on to a relationship that you sense is not going to work out.

22. FRIDAY. Easygoing. Partnerships should be much smoother today. A loved one may be able to help you further some of your more important aims and ambitions. Power struggles which have been putting a strain on an ongoing relationship are now disappearing. Social events generally are apt to be enjoyable. Single Virgo men and women looking for romance may find it locally at an event being hosted by a neighbor. Someone who has been difficult to contact recently is apt to resurface on the social scene. Enjoy catching up on all the news. A good friend may be planning a move that will bring you closer.

23. SATURDAY. Stressful. The weekend may not get off to the most pleasant start. There is apt to be tension in your partnership, probably due to financial difficulties. If your mate or partner has been overspending, you are likely to find out now. Try not to be too harsh; maybe there is a good reason for the temporary excess. If your loved one has been waiting for news about a potential pay raise or inheritance, you may receive word now. However, the amount may not be as much as expected. It is in your best interests to try to live within your current means. Much as you want the best for both of you in the future, some belt-tightening is needed now.

24. SUNDAY. Demanding. Be cautious and careful if you have to handle any legal matters. If you are reading over a contract or other documentation, confer with a friend or family member who understands the language. It is possible that there is some misrepresentation, but it could be so subtle that you are not aware of it. You can look forward to a promising development in a personal relationship this evening. If you have been involved in a casual romantic relationship, your partner may now want to move to a more permanent level. Contact with a good friend is also likely to be rewarding. Their news could be an eye-opener for you.

25. MONDAY. Disturbing. A quarrel could escalate into a threat of legal action by the other party. As a Virgo you tend to worry about even a minor problem. Before you get too concerned, check with an authority to find out if a lawsuit is actually justifiable and if it can force you to court. If so, it may be wisest to do what is necessary to smooth over the situation, even apologizing although you do not feel that you are to blame. Otherwise, let sleeping dogs lie. There could be word from someone you have not seen in a long time. This is a favorable time to plan a reunion. Try to get to know a neighbor better.

26. TUESDAY. Mixed. Virgo students may want to spend a good part of the day concentrating on research, writing, and memorizing. You may also enjoy some reading purely for pleasure. It may not be easy to get your ideas in focus all at once, however, because there are conflicting views. For now, concentrate on taking notes. Someone on the work scene may be quite aggravating, coming up with all sorts of excuses for why certain work cannot be done or why a deadline cannot be met. It is up to you to inspire this person with some added confidence; secretly they may be so afraid of failure that they are unwilling to even try.

27. WEDNESDAY. Changeable. Today is apt to be a series of stops and starts, especially in the morning. If you need written approval before beginning a certain course of action, there may be more than one channel you have to go through. Keep focused on the desired result. At the end of the day, despite the bureaucracy, you should have made good progress. It is important now to play by the rules. There could be an unusual career or promotional opportunity coming your way. If this relates to freelance work, juggle your schedule to make time for it. You never know what else may develop as a result of a new contact.

28. THURSDAY. Manageable. Avoid the temptation to ask the boss or another authority figure for a favor. It is possible that others see you as pushing your luck and demanding too much. Be sure to keep to your word and honor even inconvenient promises. You could create quite a scene otherwise, which will be more emotionally upsetting than it is worth. Although you may wish for a more comfortable life at the moment, you have to work hard for every penny. Take heart, however. In the not too distant future, the efforts that you are putting in now will start to pay off in unexpected ways. Keep your personal spending within tight limits; a new budget might help.

29. FRIDAY. Fair. This is a favorable day for dropping in on friends or calling to see how they are. Any get-together with close associates should be enjoyable. Also be in touch with individuals you have not seen for a long time. You may have forgotten just how inspiring one particular person's company can be. The same is true of activities which you have allowed to lapse. Include a group of friends in your social plans for this evening or for the weekend. It can be entertaining to watch television, but you can experience a complete change of perspective at a theater or sports arena. Focus on the big picture.

30. SATURDAY. Variable. Today provides an interesting mix of business and social affairs. Even though the working week has come to an end for most people, it may not be over for you, especially for Virgos who are self-employed. Meetings of all kinds, whether purely social or business oriented, can produce satisfying results. One or two could run late, however, so allow yourself ample time between engagements. For Virgo business people anxious to make a good impression on potential new clients, this is a starred time for special entertaining. Pull out all the stops to make people take notice of you.

31. SUNDAY. Disquieting. You may get the feeling that loved ones are not being totally upfront with you. Be careful how much you pry, however. If you intend to press for answers, keep in mind that some people are more sensitive than may be obvious. A colleague who comes crying on your shoulder may want sympathy, not answers. As a Virgo you can sometimes be flattered when others turn to you for help, but be alert to what might really be going on now. It is possible that this person is using your sympathy in order to try to obtain some information from you which is strictly confidential. Be kind, but do not be taken in by underhanded approaches.

NOVEMBER

1. MONDAY. Calm. Someone who is working behind the scenes on your behalf is likely to do you a few favors. This is a useful day for catching up on neglected tasks which have been put aside for far too long. The atmosphere at work should seem warmer than usual, with people taking time to look out for each other. For Virgos who have been temporarily out of work, now is a good time to renew efforts to find another job. Get back in touch with an agency that helped you in the past. If you have moved, a potential employer may have no way of contacting you. Be sure to dress conservatively for an interview or meeting.

2. TUESDAY. Variable. This is another helpful day for completing neglected tasks so that you are ready for new starts. You may surprise yourself at the amount of work you are able to get through. Any matter which requires close cooperation with other people needs to be handled with care. Others are apt to be sensitive about your attitude. As a Virgo you have a tendency to sometimes be critical. Because of this, try hard not to allow this to show through in any conversation you have or any letters that you write. Discussions relating to property matters can be difficult. You may have to work hard to understand a banker's jargon and understand exactly what is at stake.

3. WEDNESDAY. Useful. If you have been feeling rather upset, today you should be able to find a way to perk yourself up. This is a good time for brightening your personal image. Treat yourself to a new outfit or a different hair style. If you are going for an interview or out to a business lunch, feeling good about your appearance can do much to boost your overall confidence. It should be easier to unleash your creativity on new work projects. The newness of what is taking place now is sure to stimulate you. Do not be afraid to push forward with your own ideas in the workplace. An influential figure is watching with interest and waiting to see what you can accomplish.

4. THURSDAY. Excellent. If you are still in the mood to improve your image, this is a propitious day to shop for new clothes. You have a good eye for color and style. Try to buy a complete outfit, including shoes and accessories. If you recently lost any property, it might be worth inquiring at all the stores and restaurants where you were and also putting an ad in the newspaper. It is possible that someone was honest enough to turn in the item. This is a good day for working up a new decorating scheme for your home. This evening you may end up feeling more positive about a get-together you have not had much enthusiasm about since accepting the invitation.

5. FRIDAY. Cautious. No matter how hard you try to be careful with your money, there are times when you end up going over the top. This is likely to be one of those days. If you do not really need to go out shopping, postpone the trip until another day so that you do not put temptation in your own path. You should be able to smooth over a relationship with someone you argued with lately. Sometimes it is through pure practical necessity that people cut through emotional red tape and take steps toward reconciliation. Do not worry about trying to anticipate what moves others may make; they are apt to catch you off guard.

6. SATURDAY. Difficult. Try to make this weekend easy on yourself. There are some individuals who will always rub you the wrong way because of a basic personality clash. Give such a person a wide berth. This is another day when the spending bug can bite you. If you go out shopping with your mate or with a friend, you may be inclined to spend less simply because the other person is there to witness what you do. For Virgo parents, children may be quite demanding today. You may need a break with purely adult company for a while. A neighbor may be prepared to do you a favor. Money due you from a friend may not be repaid as promised.

7. SUNDAY. Uncertain. You may not be in a position to make definite plans or commitments at the moment. Be honest about this rather than making any promise you may not be able to keep. If you are unattached, it can be difficult to get a new relationship off the ground. You may suddenly become tongue-tied in the presence of someone you find attractive, or when they call you on the phone. This is not the time to try to explain yourself. Instead, try not to worry too much about making a good impression. Just be yourself and act naturally. Chances are the other person is just as nervous as you and may be harboring the same doubts.

8. MONDAY. Sensitive. A new relationship may be slow to get off the ground, perhaps because both of you have work or family commitments. This is a favorable day to try to arrange to spend time together. It is possible that you will discover that you have more in common than you originally thought. In your business dealings it may be necessary to have more discussions than you anticipated, particularly in relation to beginning a new project. If you are not looking sufficiently to the future, others may have a curious way of reminding you to do so. Sometimes it is not a bad move to be a little impatient; let your feelings show.

9. TUESDAY. Satisfactory. As a Virgo you tend to function best when you are given clear guidance and then left to get on with the job. Today you may receive more of a free rein than usual. Do not hesitate to try out new working methods. Although what is tried-and-tested may be safe, you will not find other, perhaps better ways if you never give them a fair trial. For self-employed Virgos, this is a time to take a few well-calculated risks. There may be a very lucrative opportunity which requires a leap of faith in your own future. Do not be afraid to take that vital step. A family gathering should be very enjoyable this evening, especially if children are included.

10. WEDNESDAY. Challenging. If all is not rosy at home this morning, do not worry too much. Any small step which you take to try to smooth over the situation should achieve desired results. If someone close to you seems moody, the subtle approach is likely to be the best way to jolly them out of it. If you work for yourself, you may be thinking about acquiring property or merging with another business. You can afford to be innovative and consider unusual propositions. The time is ripe for expanding into new territory. If you work from home, consider sharing office space or hiring a professional telephone answering service.

11. THURSDAY. Buoyant. This is a day for thinking big in all respects. Self-employed Virgo people may now be in a position to afford to expand. If you have tended in the past to take on more work than you can comfortably manage, think carefully about how to organize in the future. There are a lot of options, and you need to be very selective this time around. It makes sense to opt for the higher earning option even if you are not totally convinced that it will be a success. New enterprises begun now are likely to prove more profitable than you expect. Keep tonight free of social engagements so you can get extra rest.

12. FRIDAY. Variable. The usual ideas you have for entertainment may seem too expensive, or maybe you want to treat yourself without going over a budget. In either case, consider what option will satisfy you while not breaking the bank. A friend may come up with some helpful ideas or even some practical support. If you are looking for a new place to live or for new office space and are concerned about the cost, it may be possible to juggle around your budget and find a way to afford what you want. This should be a satisfying end to the working week if you get together socially with colleagues this evening.

13. SATURDAY. Stressful. This can be quite a difficult day unless you stay in tight control. For Virgos who are in business, working relationships may be going through a more than usually demanding period. It may be a good idea to offer incentives, however small, in order to try to raise general morale. This is not the best time to bring up sensitive issues; you could end up creating further friction. In a close personal relationship you may not be able to resist saying what is on your mind. It could be important to discuss plans for the future no matter how wary you are of tackling the subject. Such a discussion could end up putting the relationship on a more stable footing.

14. SUNDAY. Unsettling. A romance which has had its ups and downs recently should be smoother today. It is likely that you will be able to talk your way through any problems or misunderstandings. Plans can be made for the future with relative ease. Arrangements relating to a long-distance trip that are upset at the last minute could be very annoying. It may actually benefit you to express how you feel in no uncertain terms. Others who are taking a lot for granted might end up taking you more seriously. Do not worry about a friendship that seems stressful just now. Keep in mind that no relationship is easygoing all of the time. If you have a sound basis, it will endure.

15. MONDAY. Fair. You can look forward to a productive start to the working week. You may need to work at a slower than usual rate, however, in order to ensure that mistakes are not made. This is a propitious day for starting a new project or even a job. You should have few problems getting along with colleagues. Be prepared to gradually learn a new technique or procedure. You are likely to achieve less by trying to race ahead or by pretending that you know it all. More experienced people, even those younger than you, are likely to be more than happy to fill you in on details relating to equipment or paperwork with which you are not familiar. Remind yourself that being professional does not have to mean being perfect.

16. TUESDAY. Productive. In your business dealings a more lighthearted attitude can work wonders. While you want to present a professional front, others can feel you are making too much of a casual situation by approaching it in deadly earnest. You can win other people's confidence by opening up a little. Although you may not like to admit to making mistakes or taking shortcuts, doing so can improve overall cooperation. After all, everyone is human with special talents and some flaws. And everyone makes mistakes. Anyone who pretends that they do not can seem a little too daunting for comfort or become a target for blame.

17. WEDNESDAY. Disconcerting. If relations with a loved one have been tense lately, do not put off a heart-to-heart talk any longer. Matters which have brewing below the surface are likely to come to a head of their own accord. As a Virgo you do not often lose your temper, but when you do you are usually precise and forceful. This makes it crystal clear that you are not joking. If you feel that your recent emotional outburst was unjustified, it is up to you to apologize and try to make amends. However, if you feel you had every right to be angry, stand your ground. Only in that way will your feelings be respected.

18. THURSDAY. Pleasant. Relations with those you are close to should be a lot easier going today. If there have been eruptions in a partnership lately, the storm should calm now. It is likely that you will receive an apology from someone whose actions or words have been out of line. A letter in today's mail is likely to be heartening. Single Virgo men and women who recently met a potential partner may receive an encouraging communication from this new person. Tempting invitations are coming your way. If you are going out on a date this evening, expect it to be quite romantic.

19. FRIDAY. Good. An unusual partnership that you recently entered into has now passed the make-or-break stage. Review all of your relationships overall, including friendships. It may have lately become obvious to you that certain individuals are staying in your life only so long as you prove useful to them. This is a time to drop one particular individual who is doing too much leaning on you. There is little point continuing any relationship that is burdensome. If necessary, make the decision to cut loose. A new commitment relating to a business interest is likely to fill you with hope for the future. This is a starred time for a merger.

20. SATURDAY. Frustrating. It is necessary to get your finances in order this weekend. If you have a lot of debts to repay, you may have to spread your money around, paying a little here and there. You could need to renegotiate payment deadlines, especially if money due you has not come in as expected. Virgo people involved in a difficult relationship may no longer want to simply drift along in the hope that things will sort themselves out eventually. You will be best off taking more positive action. You may even decide to issue an ultimatum in order to find out if any real future commitment is possible.

21. SUNDAY. Rewarding. A joint partnership, whether relating to business or to your more private life, should be going from strength to strength. This is a favorable day for enjoying more of the good things in life. A raise in pay for you or for your mate may allow you to indulge in luxuries which you could not previously afford. You may feel an urge to get away together for a change of scene later in the day but not know where to go. Put your heads together and you are bound to come up with a good idea. Try not to set off too late; the traffic may be unpredictable and a restaurant or theater very crowded.

22. MONDAY. Disquieting. This is one of those days when you are likely to be very restless. If you are going on a long trip, the change of scene may do you good. However, there could be more delays to contend with than you expect. If you are driving, the trip could turn out to be especially tiring. It might be better to take public transportation if you have the option. There will be a number of routine matters to tie up before you can get out of town. You could spend a lot of time talking to people but elicit little information from them. You have to work hard to make your point in order to get the results that you want.

23. TUESDAY. Changeable. If you concentrate firmly on what you want to achieve, you should be able to make a dream come true. This is not one of your easier days, however. A work superior or other authority figure may not give you the approval or recommendation you seek. Do not give up at the first obstacle, however. Some people can be talked around to see things your way if you are prepared to humble yourself a little. Sometimes a formal request for help can get lost amid the bureaucracy. Be prepared to try a more personal approach, which should produce much more positive results. Use humor to ward off an argument.

24. WEDNESDAY. Lucky. If you have been thinking about trying to change track where career matters are concerned, this is a good day for taking the first step. Authority figures are likely to give you the support you need. If you are concerned about conditions at work which affect both you and fellow employees, this is a favorable time to speak up about them. You may be surprised at how effective you can be when you focus on resolving a problem rather than just complaining about it. News which comes your way concerning a property matter or proposed move is likely to be encouraging. People could be more agreeable than you expect.

25. THURSDAY. Enjoyable. Family matters are likely to be quite smooth on this Thanksgiving Day. If you recently asked a loved one for a special favor, you are likely to be feeling confident of the result. You may have enough time to get down to some basic fence mending among family members. Decide which problems can be put off for the near future and which should be ironed out immediately. This can lessen pressure on you personally. Conditions favor making plans for a get-together next month. You may discover what you need to know simply from noticing how different loved ones are responding to one another.

26. FRIDAY. Mixed. All of your relationships are likely to be quite easygoing and agreeable on the whole. It may be necessary, however, to take more time to show others that you care about them as individuals. Because doing so comes easily to you, do not rush through the preliminaries or someone may feel that you are talking down to them. This is a favorable time for working as part of a team. You should be able to make more progress by cooperative effort than you would through working solely on your own. A social event this evening should go well and could prove useful for linking up with new friends or potential clients.

27. SATURDAY. Variable. You may be inclined to dwell on the past. Something you see, hear, or smell could remind you quite vividly of a previous experience. If it was a negative experience, try not to dwell on it too much. Matters that make a strong impact cannot always be completely forgotten, but you do have the option to put negative thoughts out of mind. There is a chance now of bumping into someone you would rather not see, perhaps when you are out shopping. If there has been stress between you, be pleasant but not overly friendly. It may be better to pretend that you do not even remember the incident or problem.

28. SUNDAY. Pleasant. Neighbors and friends are likely to be particularly cordial. If you need a favor of some kind, now is a favorable time to ask. Generally try to take life at a slower pace. You may have to go on a trip, but do not make it hard on yourself. Allow enough time so that you arrive in good spirits. If you need a bit of cheering up at the moment, a shopping expedition could be the answer. So long as you can afford to splurge a little, doing so can perk up your spirits. If you are sometimes called in to work on weekends, this could be one of the days when you have to do so at short notice.

29. MONDAY. Confusing. You are likely to be happiest if you can make time to take care of neglected tasks. The earlier part of the day is best for this. You also may need to get personal telephone calls out of the way; if you work, you should be able to make some calls while the boss is out of the office. Your family may be more demanding on your time than usual. A burden you would rather not have, such as organizing Christmas activities, may fall on your shoulders. If you have not chosen to do this, at least put up a small fight. Keep in mind that people will only attempt to impose on you if you allow them to do so.

30. TUESDAY. Fair. If there have been underlying, difficult issues left undecided in your family, they could come to a head today. Do not hesitate to speak your mind. Sometimes you can be amazed at the depth of your own feelings. Others, too, may be taken aback if you suddenly blurt out exactly what you are thinking. However, it can sometimes be the one surefire way to clear the air and achieve something positive as a result. If your energy is ebbing due to an overload of work, a change of scene might help you pick up steam. Try going for a walk at lunchtime, for example; a breath of fresh air can also do a lot to restore your perspective.

DECEMBER

1. WEDNESDAY. Cautious. Money matters need careful handling if you are to avoid depleting your reserve funds. You are likely to put yourself in a stronger position by saying little rather than trying to explain the smaller details of a complex situation. In a close personal relationship, it is vital to respect the confidential nature of what you are told. A contract or agreement which you are about to sign may have hidden clauses which require further explanation. Question anything you do not fully understand. An associate with subtle and creative ideas is someone you can trust to turn a situation around in your favor.

2. THURSDAY. Satisfactory. This is a useful day to make a start on your holiday shopping. You can fulfill most of your shopping needs in one trip to a large mall. You may be able to negotiate a good deal if you are buying anything in bulk. Continue to keep a watchful eye on your spending; it can be all too easy to run up a large credit card bill in a short time. You may also find yourself more easily seduced by clever salespeople who are determined to sell the latest gadget or craze. Discussions with your family should prove rewarding even if you are hashing out a difficult problem or situation.

3. FRIDAY. Changeable. This is another day when you may be tempted more than you intend. Carry only a small amount of cash, or leave the credit card with the higher spending limit at home. This should make it a lot easier to avoid impulse buying. If you are negotiating a business deal at the moment, it is in your best interests to drive a hard bargain. As a Virgo it can be difficult for you to sell yourself or to take control, but this is what you should be doing. Otherwise you are apt to come out with a deal that will not make you satisfied for very long. Be prepared to blow your own horn and strut your stuff.

4. SATURDAY. Frustrating. The inability of other people to make up their minds and commit to specific arrangements can be infuriating at the moment. Although they may have genuine reasons for this, you may feel it is necessary to issue an ultimatum. This could be the only way that you can really plan effectively. Guard against making any promise that you may not be able to fulfill, especially when other people are issuing the invitation. It is possible that work colleagues may be in touch today, keeping you talking a long time about matters which have little to do with you. Try to cut the conversation short with a promise to continue the discussion on Monday.

5. SUNDAY. Variable. You are likely to have a choice of social activities. One may involve a long-distance trip, and therefore more effort, than the other, but that is the one that is apt to turn out to be the more interesting option. Self-employed Virgos need to sort out paperwork or contact people only available on the weekend. Expect one or two distractions which interrupt your concentration and tear you away from this. It is best to spread your time and energy around since you may find it difficult to concentrate for any length of time on anything that is detailed or in depth. Keep evening plans simple and relaxing; get to bed early.

6. MONDAY. Successful. This is a positive start to the working week. Casual conversations which occur early in the day could help you elicit information which you have been trying to get for some time. You can now bring together a number of plans which have been on the back burner. Be careful about the kinds of commitments you make today. Other people may take you strictly at your word although you may only be making loose promises. A friendly get-together this evening should be quite intimate and uplifting. Try to include a neighbor who is almost a part of your family circle.

7. TUESDAY. Useful. If you are at home for a part of the day, this can be a good time for decorating and for repairs which you have been putting off. If you are trying to get negotiations concluded, make specific appointments with the people involved. There could be a flurry of activity at work. You can finish up a tedious project if your put your mind to it. This evening you may want to opt out of a social meeting in favor of relaxing at home. It should also be a good time for impromptu entertaining, perhaps inviting some friends for coffee and dessert. Keep looking ahead; let go of the past.

8. WEDNESDAY. Confusing. If you are looking for a new home, check the local newspaper. You may find a lot more options than you expect. Real estate agents who know you are looking are likely to deluge you with property details. Be ruthless in deciding which properties you will view; it is unlikely that everything you see will be suitable. It is important to be more sensitive in dealing with neighbors and relatives. Because there may be some confusion over a matter which you want to discuss, be sure to make yourself crystal clear in your initial explanation. Avoid confusing a situation by going into too many details.

9. THURSDAY. Rewarding. This promises to be an easygoing yet rewarding day with numerous opportunities to go out and to be entertained. Certain people may be starting holiday celebrations early; join in enthusiastically. Whether Christmas festivities or other celebrations, you should find that your social life picks up now. If you have been thinking about trying a new sport or hobby, this is the perfect time. For unattached Virgos, a romantic opportunity may arise this evening through a local event. Do not hesitate to make the first move, keeping your conversation on the light side.

10. FRIDAY. Mixed. A romantic attachment is moving from strength to strength. Issues which have been a problem between you can now be quite easily cleared up. You may both be prepared to make a solid commitment for the future. In the workplace all may not be smooth. There could be an argument with a difficult associate who is seeing a situation from a broader perspective than you are. If you suspect that you may be suffering from tunnel vision, it is in your best interests to put yourself in the other person's shoes. Probably you both need to adjust your outlooks slightly and find common ground so that you can work together.

11. SATURDAY. Unsettling. You may be frustrated with the attitude of someone who is not willing to go along with your plans. If you are involved with a new partner or colleague, you may be starting to discover some prime differences of approach. However, just because you have a difference of opinion, do not assume that everything will be permanently wrong between you. One argument does not have to signify the end of the relationship. It is necessary to try to be somewhat flexible in your approach. As a Virgo you yearn to have everything worked out to the tiniest detail. Sometimes, however, it pays to go with the natural flow.

12. SUNDAY. Variable. You may not be in the mood for doing household chores. However, your sense of needing to have everything in good order could be the impetus to getting those tasks done and out of the way. You are sure to feel better after a general clearing out around your home. Getting your closet in order might turn out to be quite therapeutic, especially if there is something which you are trying to get out of your mind. A family get-together could be quite special. If you have been waiting for the right moment to discuss a private matter with someone close to you, this could provide the perfect opportunity.

13. MONDAY. Good. This is a highly positive start to the work-week. At work, aim to deal with one job at a time. You need to prioritize since there could be many demands on your time. Think about the future; this is the perfect day for making long-term plans. As a Virgo you sometimes find it difficult to concentrate on anything but the details of life. Today, however, you should find it easier to see life from a broader perspective. Make an effort to be more charitable toward work colleagues. Someone who does not seem to have their mind fully focused on the job may have private concerns that are distracting them. A shoulder to lean on may help.

14. TUESDAY. Difficult. This is not the best time for trying to mix the company of friends, neighbors, and family members. However, if you have such a social arrangement already planned, go ahead. If individuals do not get along, there is no need for you to take the blame personally. If you are contemplating an impromptu get-together, aim to keep it small and intimate. If you recently became involved with a new romantic partner, do not be in too much of a hurry to escalate the relationship. You need to get to know each other better before making definite mutual plans for the future.

15. WEDNESDAY. Disquieting. Unattached Virgos anxious to meet a new partner may be in luck. Early holiday gatherings at work or in your neighborhood may be your key to meeting that special person. You could find yourself in the middle of an awkward situation involving family members. If you are taking a new friend to meet your family, do not necessarily expect everyone to take an instant liking to each other. Although you naturally hope for this, someone is likely to say just the wrong thing at the wrong time. Your best bet is to be supportive and do whatever you can to smooth things over. Maintain a sense of humor no matter what develops.

16. THURSDAY. Mixed. The responsibilities of your home and family life may be weighing heavily on you. You may have to take time off from work to sort out a difficulty. Life in the workplace is apt to be quite busy; it is possible that you have to cover for an absent colleague. What you cannot do today is be in two places at the same time. If there is an opportunity to delegate some of your work to a colleague, do so. The up side of having to put in more time at work could be that you receive a bonus or overtime pay just when you need it most. Select the best of available options.

17. FRIDAY. Buoyant. You can make excellent progress with a joint venture. If you have been waiting for confirmation of an impending deal, it should come now. However, take nothing for granted. Things are likely to change by the hour or minute, but the basic arrangement or agreement should be set firmly in place today. It is unlikely that other parties will go back on their word no matter how the details get worked out in the end. You should find it easier to handle home-based responsibilities this evening, with family members available to share the tasks and make light work of them.

18. SATURDAY. Misleading. Although you should be cautious about chastising someone for their recent bad behavior, you need to find the courage to say something in order not to condone it. Sticking your head in the sand is unlikely to solve anything and will probably only prolong the inevitable confrontation. Important developments are likely in relation to a contract under negotiation. It may seem as though everything suddenly comes together. Home and family life should be especially rewarding this evening. Be careful, however, in discussing religion or politics. Someone's prejudice may turn out to be their driving force.

19. SUNDAY. Difficult. You may bump into someone you usually find hard to tolerate. Be prepared for an intellectual discussion which does not really interest you. Also avoid gossipy neighbors. Your best bet is to give these people a wide berth, or at least cut your conversation short. If you need to produce written work, you could find it hard just making a start. Once you can get over that, however, you should make good progress. It may be helpful to work in the library so that you are not distracted by visitors or telephone calls. Nothing should be taken for granted in a new friendship or romance. If you break a date, you may be seen as breaking off the relationship.

20. MONDAY. Rewarding. You have good reason to pat yourself on the back and even boast a little about your current achievements. In addition, chances are that your results speak for themselves. There could be some kind of reward or acknowledgment coming your way. Today should be fairly easy, with much going your way. There may be an unexpected yet pleasant invitation. Someone could even be in the mood to throw a surprise party. Be confident that you will be able to tie up important outstanding work before the holiday celebrations are fully under way. Cooperation is yours for the asking.

21. TUESDAY. Disquieting. This can be a productive day in the workplace if you are willing to come to grips with a long-standing problem. With Christmas so near, you may not feel that you have the energy to devote to unraveling difficult problems. However, if you can muster a little enthusiasm, you should be able to put one huge problem behind you once and for all. Work superiors may apply extra pressure just when you need to take care of a personal matter. Try to keep cool and calm. If you deal with one issue at a time, you can do all that is expected of you and keep everyone happy.

22. WEDNESDAY. Variable. The pressures that kept you hopping yesterday are likely to lift today. The boss or another higher-up finally understands that you only have one pair of hands. Requests you made some time ago for updated equipment or extra assistance may now be granted. Even though Christmas is just around the corner and people are geared to festive activity, this is still a propitious day for a job interview or promotion discussion. As a result of the festive atmosphere, prospective employers may actually be more affable and easy to talk to. It is not smart to try to mix friendship and romance this evening.

23. THURSDAY. Happy. Any gathering involving friends is likely to be good fun. For Virgo professionals, this is an excellent day for entertaining valued clients. You may pick up more information in a restaurant than at all those previous boardroom discussions throughout the year. To make a special personal dream come true, you may have to travel farther afield than usual. A group night out is sure to be memorable. For Virgos who are romantically unattached, someone interesting may be a guest at a social gathering and make it a point to meet you.

24. FRIDAY. Satisfactory. On the whole this should be a satisfying end to the working week. Do not be too disappointed if you cannot tie up every single problem before the holiday. If you still need to purchase gifts, a last-minute shopping trip should be quite successful. Going out with friends or colleagues is the perfect way to celebrate. If you intend to drive, however, be careful about how much you drink. Enlist the help of family members to finish up gift wrapping or to help with some holiday cooking in advance. Be generous in giving a donation to a worthy charity on this joyful Christmas Eve.

25. SATURDAY. Merry Christmas! This may turn out to be a quieter Christmas than you expect. Relatives who would have a long way to travel to be with you may cancel out at the last minute. With fewer people around, there should be less for you to do. If you are feeling tired from having worked so hard to get tasks finished during the week, enjoy the chance for a day of rest. Close-knit family members are likely to be in touch if you are not spending the day with them. Catch up on all their news despite long-distance phone charges; consider the call a gift to yourself.

26. SUNDAY. Pleasant. Take a back seat today. Let other people do the entertaining. Your social activities should be pleasant, so long as you do not have to mix too much with colleagues. Put the working world well behind you this weekend. Neighbors who are intent on providing a good time may invite you to a noisy party. If it is really not your choice, you can use the excuse of tiredness and slip away quietly without anyone objecting too much or probably even noticing. You may have the sense of finally putting a chapter of your life behind you and being ready and willing for a new start.

27. MONDAY. Challenging. You should be feeling especially positive about all that is ahead of you. This is an ideal day for focusing on your main objectives for the future. If you go out socially, you are likely to be the center of a lot of attention. You are in the mood to enjoy the limelight now that you have had a few days of rest. For unattached Virgo men and women in particular, this could be the key day for meeting someone special. Try not to spend a lot of time at home. A walk should be invigorating. If you are working today, you should make excellent, fast progress and a lasting impression on higher-ups.

28. TUESDAY. Useful. Spend some time contemplating how you can achieve your dream in the future. Through joint efforts you may be able to make the greatest progress. You may instinctively feel that someone who comes into your life now is the right person to team up with. Trust your inner voice. If some criticism is being leveled at you, you may want to prove yourself to family members or colleagues. Try not to let what other people think matter too much to you. Now is the time to maintain your self-esteem and look to the future with renewed confidence. You have a lot to look forward to and a lot to offer.

29. WEDNESDAY. Fair. Do only what is necessary today. Money could be in short supply after the expensive holiday period. It could become obvious that you or another family member, perhaps a child, needs new clothing or shoes. You do not have to purchase everything all at once, however. It is a good idea to put together a long-term budget, which will help you spread the costs. It is also possible that you can pick up a few useful items in the sales which have already started. You may have to cover any significant expenses with your credit card, but try to pay it off in full as soon as possible.

30. THURSDAY. Manageable. If yesterday you were concerned and worried about money matters, today could give you a whole new perspective. There is likely to be a pleasant surprise or bonus affecting your finances. Or an investment made some time ago may finally begin to pay off even if you did not expect it to be a money-maker this year. If there is something important which you need to buy for your home, it might be possible to borrow it from a family member or trade for it with a friend or neighbor. If the item will benefit two of you, it is likely that you can arrange to share the expense.

31. FRIDAY. Tricky. With all the sales going on now, it can be tempting to spend beyond your means. Keep in mind that sales are intended to get you to spend, although the emphasis may appear to be on saving you money. Besides, buying at sales may cause you to make compromises that you might otherwise not be willing to make. It might be a lot more rewarding to set your sights on an item you really want to own, then come up with a long-term budget to pay for it. A friendly social gathering is the best way of bringing in the New Year. Consider staying overnight if you do not want to travel in the wee hours.

VIRGO
NOVEMBER–DECEMBER 1998

November 1998

1. SUNDAY. Mixed. A personal relationship that is going through an up and down period can make life tense for you. It can be hard to gauge someone's mood from one moment to the next. Paying closer attention to their needs could help draw them out; this is a time to listen rather than talk. However, if someone is being continually difficult, leave them to their own devices. It may prove impossible to resolve certain issues without direct confrontation. If you cannot win someone over to your way of thinking, at least attempt to reach compromises. If a work worry is weighing on your mind, talk it through with someone whose judgment you respect. Some outdoor exercise can alleviate a stress headache later in the day.

2. MONDAY. Quiet. In your business dealings this is a good day for sorting out financial matters of all kinds. Virgo entrepreneurs may come across a new venture which would be worth backing. An investment made at this time is likely to prove lucrative. In your personal life this is an important day. You can gain deeper insight into the psyche of someone who is becoming increasingly special to you. A casual relationship can now become more serious as you win increasing trust and respect. Discussing your feelings and exchanging confidences with this person can lead to greater intimacy, which should be satisfying for you both.

3. TUESDAY. Uncertain. At work you are likely to be caught up in matters which require total concentration and dedication. This is likely to force other responsibilities out of your head. Make a point of checking your calendar for any appointment or task which may have slipped your mind, then reschedule them for a time when you are under less pressure. If you can afford to lend some money you may want to bail a friend out of a financial crisis. Make sure, however, that the terms of your loan are clear from the very beginning. Before bringing up a sensitive issue with a co-worker, it could be helpful to first write down your thoughts, opinions, and proposed solution.

4. WEDNESDAY. Good. This promises to be a rewarding day at work. If you are part of a team, it is important for everyone to pull their own weight. Avoid doing more than your fair share of the work just because you do not want to make waves; voice your objections, strongly if necessary. Written work can take up a lot of time, especially if you are proposing a new idea or plan. For Virgo students, studying of all kinds can be satisfying; a new subject can capture your imagination and prove to be of great interest to you. This is a good time to sign up for an evening class to find out more about a certain topic; you could extend your social circle at the same time.

5. THURSDAY. Disquieting. You may face the day with a sense of weariness. It can seem that a superior has unrealistic expectations, either of your abilities or your efficiency. Avoid getting involved in a dispute of any kind unless you have hard facts to back up your views. Keeping a diary can help prove just how long certain tasks take and how you are using any spare time. Although this is a difficult period if you are trying to learn a new skill, do not be tempted to give up out of frustration. Your enthusiasm may well return and your skill increase dramatically if you just stick at it. Guidance from an older workmate can be helpful.

6. FRIDAY. Difficult. This is a difficult end to the working week. You you are apt to be at the beck and call of superiors. It is important to stay cool if someone is piling on the pressure. Only by thinking clearly can you deal with the day's problems or meet a deadline. Organize your time or it could easily slip through your fingers. There is a risk that a promise made to you earlier in the year may be broken. This could lead to questions about trust and respect. Having to accept that someone is not as reliable or as caring as you thought could cause you some painful moments.

7. SATURDAY. Calm. On this quiet day you almost certainly need some time to yourself, so keep your social plans to a minimum. You may want to meet a friend for lunch, then have the rest of the day to yourself. Focus your thoughts on your long-term future. Think about what you want to be doing or where you would like to be at this time next year. Only you know whether you are on course. Setting small goals on the way to your main aims in life can be helpful. It is time to bury the hatchet if you recently argued with a friend. Be the first to apologize even if you were not totally to blame.

8. SUNDAY. Excellent. This is a favorable time for celebrating a birthday or anniversary. Throw the doors open for friends and family members; the more the merrier. Generations should mix easily, so do not hesitate to include children in your plans. A new romance should be living up to or even beyond your expectations. Conditions favor introducing a new partner to your friends and family. If you are unattached at the moment there is a greater chance of meeting a new romantic interest, most likely through your existing social circle. For once you could be pleased when a friend plays matchmaker. Someone from a different country or culture could be the perfect match for you.

9. MONDAY. Changeable. If you have no pressing work to attend to, take the day off so that you have a long weekend. Working from home can be more productive than going into your usual place of work. You should find it easier to settle down to the day's tasks if you minimize the chance of interruptions. Virgo managers can benefit from spending time with staff members on a one-to-one basis. You may be able to talk someone out of quitting if you give them extra practical support and encouragement. A family member could have good news to share. An evening spent with loved ones can be enjoyable if you focus on the future and do not bring up the past.

10. TUESDAY. Buoyant. A working relationship that has taken a long time to build should be particularly successful today. Both of you may realize that you make a good team because one is strong in areas where the other is weak. There is very little that you cannot accomplish between you. A new business partnership or merger finalized at this time is likely to prove rewarding. If you are going on a job interview or are attending a special function, take extra trouble with your personal appearance. First impressions could prove very important. This can be a particularly productive day for Virgos who make a living as writers, editors, or typesetters.

11. WEDNESDAY. Happy. If you are making plans for a winter vacation, work out the finances carefully. Keep in mind that there are always hidden extras; you might be underestimating the total cost. Investigate cheaper alternatives before committing yourself. Friends who are better off than you may assume that you will join in on certain social arrangements. If these are clearly beyond your means, say so. Do not let someone pay your way or give you a loan if you suspect that there may be strings attached to their offer. Meeting up with an old friend can be fun; you could wind up talking late into the night.

12. THURSDAY. Stressful. Someone who is being unusually friendly or cooperative may have an ulterior motive. Guard against being manipulated in any way. Do not take anyone or anything at face value. A little skepticism could stand you in good stead at the moment. Virgos who are unattached should be wary of being swept off your feet; someone's charm may be only superficial. Think twice before beginning a romance with someone you work with; you could easily become the object of gossip despite your attempts at discretion and secrecy. Hostility from a rival in love can be upsetting; ask yourself if the prize is worth the battle.

13. FRIDAY. Fair. The wisest counsel can be your own. Your Virgo powers of intuition should be totally reliable; be guided by what feels right. In your business dealings keep your latest plans to yourself until you are ready to go full steam ahead. In this way nobody can push you into a premature or hasty decision. An ace up your sleeve can be your best weapon when it comes to taking on rivals. If you are single but have your eye on someone new, do not make your interest too obvious. Subtle signals are the most effective way of stirring their interest; you can then be the pursued rather than the pursuer. Gambling of any kind should be avoided.

14. SATURDAY. Stimulating. The early part of the day may bring word of someone you lost contact with a while ago. Whether the news is cause for celebration or commiseration, this is a good time for getting back in touch. Your willingness to heal the rift is almost sure to be reciprocated. Shrug off any grudges or grievances which came about through a petty argument. You will feel much better about yourself if you forgive and forget. If you are in the mood to go out tonight, try a new restaurant or social club rather than sticking to your usual haunts. You could discover exciting new faces. This is also a good evening for hosting an impromptu party.

15. SUNDAY. Good. This is one of those picture-perfect Sundays when you can just relax and feel at peace with the world. Your family and friends should let you do as you choose; one or two may even go out of their way to spoil you or spring a surprise treat on you. Even if you feel physically lazy, you still want some intellectual stimulation. Seek out the company of people who share your interests. Someone who can always contribute to a conversation no matter what the subject may be especially fascinating to you. Single Virgos can be attracted to someone who openly challenges ideas and makes everyone think.

16. MONDAY. Deceptive. The day gets off to an easy start, but do not be lulled into a false sense of security. Pressure in the workplace is likely to mount as the day goes on. You may be called upon to make snap decisions in the absence of a superior. In your business dealings you could come up against someone who has more power than you, and they will probably not hesitate to wield it. Your best policy is not to show that you feel intimidated. Keep your cool and you should be able to think on your feet. Guard against spending money too freely. Some unforeseen expenses are coming up that could require paying in cash.

17. TUESDAY. Variable. Today's mail is likely to include one or more bills. If you receive a final demand for payment, try to settle it today. If a bill is much larger than expected, you may be able to extend the payment deadline. Try not to let money worries depress you; anxiety only makes you feel bad without solving anything. Think practically. Prioritize your expenses. Many of the day's tasks are apt to be unchallenging or dull. This is a day when you can achieve the best results by putting your nose to the grindstone. Whatever you put aside today will still have to be tackled at some point; you might as well clear the decks now.

18. WEDNESDAY. Satisfactory. If work has been nothing but trial and tribulation recently, things should take a turn for the better now. This is an auspicious time for fresh starts of all kinds. Do not struggle on with work which is confusing or flawed. Ask a colleague for help; a fresh perspective could be all that is needed. This is a lucky day for Virgos who are taking a test. Sign up for lessons if you have need to learn new skills or brush up an outdated ones; it could open up new possibilities for you. Someone close to you may be set on spoiling you this evening. Enjoy their attention without making any promises to them.

19. THURSDAY. Fair. Someone close to you may be talking about taking a course of action which you consider unwise. It would probably be best, however, to keep your misgivings to yourself for the time being. Give your opinion in diplomatic terms if you are asked for it; keep in mind that everyone has to learn from their own experience. Do not give up if you are house hunting. You could find the right place just when you are becoming discouraged. If you are renting a home or office, make sure that you have everything in writing. This should include a full inventory as well as a lease and a receipt for your deposit.

20. FRIDAY. Tricky. You may be offered the chance to travel, maybe in connection with your work. Although this might lead to some disruption in your usual routine, consider the proposition carefully. If you turn it down you may later regard it as missed opportunity. Jump at any chance to expand your horizons, whether this is visiting a new part of the world or broadening your mind. Vocational courses designed to improve your work skills can be challenging but also life changing; do not let fear of failure be the reason for holding back. This is a time to try anything new that appeals to you. Friends make the best companions tonight.

21. SATURDAY. Variable. If you have a busy working life, try to devote today to your family. Someone is waiting for a chance to discuss an important matter with you, but if you are always preoccupied you may come across as uninterested. Make a point of encouraging intimate conversation with loved ones. If you are self-employed you may have reached the stage where you are prepared to turn down work which would take up too much of your personal time. Keep in mind that money is not everything. If you are entertaining at home this evening, expect one or more guests to be late or even not to show up at all.

22. SUNDAY. Tranquil. This promises to be a lazy Sunday. Keep domestic tasks to bare essentials. You may not want to wander far from home. If weather is bad, the prospect of staying warm and dry indoors can be far more tempting than any social invitation. Do not allow yourself to be dragged away from home unless it is an invitation you really cannot refuse. If you live alone, you may want to invite friends or family members for a meal later in the day. Cooking for others can be satisfying. A new romance can blossom by spending more time together. You may discover that you have even more in common than you at first suspected.

23. MONDAY. Disquieting. Work which requires creative skill can be especially challenging. Bounce your ideas off other people, but guard against collecting too many opinions. If you listen to everyone and anyone you run the risk of making a project more complicated rather than clearer. If you are working with children, vary planned activities more than usual. Abandon any material which is clearly failing to capture their interest or imagination; you can always rework it into a better format at another time. Friction at home this evening can be upsetting even if you are not directly involved. It may take a while to discover what the real issues are.

24. TUESDAY. Fair. Work is more likely to be a pleasure than a duty in the earlier part of the day. You may be given more interesting tasks than usual. Be prepared to take on a new challenge, especially of an artistic nature; it could lead to rediscovering your creative talents. This is a good time for learning to play a musical instrument. Writing poetry or prose can also be a satisfying pastime. Your usual routine is apt to be disrupted this afternoon. There is a good chance of having to put in some overtime at work. If you have to cancel out of a social arrangement, try to give your host as much advance warning as possible.

25. WEDNESDAY. Good. The morning is the easier part of the day. Run-of-the-mill tasks are likely to take a lot of time, but you may welcome the chance of not being under too much pressure. If close concentration is not required, listen to some music or to a radio program as you work. If you are unemployed at the moment this can be a lucky time for securing a part-time or temporary job. Although it may not suit your wishes exactly, getting a foot in the door could lead to other opportunities in the future. This evening is a good time for entertaining at home. Imagination can make a little food go a long way.

26. THURSDAY. Mixed. Take extra care not to annoy or anger a family member. Be thorough in all that you do, especially when it comes to cleaning up. Cutting corners may seem like a good idea at the time, but you may later wish that you had taken the trouble to be more particular. It appears that someone is trying to catch you off guard and at a disadvantage. You need to have answers at your fingertips if you want to come out on top. Try to duck out of a serious discussion if you feel that you are not sufficiently prepared. Any health problem at the moment is likely to be a result of overdoing. Try not to make too many social visits on this Thanksgiving holiday.

27. FRIDAY. Demanding. This is a demanding end to the working week. You may realize that you have bitten off more than you can chew. Do not struggle on with a project which has turned out to be too complex for you to handle alone. If you cannot get the assistance or advice you need, put it on the back burner for now. Meeting a deadline can be touch-and-go. You might be forced to admit that you have not used your working hours as efficiently as usual this week. At least you can learn from your mistakes. If you analyze how or why something has gone wrong, you are less likely to repeat the error in the future. Virgo shoppers can pick up some real bargains in clothes or household accessories.

28. SATURDAY. Fair. As a Virgo you like to be well organized in advance. This is a good time for planning your holiday shopping. Find out what friends or family would like as a gift. One advantage of getting an early start is the chance to spread the cost, especially if you are buying for a lot of people. A romance which has been going slowly downhill may finally come to an end. You are bound to feel a sense of loss, but making the final decision can also come as a relief. Remind yourself that it is better to be single than in an unhappy or undermining relationship. Restarting your own social life can be easier than you imagine.

29. SUNDAY. Exciting. You should feel very much in tune with the world and all those around you. Even someone who is normally difficult to talk to may suddenly take your side regarding a personal issue. You may realize that their opinion of you is much higher than they had previously led you to believe. It is in the Virgo nature to be self-critical; today's boost to your self-esteem can do you a world of good. Accept an offer of a day out even if you are inclined at first to turn it down and stay home; you could be glad that you made the effort. A money problem can be solved unexpectedly when a relative steps in with a genuine offer of help.

30. MONDAY. Unsettling. The last thing you need is to brood over an argument or misunderstanding. The other person involved has probably already forgotten about it, so try to do the same. You could have made the situation worse in your own mind than it really is. Your positive attitude is bound to rub off on those around you. You may have been taking certain individuals far too seriously. A lighter touch can improve both your professional and personal relationships. Finding your sense of humor when a situation threatens to blow out of proportion. Avoid making vacation plans until you are sure you can arrange the time off. Get to bed early tonight.

December 1998

1. TUESDAY. Manageable. The new month gets off to a satisfactory start for Virgos. Some work matters may be causing you more trouble than usual, but there is little that you cannot handle once you get down to it. If you are involved in litigation of any kind there could be an unexpected setback. Heed advice from your lawyer or other professional adviser; they are the experts, so put yourself in their hands. This is a favorable time for Virgos who are buying or selling property. A transaction could go through much more quickly than you anticipate. Be suspicious of anyone who tries to rush you into making a decision or signing a contract.

2. WEDNESDAY. Productive. This is likely to be a busy day but a productive one. Get an earlier start than usual. Extra advance preparation for an important appointment could prove invaluable. If you are spending more and more time at work, ask yourself if you are taking advantage of offers of help or trying to do it all yourself. This is a trap which is easy to fall into for the industrious Virgo. Try to ease your workload. Do not take on any new responsibility until you are satisfied that your current work is under control. Trust a colleague to be as efficient as you are. Do not risk flirting if you are already attached; you could arouse jealousy or disappointment.

3. THURSDAY. Variable. In your workplace, changes taking place at the managerial level may disrupt your usual working routine. A new boss can be difficult to get used to; it may be a case of a new broom sweeping clean. Your best approach is not to resist change; your working life will benefit in the long run. Make an extra effort to prioritize your tasks. Lack of organization can lead to underachieving. Avoid offering to help a colleague if it means that your own work would suffer. Devote this evening to domestic chores. Putting your home in order can be therapeutic for the neat-loving Virgo nature. Clutter is sure to upset you and can have a negative impact on your current mood.

4. FRIDAY. Slow. Although this week has had more than its fair share of ups and downs, the dust should settle today. Pressure at work is likely to be considerably reduced because some tasks are taken off your hands. Someone who has been breathing down your neck should now leave you to work at your own pace. There may be time for a long lunch with a friend or colleague. If you are going away for the weekend, aim for an early departure so that you miss the rush hour. You may need to cancel out of social event this evening if it is beyond your current financial means. If someone offers to pay your way, make sure that there are no strings attached.

5. SATURDAY. Mixed. If you are unemployed you may get a lucky break today. There is a greater chance of picking up some temporary work of a seasonal nature. If your work involves serving the general public you could receive higher tips. If you have been arguing with an older relative, this is a favorable time for a fresh start. Many of your differences may be due to the generation gap; show tolerance and understanding and you are more likely to get the same in return. A family problem can be solved quite easily if everyone is prepared to sit down and talk about possible solutions. Entertaining at home can be more enjoyable than going out.

6. SUNDAY. Satisfactory. You are apt to have more energy than those around you. Family members and friends may look to you to get things organized. Be prepared to take the lead, and hope that others will follow. Family duties should not be shirked. If you are visiting your partner's relatives, you can boost your popularity by being extra charming and entertaining. If someone seeks your advice, make a point of speaking the unvarnished truth. This is not a time to say just what someone wants to hear. A child may need extra discipline, but make sure that it is tempered with love. It is important to fulfill a promise even if it is inconvenient to do so.

7. MONDAY. Fair. This is a busy start to the workweek. Be prepared for a constant stream of drop-in customers and telephone calls. It may be hard to get rid of someone who outstays their welcome. This is a time to get on top of administrative tasks such as bill paying and letter writing. Virgo business people may be more effective in the office rather than on the road. You can tie up a lot of loose ends over the telephone rather than arranging face-to-face appointments. This evening favors a quiet night at home. Get to bed early to recharge your batteries.

8. TUESDAY. Fortunate. In the workplace a lot of time can be taken up with confidential discussions. If you work in a managerial capacity, someone may need to talk to you off the record. You can solve problems if you refuse to be bound by red tape. Do not hesitate to bend a few rules to your advantage or someone else's. An occasion which requires you to be in top form should be enjoyable; you are likely to enjoy yourself. Keep in mind the saying that charity begins at home. Someone close to you may need some financial assistance but feel awkward about asking. Offer to help if you can. A lottery ticket could be lucky for you.

9. WEDNESDAY. Sensitive. You are likely to be more sensitive than usual to comments or criticisms directed at you. However, listen carefully to what others have to say; you may realize that they have a valid point. There is a greater risk of jumping to wrong conclusions if you react too quickly or too emotionally. People may bring their problems to you. Taking on someone else's pain can be wearing; establish your own boundaries so that you do not become overwhelmed. Guard against possessive behavior if you are in a new relationship. Emotional security grows best if you allow one another enough space. Relax and be yourself and you are sure to make a lasting impression.

10. THURSDAY. Disquieting. The day may get off to a somewhat chaotic start. It may be harder than usual to get up on time. A telephone call or a visitor can make you late for an appointment. In your business dealings you may not feel that you are on firm ground, but pinpointing the problem may not be possible just yet. There is more information to come which can put matters in a different light. Delay making any binding decision until you are sure of the way you want to go. If you have a hair appointment do not be tempted to change your style or color too drastically. Use a stylist who is known to you or who comes highly recommended. New shoes or boots can be a worthwhile investment.

11. FRIDAY. Difficult. This may not be a productive end to the working week. You could be hampered by constant distractions or interruptions, making it harder to give full concentration to matters at hand. You may be approached by company looking for someone with your special expertise. Although it can be flattering to be head-hunted, make sure that your final decision is based on all aspects of the work being offered and not by the financial benefits alone. Put job satisfaction on the top of your list of priorities. Plans for this evening may be canceled on short notice. Have an alternative in mind to avoid sitting home alone.

12. SATURDAY. Successful. This is an excellent day for shopping. The malls may not be as busy as you fear, allowing you to quickly move from store to store. Inspiration can strike when it comes to choosing a gift for someone who is normally difficult to buy for. If you have a large family you may want to agree on a price limit on presents so that you keep costs within reason. This is a good time for taking advantage of credit offers in the larger stores as long as it is interest-free. This evening favors hosting a party. If you prefer not to cook, food to go from a favorite restaurant is sure to be a hit with your guests.

13. SUNDAY. Mixed. The effort that you have been putting into a special relationship is now starting to pay off, but you still have some testing times ahead. Certain issues are still difficult to address openly and honestly because you fear rejection or criticism, which is every Virgo's nightmare. Let yourself off the hook for a while; a better moment may present itself toward the end of the month. Give special thought to holiday presents for older relatives; you could come up with original ideas sure to please them. Browsing around a secondhand store can be fun and lead to some unusual gifts. Or buy through a charity fund-raiser.

14. MONDAY. Changeable. The beginning of the workweek is a good time to refigure your budget for the remainder of December. Work out how much you can afford to spend on gifts and cards. Remember hidden extras, such as the cost of mailing packages and greeting cards. Set aside some money for cab fares on occasions when you cannot use public transportation and do not want to drive. Morale in the workplace is likely to be high. The holiday season puts most people in a good mood. In general chitchat you should guard against joining in on what is clearly gossip; your words could easily be repeated out of context. Social invitations are apt to be plentiful; acknowledge those you cannot accept.

15. TUESDAY. Exciting. Opportunities to earn extra cash are plentiful, but you may not see the benefits for a while. You are primed to spend money liberally rather than to save; money is likely to go out just as fast as it comes in. You may find that you are spending much more on your social life than usual; enjoy this extravagance rather than feeling guilty about it. This is a good time for a reunion of any kind. Meeting up with old school friends or former workmates can be fun for all. Single Virgos should pluck up the courage to ask someone out; you could be glad that you did not wait a day longer.

16. WEDNESDAY. Rewarding. Mail might bring a stack of holiday greetings. In the business world this is a good day for sending presents to valued customers as well as people whose business you would like to cultivate. Placing orders now for any gifts which are difficult to find at the last minute could save you a lot of time. This is also be a favorable day for purchasing advance tickets for a Christmas show or songfest. In your personal life the evening favors intimate conversation. If you are at home with family or friends, switch off the television in order to create the perfect atmosphere for talking and listening.

17. THURSDAY. Fair. If you still have cards and gifts to buy, purchasing them from a favorite charity is a good way of making a donation. If you have cards or packages going abroad, send them off without delay in order to guarantee that they arrive in time. In the workplace this is a busy day. You have to keep your nose to the grindstone if you are going to catch up with routine tasks as well as new matters which require urgent attention. This is not a night to sit at home. Accept a social invitation from someone you know through work, or go along with your partner to a party. The approach of the New Moon holds promise for Virgo finances.

18. FRIDAY. Satisfactory. If you are trying to buy or sell property there could be progress in the right direction. Do not hesitate to put pressure on the decision-makers. In this way you may be able to complete the transaction before Christmas vacation. For professional Virgos, work pressures should be easing. You can now afford to put family life at the top of your list of priorities, especially if you have young children. Enjoy an evening at home decorating the tree or wrapping presents. The spirit of goodwill is rubbing off on you. It can be a relief to make your peace with someone you have been bickering with for a while.

19. SATURDAY. Calm. Make necessary phone calls to sort out your Christmas vacation plans. Married Virgos need to work out how to include both sets of relatives in holiday festivities. It should be easier to reach compromises so that everyone is happy and content. Because this is the last shopping weekend before Christmas, hunt down any gifts you still need to buy. Finding the right one for someone who is usually difficult to buy for is likely. This evening is excellent for a small party. An intimate gathering where you know most of the other guests and can converse easily should suit your mood.

20. SUNDAY. Variable. You are probably not in the mood to sit home all day. If you have not made any advance plans, call your circle of friends or family. You could be invited to join in their plans, or you may want to make suggestions of your own. The time of year may be putting extra strain on your finances. Work out exactly how much you have to cover all the things you still need to buy, then figure out where it is possible to cut back. If you have small children you may find that other members of the family will be extra generous. A grandparent or other relative may insist on giving a donation toward an expensive gift sure to be the highlight under the tree.

21. MONDAY. Confusing. The workweek is unlikely to start off the way you would like. Both your physical and mental energy are at a low ebb. You may not feel equal to creative or intellectually demanding work. Try to stick to routine tasks which do not require much effort. Also go out of your way not to put a colleague under extra pressure. Only delegate work if you really have no. A choice gift for a child may be more expensive than you budgeted. Shop around; you could find the same item at a cheaper price in a store having a sale. Avoid alcohol this evening, especially if you have an important day tomorrow and must have a clear head.

22. TUESDAY. Difficult. Virgos are likely to be under a lot of pressure in the workplace. If someone has unrealistic expectations, now is the time to say so; point out that you only have one pair of hands. This is not a favorable day for finalizing business transactions of any kind. A certain individual may deliberately be painting you a false picture. Nor is this the time to put your faith in anyone who has not already proven their reliability. Read the small print of any document which requires your signature, especially in relation to transactions concerning property. If you are seeking a mortgage or a personal loan, shop around for the best interest rate.

23. WEDNESDAY. Good. You may get the chance to earn some extra cash. Although this probably means that some of your personal plans are disrupted, the financial peace of mind makes temporary inconvenience worthwhile. If you are out shopping it could be helpful to patronize smaller stores. Local shops may be good hunting grounds for original gifts. This is a good day for a Christmas party with your workmates. In a festive atmosphere you may get the chance to know a co-worker or a superior better. This evening is a good time for putting the finishing touches to your own holiday preparations.

24. THURSDAY. Fair. This is a particularly busy day for Virgos who have to go into work. Covering for colleagues who have already started their Christmas vacation could lead to extra pressure. Make a point of refusing additional responsibilities which the boss tries to foist upon you. There is no reason you should suffer because of their lack of vision or poor organization. Putting in overtime now will not please your loved ones. Children should have priority this evening. If you are going out but cannot find a babysitter, you may be able to take youngsters with you to a friend's party or to a restaurant. But get home early to celebrate Christmas Eve with carols and traditional tales.

25. FRIDAY. Merry Christmas! Enjoy a leisurely start to the day rather than hurrying through the fun of opening gifts. All the organization which has gone into making this the perfect Christmas is likely to pay off. Relax and let the day unfold. This can be a particularly special time if you have young children in your home or visiting you. Their excitement can lend extra spice to the festivities. Being with your partner can also make for a magical day. A loved one is determined to spoil you; you may feel a little overwhelmed by their generosity. After dinner is a good time to linger at the table and talk over old times. The party mood is likely to stay with you late into the night.

26. SATURDAY. Mixed. Virgos are known for being health conscious. To shake off the ill effects of a late night or too much indulgence in food and drink, get some exercise, such as going for a walk. You may prefer to go alone if you have been socializing nonstop. You can almost certainly benefit from having some quiet time to yourself. Later in the day favors visiting relatives or friends who did not spend time with you yesterday and for exchanging gifts. If you are driving, be alert to prevent an accident; do nothing in haste. If a loved one is away, you are apt to miss them more acutely today. Make special plans for their return.

27. SUNDAY. Stressful. If you have been hosting houseguests you may find that the work involved is beginning to take its toll. Keep in mind that you do not have to wait on them hand and foot; let them fend for themselves for a while if you need a break. Ask for help with cooking or clearing up if no one volunteers. Avoid being cooped up in the house all day. Friction between certain family members may surface if there is not enough to do or if they spend too long in each other's company. Do not forget to make a promised telephone call; someone is waiting to hear from you. Check your finances to determine if you can accept an invitation that involves buying a special gift.

28. MONDAY. Demanding. If you are back at work do not expect an easy ride. There is apt to be a lot to do. Get down to it as quickly as possible or the day could be over with nothing accomplished. If you are at home, restore your home to its usual Virgo neatness now that the festivities are winding down. Avoid making too much work for yourself; straighten up rather than actually cleaning. If you are traveling a long distance later in the day, be prepared for a tiring journey. You may arrive at your destination later than scheduled. Keep social plans to a minimum this evening; recharge your batteries by getting extra rest.

29. TUESDAY. Pleasant. If you have young children this is an ideal day for taking them to a movie or to a child's theatrical performance. Adults should enjoy the occasion too. There may be a choice of party invitations; opt for the one where you will know most of the other guests. This can also be a favorable time for hosting a get-together. A lunchtime party may suit you best if you want to mix the generations among your family and friends. If you have to work, the morale among co-workers is likely to be high. A difficult task can probably be put on the back burner until next week. Unattached Virgos are likely to meet someone romantically interesting from a different country or culture.

30. WEDNESDAY. Sensitive. Professional Virgos are unlikely to be able to finalize any business matters. However, this can be a good time for preparing for an important meeting which is coming up soon. Meticulous advance planning could pay dividends. If you are unemployed and feeling anxious about work prospects for the coming year, consider retraining. Do not rule out returning to school. Although you need to provide for your immediate needs, this is also a time for thinking long-term. If there is a conflict for tomorrow night, try to resolve it today so that everyone is informed and not kept wondering. It is not too late to buy a new outfit for a gala party.

31. THURSDAY. Promising. Even if you have to work there is a good chance that you will be able to finish earlier than usual. Try to dispense with routine chores this morning. The sociable mood of the day will soon be upon you. Take time to reflect on how you have grown during the last twelve months. Resolutions for the new year are likely to center around career issues, especially if you want to increase your earning potential. Distinguish between what other people expect of you and what you want for yourself. Dress up for a formal party this evening. If you cannot be with someone special at the stroke of twelve, keep them in your heart and thoughts.

Having A Good Psychic Is like Having A Guardian Angel!

Love, Romance, Money & Success
May Be In Your Stars....

Get a **FREE** Sample
Psychic Reading Today!!!

1-800-799-6582

Let The Stars
Guide You To
The Future...
Where Love, Money and Success are waiting for you!
Find Out How to Get A FREE Sample Psychic Reading Today!!!
1-800-841-7648
For entertainment purposes only. Must be 18+. First 3 minutes FREE.

FREE
Love
Advice

Does he really love me?

Will I ever get married?

Is he being faithful?

Call To Find Out How To Get Your

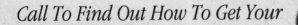

FREE Sample
Psychic Reading!

1-800-869-2879